Sophia Sutras

Introducing
Mother Wisdom

Sophia Sutras

Introducing
Mother Wisdom

by

Carol E. Parrish-Harra, Ph.D.

SPARROW HAWK PRESS
Tahlequah, Oklahoma

Cover Art from original painting by Kim Laird, www.kimlaird.com
Editor: Lee Warren
Type composition and book design: Michelle Killian Robertson

Library of Congress Cataloging-in-Publication Data
Parrish-Harra, Carol E.
Sophia Sutras Introducing Mother Wisdom
A guide to the emergence of the Divine Feminine, including guided meditations; by Carol E. Parrish-Harra.

ISBN 0-945027-25-7: $24.95
Library of Congress Catalog Card Number pending.
1. Spirituality, 2. Sophiology, 3. Ageless Wisdom

Books by Carol E. Parrish-Harra, Ph.D.
Adventure in Meditation: Spirituality for the 21st Century, Vols. I, II, & III
How to Use Sacred Space for Problem-Solving and Inner Guidance
The New Dictionary of Spiritual Thought
The Book of Rituals—Personal and Planetary Transformation
The Aquarian Rosary—Reviving the Art of Mantra Yoga
A New Age Handbook on Death and Dying
Messengers of Hope
Reflections

Manufactured in the United States of America

DEDICATED
to
THE CALL OF WISDOM

*What Wisdom is, and how she came into being, I will
relate: I will conceal no mysteries from you, but trace
her from her first beginnings and bring the
knowledge of her into the open.*
—Wisdom of Solomon 6:22

and
To the many Wise Ones
who know her well.

Contents

Editor's Note: Unless otherwise noted, the scripture quotations contained herein are from the New Revised Standard Version Bible, © 1989 by the Division of Christian Education of the National Council of the Churches of Christ in the U.S.A., and are used by permission. All rights reserved. Also unless otherwise noted, specific word etymologies are taken from the Merriam Webster's Collegiate ® Dictionary, Tenth Edition, © 1994 by Merriam-Webster, Inc.

Acknowledgments

It is my pleasure to acknowledge the professional support I have received from a number of others who love Sophia even as I. First, I thank the Board of Governors, both past and present, of Sancta Sophia Seminary. Your dedication to the seminarians and faithful encouragement of my efforts through the years has been, and is, invaluable. I am much indebted to each of you.

Lovingly, I appreciate the talent of artist Kim Laird who gifted the striking Sophia painting found on the cover. When I first saw the depth revealed by the potent color and design of this work, I knew this should be its role. Both the beauty of the art and the generosity of Kim's heart touch me deeply. It is my delight to share her powerful artistic interpretation of Sophia in a more public way.

Likewise I express my appreciation to editor, Lee Warren, for both her attention to details and the contribution of her own poetry in Sophia's honor. As well, I acknowledge my appreciation to graphic artist Michelle Killian Robertson for her artistic expertise. She has worked diligently to create a design throughout the book reflective of the beauty Sophia represents.

I proudly acknowledge the talents of my co-workers as together we celebrate Sophia in our midst.

*I*ntroduction

There is for all one entrance into life, and one way out. Therefore I prayed, and understanding was given me; I called on God, and the spirit of wisdom came to me. All good things came to me along with her. . . . I rejoiced in them all, because wisdom leads them; but I did not know that she was their mother.

—The Wisdom of Solomon 7.6–12

*W*hat a task: to describe the indescribable, to define the illusive divine feminine. A breeze, a touch, a thought waiting just beyond the edge of mind, a poem only stirring, or love waiting in the shadows—each is true as our lives echo her whisper and her joy. We delight in her mirth as we experience wit, humor, and pleasure. She walks with us in our pain, silently adding the strength of her presence to our struggle. *She who dwells within*[1] is always present just as is the air we breathe, and she is just as difficult to explain. Whether called Sophia, Wisdom, the Divine Feminine (to list only three of her many names)— regardless of heritage, history, or culture—the archetypal matriarchal force, moves unrestricted through all traditions, ever resistant to limitations and human preferences.

To try to capture some few of her infinite aspects, our approach here is to consider specific related sets of attributes in separate sutra-like chapters. Borrowing an Eastern application of the term *sutra*, we intend each chapter to be a primer, a short, clear explanation of a concept that is

---

1. *She who dwells within,* also known as Shekinah. In the traditions of Judaism and Kabalah, the divine feminine that awaits within to activate expressions of wisdom, inner knowing, and protection: a source of grace and blessings, the bearer of divine creativity, the luminous presence of God. —Carol E. Parrish-Harra, Ph.D., "SHEKINAH," in *The New Dictionary of Spiritual Thought,* expanded 2nd ed. (Tahlequah, OK: Sparrow Hawk Press, 2002), 261.

a compelling idea in its own right. The greater value of the sutra, however, is that it is also a component within a more comprehensive philosophy.

This brings us to a second application. Transliteration of *sutra* from the Sanskrit is "thread." It is mother to the Latin *suere,* "to sew," which in turn is the root of our English word "suture," meaning "to stitch together."

Each sutra, then, is like one part of a garment—a sleeve, a neck facing, a pocket, or so on. By itself, each piece cannot do much, but sewn into its proper place it contributes to the function of the whole. Likewise, the whole without every part is not perfectly serviceable.

These sutras are bits of wisdom arranged in such a manner as to help us gain a new comprehension of the long-hidden feminine nature residing beside the masculine within the ineffable Source of Life. Through one experience at a time, mystical cognition grows. As priceless bits are stitched together, a new perception gradually forms.

To introduce the divine feminine calls for a name that both acknowledges inner knowing and reflects the many facets of her nature. The time is ripe to unveil her mysteries. Her omniscience prompts us to call her by one of her many names: *Sophia,* translated long ago as "Wisdom." We cry out, "Sophia, where are you? Mother, where do you hide?" Ancient texts, Bible passages, indigenous references, inner experiences—all speak of her.

> *There is overwhelming archeological and historical evidence that during a long period of prehistory and early history both men and women worshiped goddesses, women functioned as chief priests, and property commonly passed through the mother's lineage.* [2]

As we explore Sophia we discover her to be multidimensional. She is: 1) an Archetype—one-half of the Creator, the All Wise One; 2) a Principle—receptivity to impressions; and 3) a Mode of Consciousness possessing qualities and attributes. By understanding such we can know these aspects of the divine without hesitancy. Present in all levels of

---

2. Leonard Shlain, *The Alphabet Versus The Goddess: The Conflict Between Word and Image* (New York: Viking, 1998), preface.

existence, part of her manifestation within human consciousness is as the psyche. Within a human being she can become lost in identification with the body and the material world.

Mother Matter is little understood but we all know matter exists and contains intelligence. This is because the feminine principle rushed forth at the moment of creation to form bodies—denser units of material substance—into which the "ensouled" life-force, or sparks of the divine, could settle.

We are well acquainted with the concept of Mother Nature—so taken for granted that she is most often undervalued, even when acknowledged. She is indeed "mother" of all—giving life is her nature. We see the feminine of all species, whether plant, animal, or human, bring forth new life. Birthing is natural to the physical female. Characteristic maternal activities are nurturing, protecting, being receptive to needs, and being sensitive to all manners of touch—physical, emotional, mental, and spiritual. Now we meet her as Sophia, who is also called the World Soul as well as the guide of humanity.

Other attributes of the divine feminine include fluidity, passivity, universality, perpetual motion, infinite patience, and endurance. When Wisdom perceived the divine thought, she immediately sought to fulfill the edict of the masculine aspect of the Godhead. The divine command, *"Let there be . . . ."* prompted creation; Spirit acted and Ether received. The "He" commanded and the "She" conceived.

The Lord created me as the beginning of his way, the first of his acts of long ago. Ages ago I was set up, at the first, before the beginning of the earth. . . . then I was beside him, like a master worker. Proverbs 8.22, 23, 30.

All that exists is in response to this sacred creative impulse. Matter is filled with sparks of consciousness which are in no way limited to humanity, nor does one need to be holy to be instinctually alive to her promptings.

Does not wisdom call, and does not understanding raise her voice? . . Hear, for I will speak noble things, and from my lips will come what is right; for my mouth will utter truth; . . .All the words of my mouth are righteous; there is nothing twisted or crooked in them. They are all straight to one who understands and right to those who find knowledge. . . I have good advice and sound wisdom; I have insight, I have strength. Proverbs 8.1, 6–9, 14.

Within a metaphysical understanding there is of necessity an interaction of male and female energies at regular intervals. These active and receptive forces revitalize all life: nature, human, and divine. The traditions of many Eastern and indigenous religions demonstrate a long standing reverence for this life-supporting interaction at all levels of creation.

Orthodox Judaism observes this very union between God and his Shekinah on the Sabbath eve, when pious Jewish couples make love. This pairing of God with Goddess is part of the earthly, homely religions of the ancient Middle East. [3]

In the Christian West, for many reasons (some of which will be discussed later), understanding of the interaction of feminine and masculine in all of life became distorted. Reverence for the divine feminine faded, becoming lost to memory for many Christian sects. Nevertheless, for those with eyes to see and ears to hear, the truth was preserved in symbols, myths, and fairy tales during the long medieval dark age, through the renaissance, the age of reason, and into the industrial and scientific revolutions. Although we are only now beginning to rediscover the true meanings behind myth and symbol, their ability to communicate their wisdom in subtle ways has never been dependent on our rational understanding.

In their article "Education for Spiritual Growth: Going beyond the Obvious," authors Sheldon and Jesse Stoff quoted these words from Albert Einstein's *The World As I See It*:

---

3. Caitlín Matthews, "Sophia, Goddess of Wisdom", *Gnosis Magazine* No. 13, (Fall 1989): 23.

I didn't arrive at my understanding of the fundamental laws of the Universe through my rational mind.

If you want your chldren to be brilliant, tell them fairy tales. If you want them to be very brilliant, tell them even more fairy tales.

The most beautiful thing we can experience is the mysterious. It is the source of all true art and science. He to whom this emotion is a stranger, who can no longer pause to wonder and stand rapt in awe, is as good as dead. His eyes are closed. [4]

For example, the rose, an ancient symbol of the divine feminine, is often associated with Virgin Mary, who became for many Christians the archetype of the divine feminine. As appearances of Our Lady, Mother of Jesus, have occurred around the world throughout history, most often she has been accompanied by roses. When Juan Diego of Our Lady of Guadalupe fame was told by the vision to gather flowers in his mantle to attest to the validity of her appearance, roses suddenly appeared blooming out of season. Mary herself is referred to as the Rose of Sharon, a heavenly Rose, and other references as well. We might recall the rose windows of cathedrals dedicated to Our Lady.

Recently, books such as *The Da Vinci Code* by Dan Brown have stirred the public to a new pitch of inquiry. Although written in novel form, Brown's story incorporates many of the teachings of the divine feminine that have been held quietly over the centuries, not shared openly, due to the persecution that so often accompanied these ideas. [5]

The rite of *Hieros Gamos* [6] described in *The Da Vinci Code* shocked many, but those who had gained an understanding of symbolism were ready to be reminded of the many traditions with some kind of sacred sexual act used to affirm the continuation of life on the physical dimension.

---

4. Albert Einstein, *The World As I See It* (New York: Philosophical Library, 1949), as quoted by Sheldon Ptaschevitch Stoff and Jesse Andrew Stoff, "Education for Spiritual Growth: Going beyond the Obvious," *the Quest*, 92, no. 2 (Mar-Apr 2004): 56.

5. Dan Brown, *The Da Vinci Code* (New York: Doubleday, 2003).

6. Heiros Gamos. "Greek for 'sacred marriage' between the masculine and feminine aspects of God. Sophia/Wisdom is portrayed as the feminine partner in this marriage."—Parrish-Harra, *Dictionary*, 121.

Various cultures exercised sacred rituals to remind their adherents of the power of sexuality and to hold it in reverence. This was scandalous to many Christian denominations, and every effort was made to wipe out any trace of such regard.

In some groups, pregnant women, even though married, were regarded as sinful. In other groups priests and nuns are required to be celibate and sexually guilt ridden. Indeed, irrational guilt associated with sexuality may rival belief in God as the primary common denominator among Christian groups.

Among the manuscripts found at Nag Hammadi, *The Gospel of Philip,* like *The Da Vinci Code,* describes Mary Magdalene as the intimate companion of Jesus. This idea is not new and is appearing in more places as new scrolls are found and translated. Scholars are re-examining her role as a favorite apostle of Jesus and she has been called both "the first apostle" and also "the apostle to the apostles" for her role as the first to see the risen Christ on Easter morning and for carrying the news of the resurrection to the others. The research of Margaret Starbird is extensive and excellent in this regard.

In this jaded intellectual era we are seeking interesting phenomena. Tired of the mere rational, many individuals seem to be ready for a mystical approach to the Christ. More and more have had personal, precious moments of inner knowing that have prepared them for the touch of spirit, or in a time of prayer have felt the presence of the divine comfort them in some way. It is not easy to articulate such moments verbally, but as we experience increased inner awareness, the feminine principle becomes increasingly important. She is the inner guide and protectress known as the Holy Spirit, or Sophia.

Having consecrated ourselves to a dedicated level of grace, we long to draw higher consciousness into our day-to-day existence to advance our individual awareness and expand our group mind. An enlightened humanity will relate in new ways to one another and to the world of nature. By embracing Sophia, becoming wise in the ways of higher realities, we will be better able to walk in right relationship to the Great Life. We can only discover our larger life-role by developing the awareness needed to enable us to detect other realities.

Now we advance to find Mother Wisdom. Unfortunately, only now are we discovering that it is She who holds much inner awareness for which we have unknowingly waited. Fortunately, we need wait no longer.

She hastens to make herself known to those who desire her. . . To fix one's thoughts on her is perfect understanding. The Wisdom of Solomon 6.13,15.

Enjoy Sophia. My hope is to make her "user friendly." May each who seeks a way to perceive the current shift of consciousness find her. She who was here in the beginning has journeyed with us through the ages, keeping vigil without recognition until we gained sufficient experience. Now, she who has been hidden, even from women themselves, is emerging more openly, crying out for acceptance. She to whom relationship is important would have all humanity be in right relationship to the greater spheres of Life.

Long life is in her right hand: In her left hand are riches and honor; hers are ways of pleasantness and all her paths are peace. Proverbs 3.16-17.

1 Tasks

Although she is but one, she can do all things, and while remaining in herself, she renews all things; in every generation she passes into holy souls and makes them friends of God
—The Wisdom of Solomon 7.27

Light, awareness, insights, aha's, perception—all are words we use to denote a new measure of understanding we gain when some formerly unseen aspect of life is illumined. With great rapidity at this historical point, such new light is dawning in numerous human minds and changing lives. As it does, there stands the Guardian, like the statue of Justice, blindfolded but not blind, loving though unrecognized, protecting though unknown.

She, Wisdom, serves within each as a mentor of sensitivity, and functions around each as the unknown Mother, preserving information for which most are not yet ready. Sophia steadfastly waits for the whole of humanity to perceive her presence and grow to return her love. As the wisdom aspect of planetary consciousness, she serves as the *World Soul.*[1]

As the Renaissance began, the church shortened the name Holy Spirit of Wisdom, to simply the Holy Spirit, assigning her to one-third of a divine trinity, and Sophia's biblical name, Wisdom, was used to designate the inspired mother of secular learning and art. In Proverbs 9, Sophia sends out her handmaidens to invite everyone to a feast at her home, the

---

1. The Earth as an entity—Mother Earth, mother matter, Gaia—is seen as the personality: physical, emotional, and mental levels of density animated by the spiritual essence or soul of the planet. A level of knowing innate within creation is the consciousness called the soul of the world or Sophia.—Parrish-Harra, *Dictionary,* 322, 323.

Seven Pillars, which came to represent the seven liberal arts—grammar, logic, rhetoric, arithmetic, geometry, music, and astronomy—that formed the basis for Western education until the sixteenth century.

Sophia's nature was subdivided into smaller archetypes including the aforementioned Justice, the three Fates, the three Graces, and the nine Muses of Greek Mythology. Each of the muses, for example, is credited as creator and overseer of specific areas of knowledge and creativity. Together, these all represent Mother Wisdom, the great archetype of the feminine principle.

THE NINE MUSES

In Greek mythology, the daughters of Zeus and Mnemosyne (goddess of memory), are the embodiment of inspired creativity, representing the perfection of learning and action. The cultivation of the Muses within humanity holds the hope of understanding true peace, justice, and ecological harmony and recreates intellectual, spiritual, and social unity. Plato's school, the Academy, was dedicated to the Nine Muses, according to Thomas Daffern.[2] Many consider Wisdom, or Sophia, to be the mother of virtues, the Muses. [3]

Calliope	*Polyhymnia*	*Clio*
politics	religion	history
economics	philosophy	education
development	spirituality	scholarship
Terpsichore	*Erato*	*Thalia*
musicology	psychology	literature
dance	love	humanities
drama	sexology	language
Euterpe	*Urania*	*Melpomene*
art	natural sciences	conflict
architecture	ecology	justice
design	medicine	global security

---

2. Thomas Daffern, British historian, poet, and professor, teaches Virtues, Muses material.
3. Parrish-Harra, *Dictionary*, 186.

With the Reformation and the Age of Reason, the divine feminine was repressed even more. Theologians ruled there was no need to venerate the mother of Jesus because, unlike her son, she was only human. Now the feminine lost all her outer power. Diminished as well was all knowledge of the sacred interaction between Earth and the kingdoms of nature, including human nature. Wisdom became alienated from most of the daily life in the Western world. Masculine mysteries gained priority as feminine qualities were stripped of value. Sophia went underground.

Even though unseen, Wisdom dissolves the line of tension between love and law, justice and compassion, grace and karma and freedom and obligation. At the same time that Wisdom is transcending duality, she is also helping individual men and women, individual societies, and individual sub-groups within societies to recognize, appreciate, and celebrate their own and each other's unique qualities.

Just as the Apostle Paul pointed out in his letter to the Corinthians, it takes a full range of body parts to make a body (see reference) (1 Cor. 12.16–26). *"If the whole body were an eye, where would the hearing be?"* he asks. Wisdom honors each individuality for itself. It is through intimate communication with that Holy Sophia within, that each man and woman, and by extension the collectives to which they belong, can become a fully developed and functional, irreplaceable, part of the very being of God.

So when we speak of healing duality, we are speaking of dissolving the illusion of separation, not homogenization of all categories into a one-size-fits-all mechanized system. Healing of duality brings unity, yes, but it is a unity of *diversity*, seeking expansion into the fullness of human possibility.

> *Equality of opportunity for women has indeed to be fought for, but equality of value can never be understood until we have learned to discriminate and accept difference. The biological difference between man and woman is never a "nothing but"; it is a fundamental difference and it does not stop with the body but*

implies an equally fundamental difference of psychic nature. No matter how consciously we may develop the contrasexual principle within us, no matter how strong our intuition of the ultimate union between the masculine and feminine elements in each individual, yet as long as we remain in our bodies here in space and time, we are predominantly either male or female, and we forget this at our peril. Disaster awaits a woman who imitates man, but even a woman who aims at becoming half man, half woman, and imagines she is thereby achieving archetypal "androgyny" will certainly be inferior on both counts. A woman is born to be essentially and wholly a woman and the more deeply and consciously she is able to know and live the spirit, the Logos, within her, the more surely she will realize this truth. One of the most frightening characteristics of our present Zeitgeist [4] is the urge to destroy difference, to reduce everything to a horrible sameness in the cause of "equality." [5]

A word of caution: this passage should not be construed as a comment either for or against homosexuality. Such is not my intent at all. We in the United States are struggling with stereotypes of what it is that constitutes a woman, or a man. Many traditionalists are hampered with inaccurate information that equates sexual preference with gender in such a way that only heterosexual people are seen as genuine. Homosexual people are seen as wanting to be, or pretending to be, something they are not.

It is said by such traditionalists that homosexuality is a crime against nature. We must remember, it was not so long ago that the same thing was said about women and blacks having voting privileges—that it was unnatural. So we see that our understanding of ourselves as human beings evolves as our consciousness matures.

The truth is that none of us can be genuine until we awaken to the reality of our personal soul nature. When that happens, our questions of who and what we are begin to settle into our private intimate knowing.

---

4. The general intellectual, moral, and cultural climate of an era.

5. Helen M. Luke, "The Perennial Feminine," *Parabola*, Vol. V No. 4 (November 1980): 11

This is a knowing each individual can only do for himself or herself. It is a knowing that confirms each individual's sacred right to be. It is a knowing of unconditional love that delivers us from feeling we must pass judgment on ourselves or other people. In the soul we know we are loved exactly as we are, and so is everyone else. This is the truth that sets us free.

A significant moment has arrived for a portion of humanity (as individual personalities) to awaken to its own soul nature. Since humanity is truly one, we need to think of this as individual lights coming on in a sleeping collective soul of which we each are a part. In this challenging era, awakening to the transpersonal nature is but a first step. Just as puberty moves us naturally from one stage of life to another, the Self-within responds similarly to the touch of the soul. Collectives of formerly passive worshipers are now stretching and asking, "What is mine to do?"

They are beginning to hear Sophia as she whispers answers to long-incubating questions. Similarly, each of us who asks this question, and all who invite Wisdom to truly guide humanity forward, are remembering the cryptic, frightening words, *"you are gods."* Dare to perceive yourself more ready than you think. It has been pointed out we suffer not as much from a fear of failure as from a fear of greatness.

Become aware of your own sensitive nature and how it longs to express more readily. Be willing to treasure insights that stir as you read or as you listen to others. Impressions begin to perk upward into the conscious mind long before we truly become aware of them. Too often, we push them aside, believing the words and thoughts of another have greater value than our own, but they do not.

Sophia calls us to a higher appreciation of the wisdom that heals duality

Sophia, nudging from within, reveals deep truths, personalized and appropriate to individual situations and moments in time. This inner prompting may be sensed as an internal verbal nudge, or recognized as an urge to act or to change, or as an intuitive impulse to be more. Whatever way, its instruction helps us find our truth.

As sensing grows stronger, we become more confident, and as we act upon the touch, however we received it, it proves itself again and again. Inner inspiration gains our acceptance gradually. We find ourselves becoming more comfortable in acknowledging impressions received from within. As we grow bolder, we respond more readily.

Dichotomies are many in human life; we are pulled first this way, then that. Even as we long to embrace the inner impressions offered, we don't know just what to do. We question ourselves and the message. We discover the gentle touch just withdraws when we hesitate too long.

Inner knowing, the mark of her presence, seems subtle and fragile at first, but we come to discover Sophia has such power that when we are more experienced and she makes herself known, we recognize her verity and her strength. We become attuned to this new comforting vibration. We come to recognize her promptings and find ourselves saying, "I know it is right when it feels like this." We recognize the unique combination of feeling and knowing as it touches us.

Knowing we experience duality daily, the Mother principle mystifies, for her grace reconciles painful inequities. She knows how to resolve these divergent pulls. She may or may not share her solution—never in the beginning. She waits to be courted and causes us to ponder, examine, and digest, knowing as we become trusting enough, we will perceive in a more enlightened way. *It is that very Spirit bearing witness with our spirit that we are children of God* (Rom.8.16).

In these days of increased threat to survival, Sophia is the protective mother of all, fierce as any mother would be, safeguarding her charges. Krishna calls, *"Abandoning all concerns of law, come to me alone; I shall liberate you . . .do not worry"* (Bhagavad Gita 18.66). This great Hindu Lord is not speaking against the law of the Vedas (spiritual knowledge) but reveals a point beyond duality. This is the wholeness. Similarly, Jesus is not against the Torah when he says, *"Do not think that I have come to abolish the law or the prophets; I have come not to abolish but to fulfill"* (Matt. 5.17).

Like the musician who must first learn keys, notes, chords, and practice persistently before she is able to express beautiful artistry, each of us, through continued application of the insights we receive, will in time develop a secure foundation upon which we can joyfully participate in the adventure of Life. Creative play is her game!

Boundaries established at a given point in time by wise ones are not to bind subjects but to construct a foundation upon which to build. The fulfillment of such principles prepares followers for the next revelation. St. Paul said, *"If you are led by the Spirit, you are not subject to the law"* (Gal. 5.18). These words have frightened many who interpreted them as a license of release from healthy self-disciplines.

We are easily intimidated by the idea of no boundaries. Led by Spirit, we each learn trust and affirm higher discernment daily. Recall, Jesus was criticized for hanging out with those rejected by the law-abiding practitioners of his religion. He made friends of the unacceptable, reached out to the dregs of his society, violated purity laws, and encouraged behavior that offended temple priests. With his open heart he dared to love and comfort and thus establish a new way.

He made friends of the unacceptable

Yet, during the early centuries of the Christian movement, invaders from the rational "right side of the tracks" plundered Sophia's home, abducting her children who were told she was no more. Literalists, in their desire to be perfect, distorted the love message, and those who embraced rules more than love-wisdom relished the pseudo-authority, the "safety," of dogma and doctrine. But the Mother of All waited to once again make herself tangible at the moment when she would be most needed.

She anticipates recognition. Must she continue to bide her time, or can the secular worlds of academic scholarship, science, and humanitarianism and the world of spirituality formerly relegated to theologians begin now to acknowledge the expanded awareness that is to play such an important part in humanity's future? Can these vital areas of modern humanity become friends at last?

2

*E*nlightenment

The field of possibility is inner: psychological, spiritual, and neurological. Awareness, according to the Qabalah, is the action of light processing information inside the human brain. It is our eyes that respond to light and it is light—inner light—that fertilizes expansive awareness in us, ergo enlightenment.

—Glynda-Lee Hoffman

*E*nlightenment—as a divine possibility—requires conscious, self-directed action at our stage of spiritual development. Two time-honored techniques, perhaps humanity's oldest, are prayer (crying out to God, invoking, also known as "calling down the power"), and meditation (entering the stillness and becoming one with it). These evoke the personal experiential awareness of the indwelling aspect of the immortal Oneness that is necessary for enlightenment; the result is gnosis, "inner knowing."

Genesis is not about a first man and woman; it is about potentiality and possibility, the properties of light now being defined by quantum physics but which have existed all along, hidden from our collective awareness because our cultural mind has been too rigid to see them. The story begins with the creation of light on the first day and follows the pattern of evolution, culminating with human beings. Later, on the seventh day, after eating the famous fruit,

---

1. Glynda-Lee Hoffman, *The Secret Dowry of Eve: Woman's Role in the Development of Consciousness* (Rochester, VT: Park Street Press, 2003), 8.

> *Adam and Eve's eyes are opened. Does this not reveal a hidden relationship, associating light with insight, outer light with inner light?*
>
> *Quantum scientists have proved that light does not behave according to the old Newtonian laws of matter. Light is a substance with its own laws, and our perception of those laws changes the perception of reality that traditional science has been built upon. This is just as true for inner light. Indwelling light has all the possibility and potentiality that quantum analysis reveals.*
>
> *Insight, because it is dictated by the laws of light, is the fire of awareness. It is the same light referred to in John 1:5, "And the light shineth in the darkness and the darkness comprehended it not."* [2]

Humanity, made in the image and likeness of its creator, is building the consciousness bridge between spirit and matter. As we become increasingly aware of our role, we aspire to be both "fully human and fully divine."[3] It is when we achieve this "at-one-ment" with both our external humanity and our innate divinity that we attain the state of consciousness so often called enlightenment. Waiting impatiently for this maturation, the entire universe conspires to awaken the human race, to release us from limitation, to enlighten us. God, the Source, Creator—called by whatever name—does not dictate *how* we reach enlightenment, only that we do.

> *The sufferings of this present time are not worth comparing with the glory about to be revealed to us. For the creation waits with eager longing for the revealing of the children of God.* Romans 8.18,19.

The universe loves us whether or not we believe it. Humanity awakens to this realization one human being at a time. Those who would resolve the challenges humanity now faces must learn to live in harmony within and with one another, as well as with the planet and all life upon

---

2. Ibid.

3. "This expression [*perfectus Deus, perfectus homo*—fully divine, fully human] occurs in the late fifth-century Latin Creed *Quicumque,* . . . The formulation reflects the Greek "Formula of Union" drawn up by John of Antioch and agreed to by Cyril of Alexandria in 433 and sanctioned by Pope Sixtus III." —Michael Casey, *Fully Human Fully Divine: An Interactive Christology* (Liguori, MO: Liguori/Triumph, 2004), 1, 315.

it. Once awakened to our inner nature, we willingly acknowledge we are still in-the-making.

> *The candle of God is the soul of man.* Proverbs 20.27

God outside ourselves, called God Transcendent, is the more common way we have come to think of Creator. As the matriarchal ways of life were usurped by masculine initiatives during the early stages of the current era, God Transcendent was deemed unknowable except through his appointed emissaries; this became the acceptable theological model for vast numbers of religious leaders. The emphasis must now shift back to the divine within, God Immanent, for us to claim our divine nature, be empowered, and mature. As this is achieved, we will develop a desired balance of regard for both masculine and feminine forces and be capable of wholistic—holy—awareness.

A Jewish rabbi (teacher) whose name in English is Jesus, modeled the gnosis of God Immanent. It was an old gnosis before he was born, but his mission was to demonstrate the reality of it in our three dimensional material world. To do so, Jesus embodied God Immanent in such a way that he did indeed become both fully human and fully divine. He spiritualized his own matter by use of the lots of vital energy of Creator thus embodying the great principle of love. This is the same vital energy of creation described in the Pentateuch as "God said . . . and it was so." This vital word, or Logos, proclaimed the intent of the Creator. The power used to create, came to be called love.

The love of the divine washes through our lives

Like Wisdom, then, Love also existed before the world was formed, and indeed was the energy used to form it. This love principle, which is the basis of life itself, came to be called Christ Consciousness by Christians, and the man Jesus became known as Jesus Christ. This is why the Christ is most commonly thought of only as a person—the historical Jesus—rather than as an embodiment of the great principle of Love.

Understanding Christ as Logos—the Word—and Sophia as the Wisdom behind the Word, our goal becomes that of merging the two into Love-Wisdom. Sophia, if acknowledged at all, is often described as a Greek goddess, irrelevant to Christianity. Her identity in the Judeo-Christian heritage is veiled by translating references to her in the Bible as the abstract and lower case word "wisdom." Thus, during the patriarchal period now rapidly closing, she has been well hidden.

Purification leading to transformation is the purgatory of the Christian teachings. Techniques such as prayer, meditation, contemplation, fasting, tithing, and so on, are well-known as spiritual disciplines, or wisdom ways. Each practice makes a contribution to the changing inner nature. Every tradition develops ways that work for its particular time, place, and culture, and each practice bequeaths much to its practitioners. Prayer and meditation practices are common to all religious traditions due to the vital nature of their contribution to building relationships between the inner and outer aspects of realities—both personal and cosmic. Through such practices, the emotional and mental natures are scrubbed and stripped of old *karma*. [4] Now the clear rays we carry within our true nature are revealed, to shine their frequencies and do their work.

Repeatedly, spiritual teachings help us realize the "I" of the personality must diminish and the "I" of the soul must expand. Listening to inner prompting is but one practice useful in curbing egotism; self-study will reveal which other techniques will be helpful for coming to peace with our personality as we learn how best to refine it.

By expanding the spiritual part of our nature and learning to use our will wisely, we strengthen our sensitivity to soul impulses. Self-chosen boundaries placed upon the personality curb the ego's influence. In time, we kick over the traces, personality acquiesces to the *Soul*, [5] and Soul

---

4. *Karma* means "to act" literally, "action, deed, or work." The inevitable order of cause and effect that governs existence at all levels. . . may be positive or negative. . . requires adjustment and/or compensation for all pluses and minuses: individual, group, and planetary. —Parrish-Harra, *Dictionary*, 142.

5. In this book, Soul with a capital 'S' indicates conscious spiritual awareness and/or the divine feminine in her roles of World Soul and overseer of both Humanity's group soul and each individual's personal soul, while a lower case 's' denotes an unawakened spiritual self and/or the group and individuals' souls in a generic sense.

20

begins to increase her power. Choosing to align with the wee small voice's inner direction for at least one task daily establishes the process in our lives. With experience, we will find it easier to trust the inner and to develop an openness to the impressions we receive, inviting the subtle influence to contribute a greater share to our new lifestyle. Thus *She who dwells within* becomes increasingly active and valued in our daily life experience.

By observing our inner promptings we become attentive to both our shortcomings and the lessons we face. In time, experience helps us release our allegiance to the God of fear and the restrictions we were taught would keep us "safe." When we were a child, we thought as a child. Now it is time to embrace the God of love-wisdom, the Great Parent who loves us exactly as we are—less than perfect. Wise teachings say the Mother of the World loves all her children, not just the good ones. We come to know this is true as we continue to struggle toward goals we have not yet clarified.

In this process, we discover that our inner self, knowing no other way to grow, creates crises and lessons. As we connect increasingly with our spiritual sense of self, we choose more wisely. By holding still and learning to wait, we avoid many struggles, or we get impressions of how to respond, not just react. As we mature, we recognize the difference between just being obedient and the power of choice. The love of the divine washes through our lives, refreshing us for new expression. We come to better comprehend both the masculine and feminine principles of the divine and our relationship to each.

We soon find we need the strong voice of insight to guide us. Subtle but clear, wisdom heals the duality of our life. In time, we come to know her as authenticity, strength, and genuine power. Sophia is at work in each level of our being. Though we may have come this far by staying with the familiar, safe patterns we knew, now as we discover our intuitive guide, we know she will sustain us through the many changes that lie ahead.

Certain qualities and skills have been well-attributed to Sophia: gentle but strong, nurturing, providing, guiding, guarding, ever-present, and all-pervading. We can image her taking form as the equal-armed cross of the indigenous traditions. She faces each direction, ever watchful as she brings moonlight and rest to those who strive. She restores with spring-time rains and summer blossoms. In the fall of our lives we see the fruit of her bounty. Then, as she walks more openly with us, we become her emissaries. Her spider-web inclusiveness supports us as we discover we are a part of the web of life.

Sophia breaks into our consciousness with helpful hints as we strive to meet the challenges of our day to day life. Becoming more conscious of inner prompting, we begin to look to her, Wisdom, to reveal direction as we seek. Respecting her direction provides the undergirding we need to ask whether old rigid reactions are appropriate, so that we can destroy crystallizations that imprison us. She connects the scholarly and the exotic, the light and the dark, without apology. Her impulses continually energize our potential. She is the guardian of the Self-within, the Mother, watching, ever vigilant.

She is revealed, distorted or pure, through all of us—not lawmaker but an indwelling sense of knowing—who meanders with her children in their wanderings. We call her "creativity" "intuition," "impulses," "hunches," "gut feelings," or "inner knowing." She lives within us and expresses through us. As divine discontent makes itself felt, a need to grasp the mystery of life becomes increasingly conscious. We begin to invite Sophia; to invoke her presence, beg her wisdom and seek her touch.

> *I went about seeking how to get her for myself. But I perceived that I would not possess wisdom unless God gave her to me—and it was a mark of insight to know whose gift she was—so I appealed to the Lord and implored him, and with my whole heart I said: . . .O God of my ancestors and Lord of mercy, who have made all things by your word, and by your wisdom have formed humankind . . .give me the wisdom that sits by your throne.* Wisdom of Solomon 8.18–9.4.

Theotokos, the God Bearer, entitled "Our Lady of the Sign"
by Sister Joan Tuberty, decoupaged by James H. Tuberty
gifted to C. Parrish by St. Clare's Monastery, Minneapolis, MN

A Time to Pause

In the 15th Century, Joachim of Flora prophesied there would be in the future a new era that would be the age of the Holy Spirit. This is the age of Sophia, in which she declares,

"I unite all things."

Sophia, the Theotokos—the God-bearer—is the inner mother we have all seen in icons with the divine Christ on her heart. The incarnating Self-Within welcomes rebirth to a new comprehension of both our inner nature and our outer world—we are born of Spirit, even as we have been born of matter. This maturing Self welcomes the Mother.

~Now please close your eyes....take a relaxing breath....turn your attention inward......After speaking each invocation, pause for a moment, then sound the OM

✳ Oh Sophia, Mother of All, grant our hearts be filled with love, compassion, and peace, no matter the circumstances of our lives.

OM...

✳ Oh Sophia, the Wise, grant to us ever wider eyes with which to see the true power and beauty of your world—our world. Let harmony and wholeness be established within all kingdoms.

OM...

✳ Oh Sophia, Mother Wisdom, grant the love-wisdom we embody to bring forth the Holy Self-Within, the Hope of Glory, that it might express well the gifts and talents with which we are endowed.

OM...

~Now, sit quietly for a few minutes, just allowing yourself to absorb the energy you have invoked....Enjoy it....Feel the presence of the Sacred embracing you, flowing all around you, bringing new vitality into your life.

~We rejoice in our physical nature, appreciating this time to pause and remember right relationship with the planet and all life upon it.

~Bask in a sense of joy and delight for all that comes to you through your endeavors.

~Feel a smile forming on your face. You are glad to be here in this peaceful inner place—glad there are coworkers to journey with you in the world of Gaia.

~Now....with heart aglow....as you are ready....bring your attention back to your role as a World Server. Let there be peace. Gently refocus on the outer world enriched from within.

~With our closing prayer, we shall conclude this intimate time in the company of the Divine Feminine:

> Absolute, Creative Source,
> your breath fills all eternity.
> I add my voice to the chant
> of your many names that
> echoes through the ages.
> Clothed in the pattern of your design,
> I am suited to the task,
> which is the reflection of your higher plan.
> As it is above, so it is below. Amen.

❈ And so it is.

<hr>

Sophia

Woman must affirm herself, and that is why the Sword of Spirit is given precisely into the hands of woman.[1]

—Helena Roerich

Long ago, certain Greek terms found acceptance in Christian usage, but her name, Sophia, too powerful to be uttered, was denied: Translated as wisdom, she continued her watch. She is life-giving; she travels with the *divine spark*,[2] creates veils of flesh to wear while experiencing this world of form, and then she dwells within, watching as companion, teacher, healer, guide, advocate, mother, and friend.

A large part of the human family is now awakening, questioning, and demanding to know the depth of its inner nature. A new consciousness is emerging—not so much intellectually, but spiritually—seeking to "know" our origins in a new way. We ask, "Where is she who gives birth; she who responds when we cry out?" "Where is she who is companion to the divine masculine known so thoroughly as Father, Lawgiver, the Great Will?" We seek her counsel. Rediscovering the divine feminine is the way to acknowledge and fulfill both the basic needs of our human nature and the innate drive to reach our highest potential. It is in her archetypal spiritual womb that we develop from the primal human seed, becoming fully

---

1. Helena Roerich, *Letters of Helena Roerich*, Vol.I (NY, NY: Agni Yoga Society, 1958) 409.

2. *Divine spark,* also known as the Monad, the spark of Divinity invested in the constitution of human beings. This true Self, a breath of the Absolute, is in no way influenced by conditional, finite personality. The immortal and eternal principle within us, an indivisible part of the integral whole. —Parrish-Harra, "Monad," *Dictionary,* 179,180.

human in order to "complete the self," or to achieve self-actualization as understood by humanistic psychologist, Abraham Maslow.[3]

Sophia challenges God's people to rise above juvenile foolishness

Her faces/facets are many. In the human, she abides as the psyche within the sensory mechanisms of the physical, emotional, and mental levels of each person. These planes are under constant reconstruction as awakened ones upgrade and purify themselves. The wisdom of the psyche is the Great Mother's envoy; as is the Soul who watches over the evolution of her child, the inner self. Sophia, the wisdom hidden within Mother Matter, the innate intelligence woven into DNA, is mate to the Father Spirit, animator of creation. Though "she calls loudly to us," according to Proverbs, Wisdom's cry has long been unheeded. Now the divine feminine once again heralds her presence, commanding attention. She—God Immanent—undergirds the developing inner nature, tending humanity so that She, Wisdom, may be partnered once more to God Transcendent, the lots of vital energy of Creator.

It is not that we need to think of Sophia as a person, but we need to think of Wisdom as the fulfilled enlightened nature. Personified as feminine, Sophia walks with us wherever we are on our journey. Her ways are inclusive and concerned with both individuals and the collective. From Proverbs we learn she is both wise and protective of her charges.

Although to many modern theologians the existence of a "Heavenly Mother" comes as something of a surprise, religious historians are discovering that belief in her activity dates from pre-literate times.

> *[In Scotland] are to be found curious ancient sites of religious worship known by the gaelic name of Annat or Annait which translates as the Mother Church. . .*
>
> *On this matter, an 18th century antiquary, Jacob Bryant, provides the following information in his magnum opus,* A New System, or an Analysis of Ancient Mythology: *"Many places were styled An-*

---

3. Abraham Maslow (1908-1970) humanist psychologist who postulated that the higher needs that appear to arise in the human being after basic survival needs are met are the result of an inner pressure toward a fuller expression of being, self-actualization, in the same natural and predestined sense that an acorn may press toward becoming an oak tree. —Parrish-Harra, *Dictionary,* 168.

nait…Some of these were so-called from their situation; others from the worship there established. The Egyptians had many subordinate deities, which they esteemed so many emanations from their chief God…These derivatives they called fountains, and supposed them to be derived from the Sun; whom they looked upon as the source of all things. Hence they formed Ath-El and Ath-Ain, the Athela and Athena of the Greeks. These were two titles appropriated to the same personage, Divine Wisdom…As Divine Wisdom was sometimes expressed Ath-Ain, so, at other times, the terms were reversed, and the Deity constituted called An-Ait. Temples to this goddess occur at Ecbatana in Media; also in Mesopotamia, Persis, Armenia, and Cappadocia; where the rites of fire were particularly observed. She was not unknown among the ancient Canaanites; for a temple called Beth-Anath is mentioned in the book of Joshua."

This is supported by Edward Kenealy in The Book of God: the Apocalypse of Adam—Oannes *(c1870) who comments on ".…the radical Ain, a pure Virgin, a Fountain; a name also for the Holy Spirit. Thus Aenon near the fords of Jordan, meant Fountain of the Sun: hence John baptized in it, or immersed in the Holy Spirit which was the Fountain or feminine counterpart of the Sun, namely the Moon, John iii.23. Ath-Ain became Athena or God's Fountain. At other times the name was reversed, and became An-Ait; a goddess worshipped throughout Asia: and by the Hebrew tribe of Naphthali, Josh. xix.38, at Beth Anath, or the House of An-Ait. From this place they had their name Beth Ani." Interestingly, in the Gospel texts, Mary Magdalene is identified as "Mary of Bethany".* [4]

Ancient societies always used feminine figures—Ma'at in Egypt and Athena in Greece—for knowledge-based work. Men were honored for their physical prowess, women for birthing the new. In Israel monotheism was well established by the time Wisdom or Sophia appeared in Proverbs (possibly as early as 6 century BCE). She was not presented as a goddess but served the purpose of aligning the God of Israel with Shekinah, the guardian of the community—she who traveled with them.

---

4. Barry Dunford, *Barry Dunford's E-Zine*, "The Mystery of the Mother Church," http://www.sacredconnection.ndo.co.uk/holyland/motherchurch.htm.

Wisdom/Sophia, acting as an agent of the divine, challenges God's people to rise above juvenile foolishness. Called "a breath of the power of God," Sophia is the Wisdom that serves as the transcendent agent for those who would embrace transformation. The path to adulthood is walked by discernment; discernment requires Sophia.

As Sophia tutors humanity in wisdom, she is able to adapt her mode of instruction to each pupil's style of learning. On all levels—physical, emotional, mental, and spiritual—learning styles arise from the various ways we see, or perceive, our world. Four of these are, 1) Sensorial—with our physical senses we see the dense world; 2) Temporal/psychological—we see a sequential unfolding of events with a beginning, middle, and end, and recognize how we contribute to or change some part of what is beheld; 3) Symbolical—we recognize symbols and impute symbolic meanings for greater understanding; and 4) Integral—in an intuitive flash or aha, we experience understanding of an idea or event as a whole.

If one wishes to acquire wisdom, one must be humble

The term "sophistication" in the sense of "wise beyond most," has been associated with Sophia from earliest times. It acknowledges those who are able to perceive and recognize the relationship between two seemingly disparate events, "this" and "that." True sophistication is humble and gentle. H. P. Blavatsky wrote that if one wishes to acquire wisdom, one must be humble—and will be even more humble when she or he has mastered wisdom. Current distortion of the term "sophistication" has come to designate a facade one creates behind which to hide the true nature. This feigned cleverness too often becomes a kind of arrogance, a pretense, seemingly admired and measured according to cultural status and false values.

It seems offensive to say we are ignorant when outwardly it seems we are at a peak period in human expansion. Yet to the yogis, the mystics, the saints who know God in a real and fulfilling way, we are ignorant, ill, at war, suffering from isolation and separation, unable to create a world of

---

4. H.P. Blavatsky, best know for "The Secret Doctrine Vols. I, II, Pasadena, CA: Theosophical University Press, 1970.

hope and joy for all people. We must re-think many areas of human endeavor.

As Sophia brings new knowledge forth, she often does so through wise ones who become de facto founders of traditions. As the first to receive new insights, they cast a kind of "light" into the darkness in which they find themselves. Thus each wisdom tradition develops its body of information to pass on to those who prove themselves worthy.

Specific techniques temper personalities and try the spirits of those who present themselves for training. These disciples in turn become initiates who add their wisdom to that of their collective to be passed on to future generations. And so Sophia tirelessly refines human consciousness as we pursue our adventure-filled journey back to her house, our true home.

4

Creation

*F*rom Christianity's Hebrew roots we access the mystery tradition called *Kabalah*, meaning "to receive." Here we learn the Creator's nature, with both masculine and feminine principles, is reflected throughout Creation. Each point of consciousness has the capacity to express actively (masculine) or to become receptive (feminine) to other influences.

As Christianity was developing, many of the writings that did not fit the ideas of the more powerful shapers of the new religion were left out of the Bible. Some of the wisdom tradition was included and some was not. If sought, much of it can be found hidden yet, in the traditional Bible and in the Apocrypha. Biblical books such as Proverbs, Job, Ecclesiastes, and Song of Solomon, as well as apocryphal books such as Song of Wisdom, and Sirach, preserve precious references to Sophia disguised as Wisdom. Whenever you read the word "Wisdom" (notice it is capitalized), say to yourself, "Sophia." She remains with us even if veiled.

We must remember, many church founders sought scriptures to substantiate their point of view. Others intentionally designed dogma to create the foundation of a powerful new institution. This comment is not made to be judgmental, but to place into context the historical struggle of those who sought to preserve wisdom as a foundation was laid, with good intentions, for the institution that became "the Church."

Mystery teachings existed from numerous schools of thought: Hebrew, Greek, Roman, as well as Eastern. As it is generally believed

Master Jesus came from such a tradition, much of that wisdom was readily accepted in the early years, only later coming to be called "apocrypha," from the Greek *apokryphos,* "obscure," and *apokryptein,* "to hide away." By AD 1100, these manuscripts began to be placed between the Old and New Testaments. As Gnostic writing (dismissed by many during the first five hundred years) is rediscovered—particularly the Nag Hammadi scrolls found in 1945—we catch a glimpse of the many traditions that contributed to the wisdom teachings then available. Additional discoveries add to our awareness. The writings of Elaine Pagels, a researcher who has translated a great deal of such material, help us realize the distortions that politicized the teachings of the early church.[1] All of these scrolls add insights to early respected and preserved teachings. Now once again, we are particularly interested in Wisdom's words.

Each religion preserves its mystical legacy for those who would penetrate to its depths. These traditions diagram worlds of energy, pathways, planes, and dimensions. Each provides a map to guide those of like persuasion toward greater realizations. The collected wisdom regarding these subtle dimensions provides symbols and impressions, transmissions and guidance for those who can connect with them.

Kabalah—the mystical, or inner, teachings of the Judaic legacy—is often called the foundation of Western wisdom. In its symbology it pictures the microcosm and the macrocosm and maps the way for the soul to return to its source. This mystical awareness, when later adapted to Christian teachings, became known as Christian Kabalah. It is widely accepted that Master Jesus was well versed in this mystical philosophy in which the Divine Feminine is acknowledged as Shekinah, *She who dwells within* (Holy Soul). This feminine nature, also sometimes called Holy Breath, is anchored deep within each of us as the human soul.

> *Many of the basic ideas and principles found in the Kabbalah are also found in Gnosticism because both were in the Eastern Mediterranean near the time of Christ. Both attach an importance to knowledge, called the 'gnosis' or the knowledge of God. This knowledge*

---

1. Consult the bibliography for a list of Elaine Pagels' books.

does not come from rational thinking but is inspired by God. As in Gnosticism, sin is not considered to be wrong doing but ignorance which separates humankind from God. The knowledge, specifically the 'gnosis', unites humankind to God—to know God is to be God. Those sharing this 'gnosis' are the elect; they are the enlightened ones who share the knowledge of God, although they may not lead perfect lives." [2]

Just as kabalists use a diagram (a map) called The Tree of Life to symbolize their conception of the way energy travels through vibrational levels, other indigenous people also often use a symbolic tree to represent life. Commonly, such a tree is depicted upside down with roots in the higher world.

Each human being is a leaf in the holy design. Roots planted in the higher world draw from the wellspring of life; the trunk is the body of universal laws through which all life is structured; the branches are the cultures or religions, with each having its own subset of "do's and don'ts" that impart the laws of life to the leaves on that branch. The Buddha was said to have stated, *"I have been shown the leaves of an entire forest, but I have only been able to convey to you the leaves of one tree."*

The Hebrew Tree of Life depicts similar concepts. Over the years, due to its aptness, the symbolism of this kabalistic Tree has become an increasingly meaningful map to other traditions as well, helping to clarify the path.

---

2. Alan G. Hefner, "Kabbalah" from *The Kabbalah: Early Cosmogonic Speculation,* [Internet], Eduseek, http://www.mystae.com/restricted/streams/scripts/kabbalah.html (accessed 7/7/05).

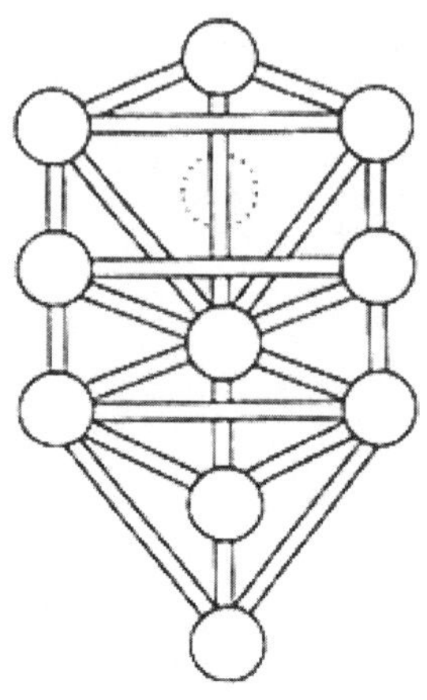

**The Tree of the Knowledge
of Good and Evil**

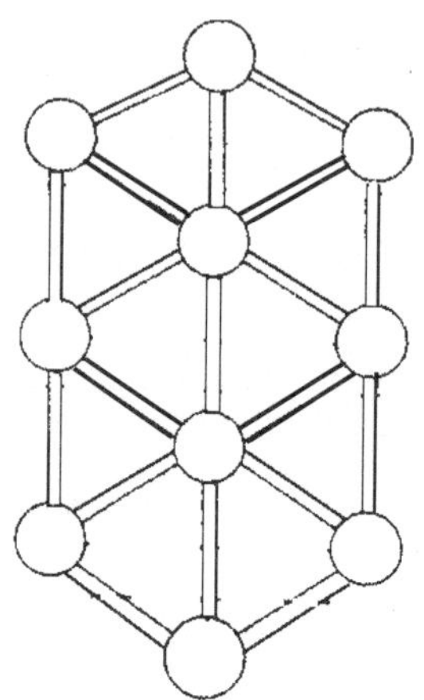

**The Tree of Life
The "perfected" tree**

She [wisdom] *is a tree of life to those who lay hold of her.*
—Proverbs 3.18

This model can be used to fit many pieces of the puzzle of life together. Mystic paths of all the world religions embody similar aspects. In any map of consciousness we find change or shifting points, whirlpools of blessings, and paths with both rewards and challenges. We encounter duality on our journey no matter which belief system we follow. For example, Chokmah (Wisdom) on the Tree of Life in the illustration expresses in a masculine way as *Abba*, (Father), but kabalists also speak of Chokmah as feminine, and the Bible personifies Wisdom as woman. The Greater Chokmah, the active potency, contains within itself the powers of the mother.[3]

Sophia was known by her Hebrew name, *Achamoth*, (Mother) from the earliest history, and was the feminine aspect of the Divine that softened and rebalanced the divine masculine. It was through this approachable feminine aspect that God Transcendent could safely interact within and among the faithful as Shekinah, *She who dwells within.* This

---

3. John Nash, "The Shekinah in Esoteric Judaism," 3.

realization of the divine feminine as not only the Heavenly Mother, but also as God Immanent, acknowledged woman as an important power (one might say, the chief executive officer) in running the household. There she continues to reflect the echoing voice of hidden wisdom.

One of the few books to be found on the market about the history of kabalistic women is *The Receiving* by Rabbi Tirzah Firestone. New and inspiring, it offers a depth of insight into a regard for the feminine not readily visible to outsiders, and builds new appreciation for Jewish wisdom ways.

> *But the rabbis of Safed did not consider divination to be witchery. They understood that consulting one's inner authority is nowhere prohibited by Jewish laws. Most important, the rabbis, unlike their Christian counterparts, were not at all threatened by the women's wisdom or the means by which they accessed it. In fact, they revered it and sought it out.*
>
> *Around the world, persecution of women has been men's way of denouncing woman's natural attunement with the non-rational dimensions of reality. Greatly feared because such information has the potential to threaten male authority, such feminine skills were, in fact, most often used by women for the purpose of healing body and spirit. But all people have access to the timeless dimensions of their souls, in which healing and wisdom are harbored. If desired, these skills can be developed by anyone, female or male.[4]*

The Tree of Life is a symbolic ladder for humanity to ascend in order to reconnect with its source. Whether we use the symbols of our own faith or the mystical map of another venerable tradition as a guide, we have more assistance than if we use none. Ultimately, any approach assigns particular attributes to be developed. The kabalistic sephiroth can be applied to human consciousness in a similar fashion as the concept of energy centers called chakras.

Christian Kabalah teaches its practitioners to develop the sephirath of the midsection, Tiphareth [Spiritual Beauty], heart of the kabalistic Tree

---

4. Tirzah Firestone, *The Receiving* (San Francisco: Harper, 2002), 218.

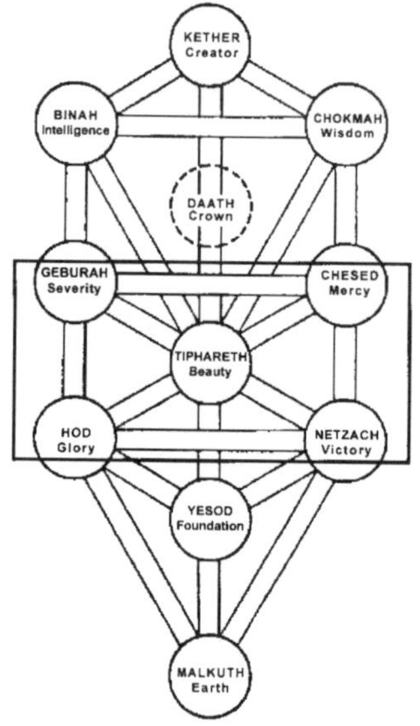

(corresponding to the heart chakra). This information could serve better if all Christians were grounded in foundational concepts of a mystery tradition; they would have a clearer grasp of the significance of things earthly than many presently do. Christians gain deeper insight into their own faith as they are exposed to Kabalah. Early disciples retained as a foundation the richness of their Judaic heritage. Rather than distorting the value of things material or natural, as is so often done today (i.e., sexuality, respect for body, attitude toward money, etc.), Christians still need to build upon this previous foundation.

As outsiders, when we look at the Jewish tradition, we tend to see its rigid, masculine priorities; however, hidden within its folds we can also find remnants of the powerful feminine that preceded it. Christianity has been called the heresy of Judaism; let's think of it as a turn of the spiral building upon wisdom already in place—topped off with new clarification about the journey.

What is now called the Christian religion has existed among the ancients and was never absent from the beginning of the human race until Christ came in the flesh. From that time on the true religion which was already in existence began to be called Christianity.[5]

A typical understanding of the kabalistic Tree of Knowledge of Good and Evil is that we are to bring heart (right column) and mind (left column) into right relationship on the central column.—"*For as he thinketh in his heart, so is he*" (Prov. 23.7 KING JAMES VERSION). On the right side of the Tree we find Netzach, "victory," (an energy center that brings warmth, inspiration and intuition, the impulse and drive of life, the

---

5. St. Augustine, attributed.

feminine principle), and on the left, we find Hod, "glory or splendor of the mind," (practical knowing, the creator of mental frames, boundaries, and limits, the masculine principle). We reconcile the duality of the world with the compassion gained as we learn to think with the heart and love with the mind.

The Tree of Knowledge of Good and Evil presents a dichotomy when compared to the Corrected Tree (another name for the kabalistic Tree of Life) of the advancing ones. The reconciliation of paradox through love when the opposites meet in the center, reveals that each becomes one with the other, creating seven centers in a direct line quite like the seven chakras of the East. The analogy of mystical marriage is used for this event. Sophia (Wisdom) delivers the higher intent, thus healing dichotomies in her own way.

5

Sophianic

It is quite easy to see those things that are opposite, quite a task to know those things that are similar, and almost impossible to understand things as they are.

—Carol E. Parrish

*E*soteric Christianity (from Greek *eso*, "within") is the most common term used today for lesser known mystical aspects of the faith. Likewise translated as "hidden," "inner," or "deep," it is that which lies concealed from view until a new depth of understanding is attained. Less well-known by the name *Sophianic,*[1] its tradition is to Christianity as Kabalah is to the Hebrew, or Sufism to Islam. We often hear these mystical teachings referenced as "The Ageless Wisdom," "the wisdom way," or "the way of the sage."

The knowledge that liberates is called "esoteric" to indicate we must go further, or deeper, if we wish to understand. This gnosis is not just information or knowledge but a field of consciousness which surpasses ordinary reason and confers spiritual liberation.

Early Christianity, as well as Hinduism, Buddhism, and others, have in common the understanding that liberation can only be gained through inner knowing. Here exists a body of perceivable knowledge based on the faith but also designed to fulfill it.

---

1. *Sophianic consciousness* was a term used by Pagan Gnostics. It referred to nature awakening to the wisdom of God. As Christianity developed, it became a Christ-centered gnosis, or knowing.

For example: all Christians are aware that Master Jesus taught love fulfills the law, but not all do the work necessary to develop impersonal, unconditional love in order to earn freedom from the law (of karma) so that they may be set free, liberated, or able to live in a healing or holistic manner.

Sophia, Wisdom, prompts humanity to become enlightened. Enlightenment, she proposes, is a higher state of consciousness, a way out of the dichotomies and paradoxes of duality. The push to ascend from human suffering and sorrow leads to new comprehension of life itself. As we broaden our perception, we recognize possible responses and means of applying them: responses that demonstrate compassion and divine sensitivity.

This mastery of human trials is known in traditional Christianity as "salvation," meaning "to heal, to make sacred." It is from the Latin *salvus*, meaning "safe," and is related to Latin *solidus*, "solid"; Greek *holos*, "whole, safe"; and Sanskrit *sarva*, "entire." We would be reminded that too often *exoteric* (outer) Christianity focuses on salvation in the afterlife, not transformation.

Jesus, the Christ, taught us how to assist ourselves—how to release ourselves from sins and fear of damnation—to heal our lives and make them sacred. Esoteric Christianity likewise accepts there is an afterlife, but has less emphasis on salvation in the future and more immediate desire for liberation, enlightenment, and/or a sense of a relationship to the Ultimate here and now.

When it is understood that accepting Christ means to embrace love as healing, we begin to bridge the separation between spirit and matter, or personality and soul. In other words, the love transmitted by Christ and the wisdom of Sophia create the awareness needed for the lesser nature to be made sacred, to be reunited with the divine. Thus, love-wisdom is a particular state of consciousness we each seek in order to become whole—holy. Salvation thus equates to enlightenment—we can now see the way.

Often identified as feminine intuition, Sophia is an awareness—an inner certainty that comes from the unknown—a touch faintly perceived. Centered in Holy Consciousness, she represents the inner urge that continuously steers humanity toward the holy. In her densest form she is psyche whose warnings from deep within struggle to emerge through layers of mental and emotional debris. Even though impulses from the highest constantly surround us, they most often evoke little response until old wounds and programming begin to dissipate.

As greater clarity is achieved and techniques are mastered, we learn we can make contact with the *Cloud of Knowable Things* [2] in the higher reality (also called divine mind). For some, the connection is like a spark that flashes, while the mind reaching upward rejoices in the point of fire it encounters for. For others this union with agape love—heavenly love arcing toward the beloved within matter—is experienced as an indescribable sensation of peace, centeredness, or unity with all that is.

No matter how the connection registers, it is most often a momentary flash, but timeless in effect. As wisdom ignites, the receiver is blessed with an infusion of wholeness. It can come as a whisper or as an aha. We could say Wisdom overshadows, as her directive races through her subject. The recipient can say, as did Apostle Paul, "*I did not receive it from a human source, nor was I taught it, but I received it through a revelation*" (Gal. 1.12). The "revelation" is a droplet from the Cloud of Knowable Things that is impressed on the mental unit.

Love itself is the evolutionary force

As we strive for a richer relationship with God, we naturally begin with simple steps which then lead us onward, assisting us to embrace higher and higher realms of thought. Wherever we begin, in our desire to become as God-like as possible, we imagine what the wise and holy would do. We then attempt to shape appropriate behavior according to our grasp of the situation and our level of developed consciousness; we aspire to evolve our heart and mind. Our inner nature rejoices as we share this love with another. Christ, defined as love, moves through our nature,

---

2. "The vast storehouse of knowledge into which flows the mind, love, and will of God from which the aspirant can receive inspiration through the awakening perceptions of high consciousness, thus finding that which is needed for the ongoing pattern or evolution." —Parrish-Harra, *Dictionary*, 54.

transforming us, acting upon us in such a manner as to prepare us for an even greater divine flow.

Heart stimulating events vibrate with a richness of *knowing* and *feeling*. Intuitive awareness flows toward this perpetually evolving center within the wise heart's domain. Saturated with love-wisdom, our sense of identity is immersed in a transcendent wholeness. While it cannot permanently remain there, once felt, the bliss of this encounter entices us to seek that contact again and again.

The first contact with unitive consciousness may not last long, but a new point is now identified toward which we yearn. Having once registered, a movement begins toward this reference. Gradually we discover how to touch into it time after time, until it becomes familiar.

We peer through the veil of *self* (the personality) when seeking to see the real *Self*,[3] the soul. It soon begins to dawn on us that our personality is not the "owner" but rather the child of our soul. This new manner of perception allows a heart-based focus to develop through which to view experience in the light of the soul. The mechanism is then in place for lessons to be learned and understanding to accrue.

Sophia—the inner knower—is the keeper of the mystical process that allows us to see the soul of the other. *"All encompassing heart consciousness possesses wisdom beyond that of the brain whose most developed function in the western world is to quantify, analyze, and judge bits of information rather than visualize the whole."*[4] For this wisdom of the heart, this divine wisdom, to be realized, one must discern the truth that is being offered from within.

In due time, sooner than most realize, the new Christianity will emerge. This Sophianic Christianity of the inner world will be formed by a balance of masculine and feminine principles of the divine. The feminine principle, now emerging within many, is awakening humanity to a turning point in spiritual evolution. What appears now to be openly alive

---

3. Self written with a capital 'S' denotes the divine or higher Self. Written with a lower-case 's', designates the personality. —Parrish-Harra, *Dictionary*, 256.

4. Carol E. Beyer, "Soul-Centered Therapy" (Ph.D. dissertation, Sancta Sophia Seminary, 2004), 28–29, from Sara Paddison, *The Hidden Power of the Heart: Achieving Balance and Fulfillment in a Stressful World* (Boulder Creek, CA: Planetary Publications, 1993), 247–252.

within some, is stirring deep within the many. The world soul itself is awakening. Thus Sophia signifies the beginning of the transformation and spiritualization of the whole Earth.

Christianity need only see Jesus as both Christ and Sophia to shift from being masculine dominated to a more inclusive theological stance. As the Master of the Way, Jesus, in becoming Christ, became Sophia as well.

> *He fed the physically hungry, taught the spiritually hungry, healed the sick, and refused to condemn the social outcasts*

*The presence of both **son** and **wisdom** Christologies in the early movement [of Christianity] affects the popular image of Jesus, the Jesus we have met before. Their presence points to gender complimentarity in thinking about Jesus, which is quite new to many people. Beyond that, they also move Christological thinking out of the literalistic framework that most often accompanies the popular image. The multiplicity of early Christological images—"son" and "wisdom" and others—leads to the recognition that this language is metaphorical. . . . . The issue is no longer believing that Jesus was literally the Son of God, but appreciating the richness of meaning suggested by the multiplicity of Christological images. He was "the Son," yes, but also the incarnation of the Word, which was also the Wisdom of God. He was the Son of God, the logos of God, and the Sophia of God.[5]*

On the cross Master Jesus met the tests of both the Godman and the Godwoman. As the Christ, he passed the tests of the masculine principle: love so great he gave his life for his message to his people. He had found the "Way" and was determined to open it to others. He fulfilled the tests of courage, daring, capability, and leadership for the masculine path, but he also became Sophia. As he beheld suffering, he demonstrated qualities of the divine feminine—compassion, universality, inclusiveness, global consciousness. He fed the physically hungry, taught the spiritually

5. Marcus Borg, *Meeting Jesus Again for the First Time* (San Francisco: Harper, 1994), 110.

hungry, healed the sick, and refused to condemn the social outcasts. He drew the little children to himself, and helped those who came to him in need. As he taught, he emphasized attitudes and principles arising from wisely applied love, not rigid, inflexible laws. He pointed out that what was important was not the outer form but the intent behind it.

From the cross he continued to exercise compassion and demonstrate service as he instructed his mother and his disciple John to care for each other. He modeled forgiveness by saying to the thief, *"This day you shall be with me in paradise,"* and by praying to God for those who were killing him saying, *"Father, forgive them. They know not what they do."*

Thus, both great courage and great sensitivity were demonstrated and witnessed. Jesus as the role model anchored both godly principles—Christ Sophia—for the heart-centered path he came to open for all humanity.

6

Mystic

All that is made bears Sophia's likeness. . .so recognizing the features of Wisdom is the name of the game.[1]

—Caitlín Matthews

As we attempt to describe the divine feminine, we must give up trying to rationally define her and shift to a kind of respectful "talking around" the meaning of Sophia. She is a mystery more easily sensed than defined, defying analytical study. She would rather tease us with a touch of insight or with a nuance of feeling than provide a rational picture. She beckons through many veils.

Metaphors are her cloak. She speaks in poems, music, art, and story; she is represented by the muses. Her media are myriad, allowing us to catch the parts we can as we learn to sense her touch and ponder hidden meanings.

Words, tending to be tools of the rational, can mask Sophia. Her truth, veiled but sensed, awaits further contact. Here she abides in the shifting light and shadows knowing both glory and disgrace. She is often "the trickster," or veiled in a dream, needing subtle perception to decipher her meaning.

OnewaytoperceivethevalueofSophiaistotrytoreadanentiresentence withoutspacesbetweenwordslikethisone. One way to perceive the value of Sophia is to try to read an entire sentence without spaces between the words. We learn that we gather meaning as we read. Spaces expedite our thought, enabling easier comprehension of the message. Spaces have

---

1. Caitlín Matthews, "Sophia, Goddess of Wisdom," Gnosis Magazine No.13 (Fall 1989): 23.

value: promoting discernment, providing relief, and allowing time to shift and integrate. The feminine in our lives provides similar benefits. We could say Sophia is the thought between thoughts.

The way of Sophia is the way of the mystic. Here one nurtures the awakening inner presence with the rich food of prayer and meditation, developing intuition, perception, and endurance for a way of life that honors the divine within. Thus personality is prepared for soul-infusion as soul increasingly becomes the director of one's life. Persistent prayer and meditation build the vessel into which soul then pours itself—the chalice or Holy Grail so longed for. All life gradually converts toward realizing soul purpose.

Many teachings initially labeled heresy were eventually accepted

It is important we recognize how frequently all of this occurs outside formal religious practice. We may begin there, but as we begin to think outside the box, we often leave our earlier outlook to search for richer food. Mystics have a way of being cast out of earlier company as they outgrow specific dogma or doctrines. Profound experiences challenge our ability to find words with which to share this developing new understanding. Often such persons describe themselves as "spiritual but not religious."

Concepts unacceptable to ruling religious authorities become labeled as heresy. Such labels are uncomfortable. To avoid them, we hesitate to consider "heretical" ideas. Individuals defined as heretics (in truth, meaning "able to choose") are those who see a different way.

As the early church developed, it soon found itself dividing into "literal" and "liberal" branches. Gnosticism—non-conventional wisdom—was understood and accepted (or not) by each adherent through listening to his or her individual inner guidance. The more structured doctrinaire style, having a hierarchy of authority, became known as Orthodox (*ortho* means "straight"). The early orthodox followed a more Middle Eastern style, adapting to the people's culture. Even today, we continue to see Greek, Russian, and Albanian Orthodox churches. In each, a national church adapted Christianity to the language and culture of local people.

As time passed, a more "literal-minded" part of the church arose, wanting strict uniformity of belief and behavior. This branch eventually became what we know today as the Roman Catholic. Two major branches of Christianity then existed until Martin Luther and other "reformers" came into being, ultimately giving rise to numerous non-orthodox, non-catholic branches.

Although each branch originally diverged from the mainstream due to an individual leader's personal revelation, each in turn developed its own system of doctrine with little tolerance for differing ideas among its members. Observing this, French Catholic writer Charles Péguy, said, *"Everything begins in mysticism and ends in politics."* [2] Inevitably, a line of tension developed between a personal mystical approach and the required unquestioning—"literal"—belief in accepted doctrines of faith. This dichotomy of spiritual paradigms continues still.

The diversity of early Christianity attracted many because it was new and different. It spoke of equality for all. In God's eyes, the early Christians declared, *"there is no longer Jew or Greek, there is no longer slave or free, there is no longer male or female; for all of you are one in Christ Jesus"* (Gal. 3.28)—a shocking but welcome idea to many, especially among the under classes. The varieties of persons attracted to such a message are legend, but before too long the organizers began to be troubled by such a plethora of ideas and such openness.

Divisions developed. Some "literalists" wanted every word (as they understood them) accepted and obeyed. Traditionalists sought ways to take the radical new ideas and weave them into the culture of which they were a part. Most believed there were several levels to the teachings: 1) a literal perspective, 2) a historical context, 3) one or more metaphorical meanings, and 4) a mystical message. The mystical perspective was the one most powerful to those we know today as the Gnostics, but the least easy for most people to understand.

---

2. Charles Péguy, *Basic Verities: Prose and Poetry* (1943), quoted in *The Great Thoughts*, George Seldes, Comp. (New York: Balantine Books, 1985), 327.

> *Without vision, without mystery, all of our fine intellectual understanding and its great values turn to dust.*[3]

For those who could grasp the mysteries metaphorically, the teachings hidden in each human journey began to emerge. The ancient words *"ye are gods"* resonated with many of these, encouraging awakened ones not to fear, neither to stall nor slowdown as barriers to "knowing" appeared before them. Their intuition pressed on and limitations fell.

It is important to realize, although many Gnostics were free from any particular approach, there were also some Gnostics within all faiths. They were "free thinkers," determined and independent, with a variety of styles—some more acceptable or more radical than others. The single characteristic shared by all Gnostics is some degree of non-conformity. Many teachings of Gnosticism found their way into early church writings and certain Gnostics themselves are known as early church fathers.

Even though many Gnostic gospels are attributed to the disciples for whom they are named, they were rejected when the authoritarian church compiled the Holy Bible in the form we know today. A few were relegated to the Apocrypha, but many were simply discarded altogether.

Some Gnostic ideas came to be labeled as heresies, and even today, as attention begins to shift toward a regained respect for the divine feminine, the term heresy once again rises to intimidate those tending toward more mystical avenues. Reincarnation, accepted in the beginning, and returning to favor with large numbers today, was considered heretical to the majority for several hundred years. Rev. Leslie Weatherhead, author of *The Agnostic Christian*, was once asked *"Can a Christian believe in reincarnation?"* to which he replied, *"Can Christian's dance? Some can and some can't."* [4]

---

3. Helen M. Luke, "The Perennial Feminine," *Parabola*, Vol. V No. 4 (November 1980): 23.
4. Leslie D. Weatherhead, *Life Begins At Death* (Nashville & New York: Abingdon Press, 1969), 71.

The phrase *amazing grace* is a good description of Sophia's nature—free and freeing from restriction—no matter which plane it is on. She is the agent of the divine, watching over the *quiescent self* [5] within, willing to go to great lengths to guide her charges with all the skill and charm Mother Wisdom can muster.

5. The human seed or soul, the quiet self deep within that contains the slowly vibrating connection to the soul. When we become centered and balanced, we can detect behind the scanning, restless survival mind (ego) another self, a quiet point—the true or quiescent, self—to be magnified as we balance our survival nature with the evolving consciousness of the subtle self, Parrish-Harra, *Dictionary*, 232.

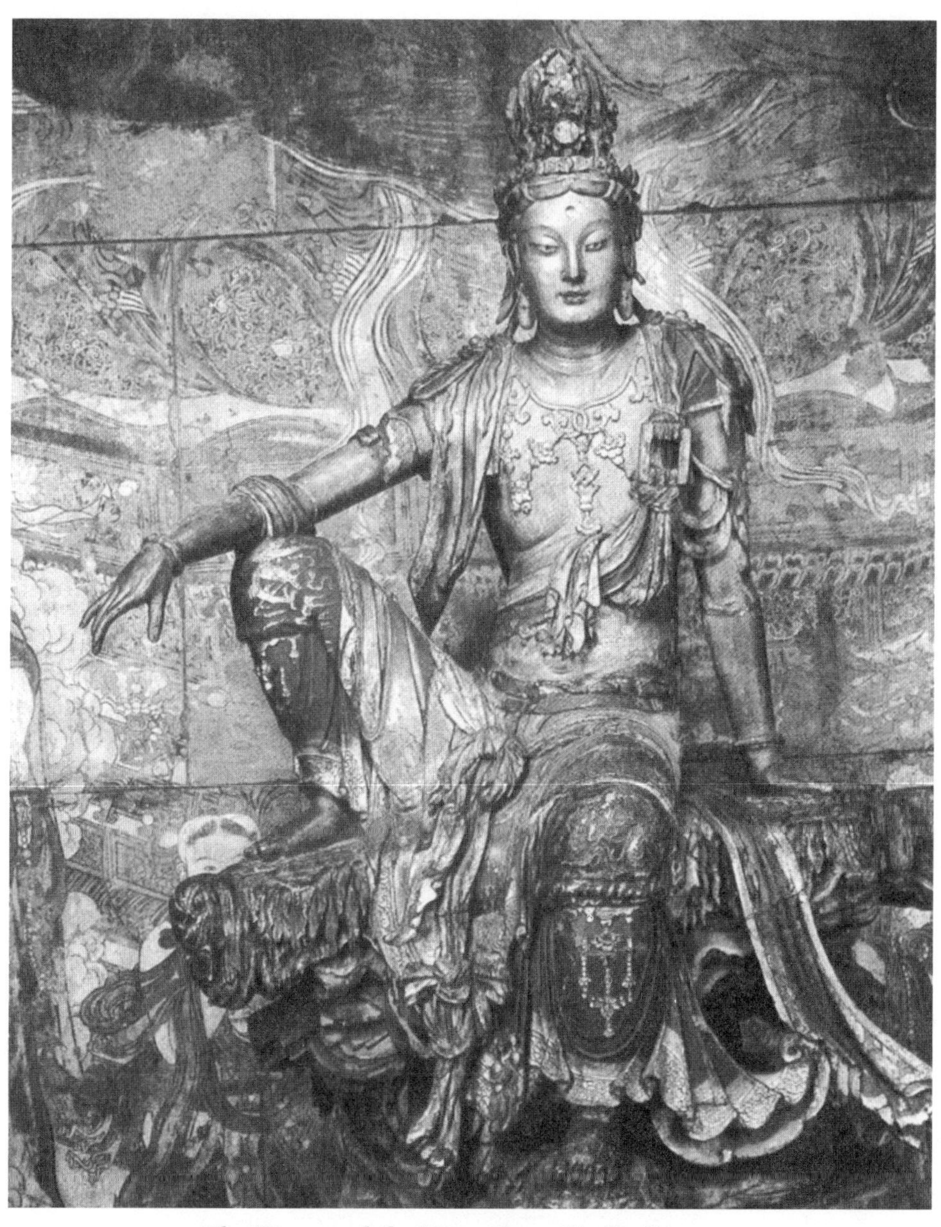

The Water and the Moon Kuan-Yin Bodhisattva.
China, 11th-12th century. Wood with paint, 95 x 65 in. Nelson Atkins Museum of
Art, Kansas City, Missouri: Purchase: Nelson Trust.
"Goddesses in Art" by:Lanier Graham

Greeting the Mother

✳ Slowly, gently, breathe in and out three times. As you relax more and more, visualize the dark night sky. Now, see the dark sky fill with twinkling stars. Just observe. Watch the stars as you focus once more on your breath.

✳ Again slowly breathe in and breathe out. This time, as you draw your breath in, let the stars grow fainter. Breathing out, hold the empty space. Hold the air out and see the black velvet sky, comfortably dark. See it deep, peaceful, and empty, as you push all the energy out of yourself.

✳ Breathe in and refill yourself with energy, prana, vitality—see the stars coming on again, twinkling and sparkling. Now breathe the sparkling light into yourself.

✳ Follow the sparkling energy through your body. Each cell glows as the conscious flow of vitality imparts fresh energy from the spiritual body into the physical form.

✳ Return your gaze to the sky. The stars are gone. They have set behind a vast dark sea, the horizon barely visible where sea and sky meet. Focus your attention at this meeting place.

✳ As you gaze, the moon begins to rise—full, round, white. See her silvery trace glistening on the waves. She hangs just above the horizon; her clear light is a pleasant soft brightness.

✳ You marvel at the beauty of the moon. Rest in this field of energy and feel her calm light relaxing you. Simply observe.

✳ Now the moon begins to change, becoming smaller but brighter—smaller and smaller, brighter and brighter, until she appears as an intensely glowing pearl so radiant with inner fire, she is hard to gaze upon.

✳ The pearl begins to expand now, becoming much larger than the risen moon. A graceful form takes shape in the pearl, Mother Mary, radiant with her own inner light. Her feet rest on a lovely rose, floating over the gentle movement of the lapping waves. Her presence comforts.

✻ As you watch, her shape changes gently and gradually into the familiar outline of Kwan Yin. With the great pearl as her backdrop, she stands on a lotus flower resting lightly on the waves. She lifts her hand in loving benediction, offering healing and hope.

✻ Once again the graceful shape begins to change; an aura of radiant light outlines yet another. In a shimmering robe, a shining halo around her head, is Sophia, Mother of Mothers. Her form shines with bliss. Wisdom emanates from her presence. Look into her eyes. Love streams from them, and her smile welcomes.

✻ Silently, whisper her names: Mary – Kwan Yin – Sophia –Wisdom – Healer – Mother.

✻ Gradually, she begins to withdraw. As she merges into the light, tears fill your eyes, and you know how blessed you are .

✻ You find yourself floating in a sea of energy. Waves of compassion, love, and wisdom wash over you. In your openness you drink in these gifts. Accept this energy now for areas of your own life where there is need for healing and renewal.

✻ We rest in the energy of the divine feminine for a few moments. Experience the gift of the Great Mother, allowing yourself to be restored.

✻ Breathe deeply. Begin bringing your attention back to the outer world. Know as you resume your daily duties you will share this energy with those whose lives touch yours.

✻ Be gentle with yourself as you become aware of the setting around you. With a grateful heart, thankful for the opportunity to receive the blessing of Mother Wisdom, return your attention to the denser world of Mother Matter.

✻ And it is so.

7

Myths

All mythological elements in the Bible, the doctrine and liturgy, should be recognized as mythological, but they should be maintained in their symbolic form and not be replaced by scientific substitutes. For there is no substitute for the use of symbols and myths: they are the language of faith. [1]

—Paul Tillich

*T*eaching myths (truths disguised within folk wisdom) are much like parables echoing through time; they persistently ring "truths" hard to dismiss. Tom Harpur, regular columnist with the Toronto Star and author of *The Pagan Christ*, explains this well:

> *The late Joseph Campbell defined myth once as: "That which never was, yet always is." In other words, a myth in the true sense of the word is a story containing a truth so infinitely precious that it can only be told by means of a story. The myth's packaging is non-historical. It is always fictional even though some historical names or places may occur in it.*
>
> *You see, history is fleeting, highly subjective, and subject to constant correction. Ask any professional historian. But, the truth carried by the ancient myths is eternal. It never changes. So, it still has incredible power to change lives today. That's why, for example, to use a phrase such as "the Jesus myth" is not to attempt a debunking of Christianity. Rather, it's a way of penetrating all the accumulated nonsense over the centuries to what the story of Jesus is really all about. It's the*

---

1. Paul Tillich, *Dynamics of Faith*, 1957, quoted in *The Great Thoughts*, 417.

dramatization of your soul's evolution and of mine. The Bible is full of myths.[2]

We, having come from the Father's house, are "gods" seeking to rediscover our divine nature

The myth of Sophia's journey from the higher planes to live as psyche within each human being has been mostly lost to Christianity. Her story is a companion tale to the Jesus Myth as to how he became Christ. Sophia as Wisdom is the companion to Christ as Love. The Christ is the main character of the story with Sophia as a sub-text because we follow the path as did Jesus. The Christ came to rescue all psyches "lost" in identification with the material world. As each human heart opens to higher love-wisdom, Sophia is found. This is the "Inner Knower" who will now guide the lost prodigal back to the true Self.

This path of Return or initiation, explained to us by Master Jesus in the parable of the prodigal son, is a teaching myth and sets the pattern for those who seek to become enlightened through the Christian Way.

Sophia, in her attempts to entice us to follow this same path of return, charms us with her astuteness. She flirts with us, seduces us, a wink here, a hint there, then another, guiding us deeper and deeper into her embrace. No wonder the rational mind (read prodigal ego) dreads her presence, condemns her influence, and calls her "sinful." This temptress reminds us that we, having come from the Father's house, are "gods"— godlings seeking to rediscover our divine nature.

"Greater works than these shall [the one who believes] do;" Jesus, the great wisdom teacher, has declared (see John 14.12). We cannot rationally comprehend or explain all this implies, but the soul as Mother persists. She uses her wiles to protect her charges. She meanders through human lives, touching, prompting, and speaking quiet words of wisdom as needed.

When threatened she can close down instantly. In the glare of rational focus, she disappears from conscious mind, reappearing behind

---

2. Tom Harpur, "Christ-centred movements precede historical Christianity," *Toronto Star*, www.thestar.com, Apr. 18, 2004. 01:00 AM, accessed at http://thestar.com on 7/4/04. See entry in bibliography for *The Pagan Christ*.

dreams, body aches and pains, even uncomfortable urges. Restricted, she stirs many tears and much discontent.

With the ascent of the patriarchal era and within that structure, the masculine principle assumed rulership of the physical world while the under-valued feminine subserviently presided over the home, the nest. Here she broods over her young. While doubts can arise over paternal claims, maternity is unmistakable. She maintains her restricted position in the deeply personal arena as the masculine claims power in the greater scheme of things. As the Christian movement became increasingly separated from Judaism, the feminine influence nursed it through its infancy.

Gnosticism was prominent as humanity moved through the closing period of the Arian age into the Piscean, (roughly 800BCE to 500CE). As structures in the known world were changing, the age-old desire to know for one's self emerged in strong ways, even as it is doing today. Mystery schools existed throughout the known world. Buddhism, Hinduism, and other venerable traditions had such schools in the Orient. In the Near East, Pythagorean, Hermetic, and Kabalistic schools flourished. In Western Europe this same knowledge was channeled through Norse, Germanic, and Druidic mythologies.

Some bold individuals penetrated deep within and found how "to know God." They discovered "gnosis," inner knowing. As national and religious authority systems were shifting, these pioneers attracted followers and often drew the ire of authorities afraid of losing their base of power. To avoid persecution or death and still be able to freely study and practice this gnosis, adherents developed secret orders.

Some, like the Essene, were less secret than others. Considered radical by the general public, they pursued enlightenment in their own manner. Others practiced healing arts or functioned as helpers or teachers, often guiding solitary seekers who in turn influenced many.

To avoid persecution or death and still be able to freely study and practice this gnosis, adherents developed secret orders

We perhaps need only to recall that the Cathars were completely destroyed because of their dedication to wisdom ways, to realize how fearful many have been of personal inner authority. As the original church differentiated itself from its Judaic roots, due in part to doctrinal disputes concerning matters of Jewish law, it continued to develop from small groups of disciples who met in the homes of the more affluent members, many of whom were women. Over time, these expanded into large public gatherings, but in the earliest years, worship centers were the living and dining areas of private homes. Few names have reached us, but history tells of women who loved and followed the Master, continuing to serve even after the crucifixion. Courageous women who served well—not just Mary, mother of Jesus, but also Anna (Luke 2.36–38), Mary Magdalene (Luke 8.2), Priscilla (Acts 18.26), and Phoebe (Romans 16.1), to name just a few—anchored for the Christian Way qualities of boldness, intelligence, and leadership. These daughters of Sophia balanced masculine and feminine qualities while modeling the ideal synthesis needed to attain enlightenment.

Masculine and feminine were split apart as the dualism of the Greek culture spread

Indigenous peoples of the world have long honored the feminine nature, keeping it present even today. Sarasvati, the goddess of wisdom and knowledge in India, is acknowledged with offerings of flowers, fruit, and incense. Gentle and graceful, she rides on the back of a peacock or swan, her sacred birds. She is depicted having four arms, indicating full use of both intellect and intuition. Sarasvati is said to have invented speech, Sanskrit, poetry, literature, and the complex patterns of higher music. Considered the Mother of the Vedas and the inspiration of the sages who listen inward for her words of wisdom, she executes what Brahma conceives.

The Maya ("maya" means "mother" in the Mayan language) still retain a sense of equal respect for Father Sun and Mother Earth with a deep understanding of the need for a balanced relationship between these mighty forces for the well-being of all. Most North American traditions, as well as other indigenous cultures, continue to honor the relationship between masculine and the feminine forces of nature.

[O]ne might come to envision Earth and her powers of creation with greater appreciation. Earth's trees and flowers become her coats of skin, while her intelligence is beyond measure as one becomes aware of her utilization of the elements of water, air, and fire. She is ever the abundant feminine caregiver for the humans living within her sphere. Even the radiations of the sun, moon, and stars are hers to implement in wise ways.[3]

Historically, in the "civilized" world feminine powers were dismissed as years passed. The two principles, masculine and feminine, were split apart as the dualism of Greek culture spread. The mysteries of masculine power are usually enumerated as courage, strength, excelling, rulership, strategy, productivity, and conquering. The institutional church incorporated these dynamics as it rapidly rose to power, while feminine knowledge—sexuality, birth, death, intuition, natural and spiritual healing, as well as creative play—were lost to most.

In writing about the differences between the masculine and feminine paths, Cynthia Avens and Richard Zelley compare them to an interstate highway and a byroad.

When we leave the highway, we immediately gain a heightened awareness . . . Whereas builders of the interstate have cut through mountains and filled in swamps to maintain the gentle gradient, the byroad follows natural contours of the land and feels closer to nature.

Just as the interstate highway represents a masculine approach to travel in its linear, rational design, so does "interstate Christianity" emphasize masculine qualities such as authority, law, and judgment in its organization, and even in its image of deity. Traveling the path of Christ, however, is like walking along a meandering bypath close to nature, where one encounters the feminine qualities of spiritual experience. The central core of Jesus's message embraced the feminine

---

3. Carol E. Beyer, "Soul-Centered Therapy," (Ph.D. diss., Sancta Sophia Seminary, 2004), 43.

*values of love and compassion and his teachings were radical essential-
ly because of their feminine nature, at a time when masculine values
were paramount in society. . .*

> *Thus the history of the [organized] church became a record of
deliberate destruction of the bypaths which had honored the feminine
values as the core of the Christian message.*[4]

Daughters and sons were punished if discovered practicing Sophianic
arts. Against all odds and out of sight in the privacy of homes, feminine mysteries of intuitive knowing, regard for dreams, "old wives tales," herbology,
and some home remedies survived as best they could as women were perse-
cuted for their wisdom.

I hunger for women as friends,

ones wise and old-in-knowing
    as the turtle
    sunning on her rock
    ancient in aliveness.

I have women as friends,
    bonded as cobwebs we are,
    tensile-strong the strands
    endured by time and sorrows
    and laugh-talk.

These women, my friends, are far-away
    scattered like seed pods by the winds,
    to the East and to the South
    to the North and to the West.

I long for my friends,
    women as wise as old turtles
    sunning on their logs.

—Dove Flowers

---

4. Cynthia Avens and Richard Zelley, "Walking the Path of Christ: The Quest for the Cosmic
Christ," *The Quest*, (Spring 1996):65–68.

8

Herstory

*I asked [Sophia] as I held the stone in my hand, if she wanted me to
write a scholarly and well-researched book about her. . .   I think I
heard her smile. "Mercy no! find me in life, in art and music and poetry which touch you; find me in nature, in its mathematics, and in the
geometry of being; find me in images, in laughter, and the heart's wisdom. Find me in your soul! Come with me and I will teach you to look
with a loving eye.[1]*

—Alice O. Howell on the Celtic Isle of Iona

George Jowett documents that some of the most vicious persecution ever recorded took place against the Celtic people
who birthed the Christian tradition of Britain. The British claim St. Paul
himself followed Joseph of Arimathea to the Isles in AD 36 some twenty
years after the Josephean Mission established Christianity there in
response to requests from the Druidic priesthood.[2] Jowett presents this
translation from a reading in the ancient Celtic Triads:

*The Lord our God is One.
Lift up your heads, O ye gates, and be
Ye lift up, ye everlasting doors, and the
King of Glory shall come in.*

---

1. Alice O. Howell, *The Dove in the Stone: Finding the Sacred in the Commonplace* (Wheaton,
IL; Madras, India; London: Theosophical Publishing House, 1988), 26.
2. George F. Jowett, *The Drama of the Lost Disciples*, 10th ed. (London: Covenant Publishing
Co., LTD, 1980), 79, 82, 85, 87, et al.

> *Who is the King of Glory? The Lord Yesu;*
> *He is the King of Glory.*[3]

In his book, *The Drama of the Lost Disciples*, Jowett continues:

> *How the Druidic priesthood knew the consecrated name so long beforehand is a mystery in itself. The name "Yesu" was incorporated in the Druidic Trinity as the Godhead. In Britain the name Jesus never assumed its Greek or Latin form. It was always the pure Celtic "Yesu."* . . .
>
> *The merging of the British Druidic with Christianity was a normal procedure, peacefully performed. Those who state Christianity was bitterly opposed by Druids speak falsely.* . . . *The Druidic Archbishops recognized that the old order was fulfilled according to prophecy* . . . .[4]

The struggle between the Roman Empire and Christians (especially the British) laid the ground work for savagery, murder, massacre, and destruction that befell the native people of the Sacred Isle both at home and abroad. Vile as are the persecutions of the twentieth century, they are brief when compared with the slaughter of the Celts that continued from the time of the Claudian invasion in AD 42, to the close of the infamous Diocletian savagery of AD 320. Numerous as were the lives lost in the purges and tortures of modern war, the loss of life is small compared to the total sacrifice of British lives during these 300 years.[5]

Stories of the bravery of Celtic warriors and their defiance rang out: *"For the first time the Romans met women warriors fighting side by side with their men in righteous combat. [Roman historian] Tacitus states that their long-flowing flaxen hair and blazing blue eyes were a terrifying sight to behold."* [6]

Few indeed realize the number of battles ignited by prejudices and fears as people met others of differing backgrounds and beliefs. The terror

---

3. cf. Procopius, *De Gothici,* bk. 3, quoted by Jowett, in *Lost Disciples,* 78.
4. Jowett, *Lost Disciples,* 78–79.
5. Ibid., 87, 88, 93, 94.
6. Tacitus, *Annals,* 14:30, referenced by Jowett, in *Lost Disciples,* 99.

of other ways of knowing has separated people for centuries. It culminated in the Inquisition, during which it is believed nearly a million women and sensitive men lost their lives. No wonder any non-rational approach went rapidly underground. Falling on increasingly deaf ears, Sophia's whispers grew fainter. Swiftly her voice faded, remaining unheard until other goals had been met.

Today, humanity's intellectual growth, facilitated by the divine masculine, is being weighed against the current desperate needs of the planet. Emphasis during the last centuries has been on the development of intellect, and graduation from innate and instinctual awareness to a rational approach is indeed a most important advancement. However, when the pendulum swings too far in either direction, nature pulls it back toward center.

The growing danger to all planetary life has initiated the return of the feminine principle into activity. Her ever-present nature has cycled into action in time to awaken evolving life to any number of threats: accidental wildfires often raging out of control; storms ever increasing in ferocity; warming temperatures with all the changes that accompany them. Now in her most protective mode, she stimulates us to survive and to protect our remaining resources. The well-being of all life is her major concern.

English scientist James Lovelock formulated the "Gaia Hypothesis" which describes the Earth as a living, self-regulating, and unified organism that defends itself from destruction as needed while it grows and constantly evolves.[7] In regard to Earth as a living, evolving entity, Sophia can be referred to as the "Soul of the World." So she has been described by Jesuit scientist-futurist Teilhard de Chardin and others, Russian Sophiologists especially. She is the very real intelligence *within* the material, as well as the non-physical animation that we know as Mother Nature. In this role she has been revered by indigenous people worldwide since earliest times.

---

7. James Lovelock, *The Ages of Gaia: A Biography of Our Living Earth* (Oxford, UK: Oxford Universal Press, 1995).

Thinking of Sophia as the World Soul or the Veiled Mother (as Nicholas Roerich called her), leads us to the challenge of seeing her not as a person, but as a consciousness. One of the finest clarifications I have seen is by Sophiologist, Robert Powell in his book, *The Sophia Teachings: The Emergence of the Divine Feminine in Our Time*. In one of the chapters, "The Three Primary Aspects of Our Relationship to Existence," he explains:

> *A mystical relationship to existence implies an opening of the heart. It is when a breath of divine love enters us. . . . Such a relationship is essential if we want to open to Sophia.*
>
> *The gnostic relationship to the world is expressed as a revelation of divine wisdom—that everything we see around us is actually a work of wisdom. . . . ["Gnostic" means] knowing on a deeper level than an abstract level of knowledge can possibly convey to us, one that has a quality of light and clarity that speaks to us from divine realms. . . . This gnostic aspect speaks to us of the opening of our minds . . . .*
>
> *The magical aspect of this relationship involves the endeavor of aligning our own will with that of the divine, in service of the good, the true, and the beautiful. Divine or sacred magic means that our own will opens to become empowered by divine will. . . .*
>
> *This book aims to explore the exciting challenge of opening up to the Divine Sophia, who can address us on all three levels— through our minds, hearts, and will.*[8]

In *Apocalypse of Peace: The Hope of the Future is Now*, Drs. Nicholas C. Demetry and Edwin L. Clonts have applied Powell's words to a symbolic representation of Sophia herself.

> *Sophia's head represents her wisdom of mind, or "gnostic" dimension, which manifests as a deep relationship to the world*

---

8. Robert Powell, *The Sophia Teachings: The Emergence of the Divine Feminine in Our Time* (New York: Lantern Books, 2001), 3–5.

through spiritually illumined knowledge and understanding. Her heart represents a "mystical" wisdom, which manifests as divine maternal love and nurturance of humanity, seeking to draw us together as one family of God. Her belly represents her "magical" function, which strives to align the human and divine will, the natural and the supernatural, so that we may share in the unfolding of her creative power.[9]

Here we see the attributes of Light, Love, and Power presented in a sophisticated manner. Though we may be unaccustomed to thinking this way, these concepts are important to our study of Sophia. Her exalted knowledge is out of reach of the intellect. To attain it we must achieve three goals:

1) We have to learn "to know" with our "inner knower."

2) We have to be willing to love freely and unconditionally, allowing our heart to be an open conduit of lots of vital energy, not a valve we turn on and off at will.

3) We must surrender our ego will to our soul's higher will in order to bring our personality into alignment with our soul.

Each is harder than we can imagine, but, hurrah!, it *does* happen. Collectively, humanity forms the mental body of the planet. As long as we stay split into "we-they" consciousness, duality rules rather than a dedication to the well-being of the whole.

Sophia calls forth the *spiritual warrior* [10] in each—a masculine sounding term that applies to everyone who engages in the battles between inner and outer, rational and intuitive, or transitory values versus eternal principles. It is an important stage that assists each to discover personal power and purpose. The demanding mother becomes fierce in defense of her inner child, the hope of glory, her progeny.

---

9. Nicholas C. Demetry, M.D., and Edwin L. Clonts, M.D., *Apocalypse of Peace,* [unpublished], quotation in Ch.2 "Creating From Stillness," referring to Powell, *The Sophia Teachings*, 3-4.

10. The spiritual warrior is the courageous part that dares to press on toward enlightenment in the struggle against the instinctual fear of the unknown within oneself that would hold one back.

The activity of the Warrior Mother is interwoven throughout creation. To illustrate this principle, which is active in both male and female psyches, we only have to recall moments of defensive fervor when danger threatened one of our children. Recognized also as adaptability, we know we *can* do whatever we must in critical moments—and we *will*!

The inner spiritual warrior is a particular space or resource we tap into whenever we stay grounded in our true nature under duress. As our world changes, we determine we can be true to whatever we sense as the "true self," or "our reason for being." We connect to the inner self with strong assurance—our spiritual practices act like batteries providing contact, direction, and insights. We are confident and surefooted. We may misstep from our path, but we rapidly correct and re-center, feeling confidence once more.

All of us have this bold self enfolded within, though we may not always be in touch with it. The more we experience and know this aspect of our nature, the more it helps us evolve into our best possible self. Certain moments call forth the attributes of the spiritual warrior within:

+ Giving birth—physical strength and bodily know-how.
+ Surviving a life-threatening accident or disease—will to live.
+ Leaving a destructive relationship—emotional power.
+ Surviving loss—courage to go on.
+ Releasing security to pursue a longed-for goal—exercising personal power.
+ Moving to an unknown country—daring and confidence.

Any of these transforming events can fill us with a heretofore unknown wonder. After the fact we are in awe of the dynamic that transformed our lives. This most natural of forces guides us through the storm.

We survive our pain and overcome negativity as we stay open to the inner prompter even though outer events attempt to impose limits on us. We acknowledge our fears and face them with intuition, imagination, and endurance. These feminine qualities shore us up from inside until the outer storms eventually subside. We discover experience transforms us. We sense an unknown companion who will, in time, become known.

Through the ages, many have personified her with a palpable sense of the "presence." Call her Rachel or Leah, Mary or Teresa, Isis or Kwan Yin—she has always been. Now, her sons and daughters are stirring the long-banked embers of the feminine within; they are fanning the sparks that warm the heart and give light to each tender soul. The sleep is over. The absent mother returns to transform our reality—to claim us as her own.

9
Grace

At the point of Grace, unconditional love becomes a natural way of life.
Grace is Sophia's middle name.

—Lee

As humanity learned rights and wrongs in keeping with the Ten Commandments, The Noble Path, and other well-defined guidelines, life was lived under legalistic forms of spiritual doctrines. It is only as individuals open their hearts and love the unlovable in *themselves*, that they are able to suspend judgment and live by grace. *I and the Father-Mother are one* then becomes a reality, enabling them to both fulfill the spirit of the law and transcend it. *For sin will have no dominion over you, since you are not under law but under grace* (Romans 6.14).

Teachings can be expressed in rational language, but loving cannot be achieved by rational intent. Transformation of the emotional nature must occur for this to be accomplished. We begin with raw emotion which, when elevated, becomes devotion; devotion in turn evolves to aspiration. New goals are set and the power of emotion is reworked and redefined again and again.

You have heard that it was said, 'You shall love your neighbor and hate your enemy.' But I say to you, Love your enemies and pray for those who persecute you, so that you may be children of your Father in heaven; for he makes his sun rise on the evil and on the good, and sends rain on the righteous and on the unrighteous. For if you love those who love you, what reward do you have? Do not even the tax collectors do the same? And if you greet only your brothers and sisters, what more are

71

you doing than others? Do not even the Gentiles do the same? Be perfect, therefore, as your heavenly Father is perfect. Matthew 5.43-48.

Adding to many Christians' challenges in overcoming prejudicial judgment are numerous instances in which translators of Aramaic writings were unfamiliar with the idioms, the metaphors and analogies, in common use. An example is found in Matthew 7.18, *"[E]very good tree bears good fruit, but the bad tree* [KJV reads 'corrupt tree'] *bears bad fruit* [KJV reads 'evil fruit']."

In Aramaic and in all the Semitic languages, the word for "good" primarily means "ripe," and the word for "evil" primarily means "unripe." When heard with Aramaic ears, those words might sound more like this: "A ripe tree brings forth ripe fruit, an unripe tree brings forth unripe fruit." [1]

Learning of this more accurate translation makes a world of difference. The tree may not be morally evil, but rather unripe: it is not developed enough to bear edible fruit. So it is with many whose process of maturing is not finished. They are not yet "ripe"; their time for enlightenment has not yet come.

Loving cannot be achieved by rational intent

As parents, we know stages of maturity bring readiness for increasingly complex mental constructs, deeper emotional responses, refined motor skills, and expanded social awareness. Wise ones understand natural errors of ignorance even as they regret to see the often painful results. Watching others learn through trial and error is seldom easy or pleasant, but it is necessary if others are going to gain authentic wisdom for themselves.

Separating every person and event into rigid categories of good and bad is as inaccurate as insisting that all thought conform to linear logic. Not only does such judgment hobble mental potential, it also short-circuits self-awareness and prevents one heart from opening to the other.

---

1. Neil Douglas-Klotz, "The Hidden Gospel of the Aramaic Jesus," *the Quest,* (Sept., Oct., 1999): 181.

One must come to see the spirit of the other amidst the struggles and be able to stay open toward the soul of the other—even when the personality is distasteful.

As we ponder the mystery of grace and what this means, we remember the importance grace holds in a caring lifestyle. To try to understand this hidden resource we have two points to consider. First, are we living the teachings of the Holy as best we can at any given moment in our lives? Second, what is grace, and would we know it if we saw it?

It may come as no surprise that peace of mind is directly related to grace. Everyone is invited to know the peace that passes understanding. The issue becomes "can we?" We can't if we only intellectualize an issue, because in order for the intellect to be comfortable, it must know the outcome before it begins the effort. Peace in the face of an unknown future cannot pass the intellect's criteria. In fact, the intellect, reading this as the peace that *by-passes* understanding, may feel quite threatened by it. Although as seekers, we gradually become aware that we are in a process of learning to trust, "Let not your heart be troubled, neither let it be afraid," is much easier to say than to do.

Grace is the ultimate answer. It is a power that draws us into a trusting relationship to the higher world. We learn to see it work in and through our daily lives, but often only after a lot of struggle. When we finally release the intellectual manipulations of our faith to a spiritual field that *sur-passes* our understanding, alignment with a daily spiritual walk begins occurring naturally.

Continued walking in this field "by faith, not by sight," builds trust in much the same way that physical walking builds leg muscle. Just as regular physical exercise assures us our body won't let us down when we need it, so by our spiritual walk, we come to a sense of security—a faith beyond intellectual belief—that we are loved, protected, and cared for.

Grace arises from the fact that the Divine (i.e., the immortal creator) has freely chosen to associate with the humanity (the mortal creation) of each of us, and has likewise placed within our humanity a spark of the original Divinity itself. This act of sharing the Divine is grace.

It brings a flow of energies, qualities, and events into our open heart/mind that we could not imagine. It sets humanity free from the limitations of the temporal, mortal, material field of consciousness. As each of us struggles with our lives, we see unbelievable solutions come to pass, far more wondrous than we could have dreamed up by ourselves. The wise old saying, *"If God brings you to it, God will bring you through it,"* speaks truly. Here the coincidences and synchronicities of the unknown weave themselves into the fabric of human-divine life.

By definition, grace is an outpouring of spiritual power that lifts consciousness into a new state of awareness. Many are the stories of individuals who, crying out for help in a moment of unbearable desperation, have received immediate assurance and a permanent awareness of the abiding divine presence.

But one need not be in a state of desperation to find grace. Embracing love, freedom, beauty, and/or joy creates a formula to invoke a new state of consciousness gifted from the higher world. This shift in our state of being brings increased awareness of formerly unknown laws underlying life.

Grace brings healing and freedom from restriction, working in a unique way appropriate to each individual life. Sometimes outer life changes miraculously. More often (and even better), it is our inner perception that changes radically. Beyond our rational understanding, what we are calling grace enters our life, and life is made new.

Grace does not avoid karma but, through continual in-pouring from the higher realities, frees us from ignorance and lack of insight. A two way stream, we can both invoke and be receptive to it. Grace, by its feminine nature, abounds but does not compel. We are always free to reject it, and by closing down, break from the accelerating momentum and return to the limitations of our own power.

Through grace, the nurturing side of God's nature—the Mother—is with us in our challenges. To receive her, there must be willingness in us to adjust, receive, or go with the flow. Here we confront the challenge of our own ego and the opportunity to adapt to a superior nature. We may have found ourselves muttering, "this could not have come at a better time," as we realize we are experiencing the divine timing of grace in action. Understanding expands, and we are renewed.

"There, but for the grace of God, go I," expresses two compassionate insights. The first is that I have done likewise and somehow escaped the damage or pain that would have ensued, and the second is that I have avoided such a fate, but I have no idea just how.

Grace as a spiritual power implies there is a force, an energy bubble or stream, outside mundane experience, which has been tapped into. Within this power-filled bubble/stream, one is lifted out of ordinary awareness into an expanded state wherein life is experienced differently.

Grace does not avoid karma

One now perceives more, and perhaps is more aware of the divine as a palpable presence or as unalterable reality. This is not a rational line of thought, but a dimensional shift of awareness. This is gnosis. This expansion of consciousness by grace that could not be forced (it can be desired) allows more grace (the outpouring of the higher world) to occur, freeing one from the restriction of the usual state of mind. This is the "lift" that allows freedom from restriction. Instead of going around in a circle and struggling to cope, now one begins to move upward in a spiral.

"Salvation" is a term the early church associated with this shift of consciousness. Rising above the duality of the material world allows one to heal the separation between the spiritual nature within and the material nature without, and trust is the result. This allows forgiveness, the ability to grasp the meaning of pain or loss with a new strength, because in the grace-filled moment, the larger picture emerges.

This was the real goal of the mystery traditions, not just to be good and/or follow rules, but to achieve a bond with the divine. Often a personal quest leads to a guide, a sage or teacher, who can serve as a mentor in assisting one to gain needed insights. Here is the significance of devouring the wisdom of the teacher at every opportunity. Receiving grace from a wiser one has changed many a person.

Wisdom teachings say persons come to the fount to drink three times before they stay with wisdom ways. The first time, they connect, but will not understand the opportunity. The second time, they awaken a temporary interest but when faced with a choice, they choose material consciousness over spiritual food. By the time the third contact is made, nothing else will satisfy.

Regardless of where we are in our connections, an inner state of grace assists certain pieces to fall into place, so life can be comprehended with a new perspective. Grace brings the courage to go on, the dedication to keep trying, and the ability to endure. "To live by grace not by law" is an affirmation for those who can hear the deeper message to begin to live differently. So will all when a higher understanding of life is realized. Having glimpsed or sensed our part in the plan, we gain a deeper acceptance of what we "already knew".

The Apostle Paul, the Gnostic, has experienced much and is a knowledgeable one when he speaks of *"his Grace which is able to build you up, and give you an inheritance"* (Acts 20:32). He says we each have an account in the higher world that allows us to bestow upon others some degree of our blessings. We can be of help to others; they can "inherit" some of our resource and it can be added to the efforts of the other. Indeed, each of us as we advance are in turn to become a blessing to those with whom we have contact.

The inheritance of grace is one of the great concepts of the mystery traditions. Saints, gurus, and prophets blessed others and called them to a higher standard. Something revealed to them changed them, they became more wise, and they were called to pass it on to those ready to receive. Grace is given to those "who have ears with which to hear." This truth rings through the ages and is true yet today for each of us. Our challenge is to recognize the resonance of truth within when we hear it.

10

Behold

Christianity subsumed Sophia and her Logos in one being. The chief architect of this construct was St. Paul, who following the lead of Philo, put the rational, masculine power of the Logos (the Word) and the intuitive, feminine power of Sophia (Wisdom) into the person of Christ.[1]
—Caitlín Matthews

In the book of John wherein Jesus speaks to the disciple John saying, *"Behold your mother,"* and to Mary, *"behold your son,"* two major truths are anchored. Esoterically, John is to represent all humanity as a collective; therefore Jesus bequeaths his mother, Mary, to each personally and all of us collectively. She receives us not just as the mother of Jesus, but as a representative of the Great Mother who receives all who turn to her. Here Mary anchors the archetype of the divine feminine, accepting humanity on behalf of the Christ.

The Christ principle (to which Jesus surrendered himself) is the reflection of the divine—both masculine (father) and feminine (mother)—principles of the greater life. Christ as love has overshadowed Sophia as wisdom in church teachings. Yet, as holy, "whole," the Christ (love) partners with Sophia (wisdom) in order for the Christ Consciousness (love-wisdom) to be realized. Thus the shrouded Sophia courses timelessly through humanity like blood through the organs of an athlete—out of sight, sustaining, guiding, and purifying the cumbersome but rich-in-potential human nature.

As the lawgiving masculine consciousness took charge, Sophia sustained the collective life so it could persevere in its quest for linear thought

---

1. Caitlín Matthews' "Sophia, goddess of Wisdom," *Gnosis Magazine* No. 13, (Fall 1989): 23.

and the development of left-hemisphere intelligence. She maintained her connection through the reptilian and mammalian brains and even now continues to retain this doorway to right relationship. She observes as each new stage of evolution brings humanity to greater maturity, but in moments of crisis when life is threatened on any level—physically, emotionally, mentally, or spiritually—she steps from the shadows to intercede. Because we are in chaos in today's tumultuous world, we are becoming increasingly aware once more of her guidance, both individually and collectively. We invoke her interaction.

In Christian approaches we have rarely thought of her, but when we did, we associated her with the Holy Spirit, comforter and advocate—she who protects, nurtures, and cares for us. We have not known her by any other name. In Eastern Orthodox and Catholic approaches the Holy Spirit remains feminine. In Protestant approaches however she was woven into a masculine trinity with few remembering her feminine qualities. Today, Sophia is stirring humanity's sleeping inner knower. Thus her presence is gaining increased significance as many become more ready to listen to the wee small voice within.

In moments of crises when life is threatened, Sophia steps from the shadows to intercede

As she reappears, we acknowledge that the golden thread that can sew many faiths and cultures together, belongs to her. In this emerging era we will come more and more under her influence, as the feminine nature of God, existent from the beginning, reasserts herself—Mother Wisdom: Sophia—eternally present, unfailingly patient, unceasingly persistent.

Christian Mystic Joachim of Flora (b. Italy, ca. 1132, d. 1202) with his visionary grasp of the unfolding of Christianity stated, *"The reign of the Father is past; the reign of the Son is passing; the reign of the Holy Spirit is at hand."*[2] She is emerging because we must re-establish our connection with her fount of life-giving mysteries if humanity is to survive.

In this, the third millennium of Christianity, we are entering a new era. It will focus on birthing the Christ-within, the hope of glory.

---

2. Quoted in J. J. VanDerLeeuw, *The Fire of Creation* (Adyar, India: The Theosophical Publishing House, 1947), quoted by Parrish-Harra, in *Dictionary*, 138.

Under the guidance of the divine feminine, we will experience the second coming of the Christ—this time to our individual lives in a deep and personal way. The biblical books of Proverbs, the Wisdom of Solomon, and the Song of Solomon best record her riches and her passionate nature. Her fiery temperament is devoted to a way of life that is far more than a mental process. We delight in her inspiration and discover how patiently Sophia invites our attention. Seeking guidance on our pilgrimage to spiritual maturity, we rejoice as we enter into a life-renewing experience with she who has been, is, and ever shall be.

Scripture teaches that God's Word set Creation into motion, at which time Wisdom was his daily delight:

> *The Lord created me at the beginning of his work, the first of his acts of long ago. . .then I was beside him, like a master worker; and I was daily his delight, rejoicing before him always, rejoicing in his inhabited world and delighting in the human race.* Proverbs 8.22,30–31

Long ago, Sophia made her home among God's children. Her presence was easily sensed and her attributes easily accessed. Again she calls to us, waiting eagerly for our response. She prompts and inspires, slipping her subliminal current through the interface of our hearts and minds, impacting us as we are surprised by thoughts that seemingly come from "out of the blue." We wonder, "Where did that come from?" or "Why did I think of that?"

Unusual coincidences happen to almost everyone at one time or another. Ancient peoples looked for and found abundant omens in nature by which they guided their decisions. Since the dawning of the age of reason, however, coincidences are generally explained away, and looking for omens or meaningful connections between seemingly unconnected events is regarded as superstitious or neurotic. Yet, the notion that there might be a universal order and interaction not limited by time, space, or obvious connections began to receive serious scientific scrutiny during the early 1900's with the advent of Einstein's theory of relativity, Jung's concept of synchronicity, and Pauli's findings concerning non-local causality.[3] What is it, then, that is responsive on the cosmic level in such a way that individual thoughts and actions of each constituent part in some way affect the whole?

Challenged to define the nature of the divine feminine, there is a need for rational underpinning to the degree it can be done; however, it can only be partially rational because it needs to be poetic as well. We come to know her most easily as a dance, a poem, music, or in stories conveying ardor more compatible with intuition than with logical exploration. Although Sophia reveals herself willingly, should we become too analytical, She simply withdraws.

[W]e may conceive of Sophia as having been hidden 'behind' Christ up until now, at least in the West. Now. . .it is possible to speak of a re-emergence of Sophia. . .to distinguish between Christ and Sophia, the Lamb and his Bride. Christ is the Logos, the creative Word, and Sophia is the Wisdom underlying the Word. [4]

Sophia will always be clothed in mystery

Icons of Sophia holding Logos on her chest reveal her as the ideal mother nurturing a less-than-mature humanity. Usually Sophia is seen as having two aspects: the higher (soul) and the lower (psyche). The higher is transcendent (all-knowing, wise) and the lesser is immanent (always present, most often hidden). Recognizing her as the psyche causes us to realize she expresses through that evasive part of the human nature not easily grasped or enclosed in specifics. In this lesser role, she is most often imprinted with human pains and fears; as individual clarity occurs and old wounds are released, psyche becomes increasingly trustworthy.

Sophia will always be clothed in mystery because the nature of wisdom is suprarational, coming from a higher reality. Designed to oper-

---

3. "Synchronicity", *Harper's Encyclopedia of Mystical & Paranormal Experience*, Rosemary Ellen Guiley ed. (Edison, NJ: Castle Books, 1991), 595-597.

4. Robert A. Powell, *Divine Sophia Holy Wisdom* (Nicasio, CA: Sophia Foundation of North America), 13.

ate outside the parameters of linear thought, she flits about, indirectly influencing us as she awaits the moment she can spring into our awareness; she flashes a quick impression, an aha, and darts away. Then, hovering at the edge of consciousness, she leaves us to ponder her gift.

Nowhere in historical religions is consulting one's inner authority considered to be sorcery, but it is a natural activity of the person who becomes one with the All. The misogyny produced by the misuse of power during the masculine era, though still strong, is at last beginning to dissipate. As new appreciation of the feminine is gained, our societies and nature will benefit.

One of the richest portrayals of the divine feminine is that of the triple goddess: young woman (maiden), birth-giver (mother), and elder wise woman (crone). Dating from the most ancient times, this model persists even today. Believed to be inspired by the stages of the moon, it has been used by many civilizations: Viking, Druid, and Greek, to name a few. The new moon waxing toward its fullness represents the maiden growing toward her ripeness; the full moon is the mother, rich and fertile; while the waning phase moving toward the darkness is the crone.

The maiden represents innocence, but exudes veiled sexuality. Her color is white representing new beginnings, youth, and a certain kind of excitement.

The mother is fertility, producing and protecting her life-giving gifts. Her color is red and she represents ripeness, stability, and even fierceness—the one who provides for her young and will fight to the death for them.

The crone is wisdom, compassion, and the death guide. Her color is black. She is old age, repose, and the gateway to death and rebirth. She is patient and waits for those who will approach, desiring her resources. Then she *"challenges us to go beyond that immature 'neurotic either/or dichotomy' stage of development to a both/and world."* Through her long hard experience she knows that *"neither the undifferentiated world of early matriarchy nor the overly differentiated world of patriarchy allows for a conscious world that can contain the opposites."* [5]

---

5. Marion Woodman and Elinor Dickson, *Dancing in the Flames: the Dark Goddess in the Transformation of Consciousness* (Boston & London: Shambhala, 1996), 49.

Similarly, the primal goddess is sometimes divided into three as creator, preserver, and destroyer. (The destroyer might be termed the recycler in modern parlance. Just as the crone completes the cycle of the physical feminine life by dying to materiality and re-entering the spirit plane, so the destroyers such as the Hindu Kali destroy the lesser to make way for the greater.) In Hinduism, the primal goddess Maha Devi (Great Mother) is represented by Sarasvati (wisdom), Lakshmi (abundance), and Kali (destroyer of ignorance and maintainer of world order). In Christianity we could think of this threefold aspect as the Holy Spirit, Mary Magdalene, and Mary the Mother.

Recall the green shamrock used by St. Patrick of Irish fame as a symbol of the trinity. Centuries earlier it represented the triple goddess— what goes around, comes around. An interesting modern replica of this three-fold imagery may be seen in the religious portrayal of Mary as Virgin, the late Princess Diana as the wounded mother suffering the dysfunction of our modern society, and Mother Theresa of Calcutta as the modern crone. Worldwide, these three images resonated with millions in recent years, affecting both men and women in archetypal ways no one expected. We have the many appearances of the Virgin occurring world wide; Princess Diana's life and death are still being memorialized; and so are Mother Theresa's. Effects of such archetypes continue to reverberate in the collective consciousness to stimulate needed change.

Athena Promachos, 1st Century B.C. E.
Museo Archeologico Nazionale, Naples.

A Moment In Time

✦ Visualize yourself seated comfortably before a window with sunlight streaming in upon you. As you watch, observe your form gradually change into that of a large, clear crystal. As the white light of the sun falls upon your crystalline form, bright streams of colored light are refracted into the room.

✦ Like the white light split into its component colors, Energy from the One Source of all Life is split into separate Rays, each having specific qualities. Daily, these Rays of energy we receive from the Source of all Life, also stream out from us, affecting life around us. Realizing this, once more picture yourself seated in that stream of light, ready now to utilize it in a more conscious way.

✦ We invoke these energies to assist us as we integrate our personality with our divine self. We commit to using well the rays of energy that bless us, that we might fulfill our reasons for this incarnation.

✦ A beam of red light falls on us to strengthen our divine will, bringing vitality into our reservoir of power and determination. Through the property of divine strength carried on the ray of red, we learn to trust our higher power, building confidence in our divine nature in the midst of human struggles.

✦ Now our mind will be refreshed by higher forces of life as we call forth rays of blue light, enabling us to embrace new ideas and to see things in a new way. This energy strengthens our connection to higher mind. Our intelligence is acknowledged as we will our mind to blend harmoniously with divine mind.

✤ Next we see the golden light of Holy Consciousness flowing down upon us, stimulating the creativity within us. New awareness of our capability abounds. We call forth imagination, play, and joy into our daily life. The eternal child within can live with us and rejoice in every level of our expanding understanding

✤ Recognizing our need for harmony, we welcome a rich green healing force to fill us. Much learning and direction come through releasing blocks, and admitting errors. The green healing light shines upon us that we may find our true way. We seek wholeness, abundance, and vibrant awareness that we may make our world a better place for ourselves and others.

✤ A gentle peach color builds within and around us as we pray, listen, and respond. We realize the powerful, creative impact of words, thought forms, and actions, and welcome this ray's help in learning to play the game of life more wisely.

✤ We hold our hearts up to the light, absorbing the rose ray of devotion into our feeling nature. We invoke clarity in dedication to duty that fulfills our purpose for incarnation. This rose ray reveals we are beings of love, releasing us from judgment, forgiving, and letting ourselves and others go free.

✤ Now we receive the violet transmuting flame, its light transforming our bodies and the physical world in which we live. This violet flame guides the cleansing in each level of our nature, allowing transformative energies to flow Earthward from the soul into the open mind, the prepared heart, the etheric body, and this physical body that is our present earthly home.

✤ Now, see your crystal-self transformed into a radiant jewel filled with light. Whether resting in the sunlight of your meditation times or busy serving, know you are always in these vibrant streams of Higher Light. So be it.

11

Worlds

When Chiti [1] playfully expresses Herself in the form of universal Consciousness, She becomes the world, vibrating and creating innumerable world forms. "It is the divine Consciousness alone, luminous, absolute, and free-willed, which flashes forth in the form of numerous worlds." [2]

—Kshemaraj

Wisdom teachings of all traditions offer similar ways of depicting the world of creation. There is an art to perceiving universal truths. We have a need to organize our philosophy of life around systematic principles, but it is important to remember that language itself is symbolic. True *knowing* is wholistic and *all at once.* Word symbols (scriptures, creeds, philosophies, poetry, story) and symbolic art, music, dance, and drama can communicate *about* universal truths, but true understanding transcends all human attempts to portray it.

Every distinct philosophy or theology has a somewhat separate set of symbols that attempt to describe the indescribable. Each system helps for a limited time, but when an individual continues to mature, she or he will graduate out of any given school of thought, even as others are matriculating into it. So it cannot be said that there is a right way or a wrong way to apply symbolic explanations to these indescribable areas.

---

1. Divine conscious energy; creative aspect of God, portrayed as the universal Mother, also called Kundalini and Shakti among other names.

2. Swami Muktananda, *Play of Consciousness: A Spiritual Autobiography*, 4th ed. (South Fallsburg, NY: The Syda Foundation, 1994), 227, quoting Kshemaraj, *Pratybhijñahridayam*, commentary on sutra 1.

87

Several systems recognize that everything exists within a continuum of vibrational frequencies. Everything is grouped into broad categories (known as levels, planes, or worlds) based on its density. The denser the matter, the slower its corresponding vibration. From slowest to fastest in ascending order, these worlds or planes are, 1) the material/physical; 2) the emotional/mental–psychological, also known as the Subtle World; 3) the Soul; and 4) spirit–monad, the cosmic participant also known as the Fiery World.

> *As I watched, thrones were set in place, and an Ancient One took his throne, his clothing was white as snow, and the hair of his head like pure wool; his throne was fiery flames, and its wheels were burning fire. A stream of fire issued and flowed out from his presence.* Daniel 7.9–10.

In this Fiery World the One Spirit divided into *monads* [3] (sometimes called "divine sparks") that descended into the lower realms to eventually become conscious of their own creative power and divine nature.

In esoteric understanding, the spark of spirit (the prodigal son—masculine) left home and descended into the nearest lower level, the plane of the Soul. The Soul level is feminine, and is the human life guardian. After wrapping themselves in Soul substance, the monads descended into the emotional/mental plane and clothed their souls in human personalities (masculine). Each ensouled, personality-clad monad then enters a physical body through which it is able to interact with the dense material world.

Although at the physical level individuals incarnate into a body which is either male or female—*"male and female he made them"*—the personality level of every human being is the "child" of soul and is regarded as "the son" (masculine) of the feminine soul. This way of talking about creation makes it clearer how it is that everyone who has a human body is a combination of both the masculine and the feminine principles. We are

---

3. An indivisible sond divine life atom. The immortal self within each living successive incarnation. . .The innermost self, the source of life and light that nurtures the unfolding soul.—Parrish-Harra, *Dictionary*, 179.

all the prodigal sons and daughters nourished by the soul as we return to the "Father's house" from which our spirit descended.

The word "father" has served as a blind (a cover) for the word "monad" down through the ages, just as "mother" has for the "soul." These were clues of our true origin preserved in symbol, metaphor, and analogy as we sought the knowledge that brings a mature understanding. The goal is to be united in a consciousness expanded by Creator's excursion into its own creation when the journey into matter is done.

The Path

Some where, some when, some why, some how—
Where? Here; Why?Urge; How?Math; When? Now—
there burst into an empty scene
a shower of sparks from the NO THING
seeking, perhaps, to find a way – blaze a trail – mount a play
to see its SELF in some new way.
"No – not just some new way," it thought,
but as many new ways as sparks that sought
to sink through ethers each more dense,
chilling SELF's fire, stilling SELF sense.
But, then, as each small sparkle flickered out
forgetting SELF in airless doubt,
Sophia's breath began to blow,
causing each cold spark to glow,
igniting in each amnesiac
Christ-fire to bring SELF's memories back,
causing each nameless spark in its heart and mind
to seek its path, and thus to find,
"SELF's Spark, I Am – SELF's Urge – SELF's Math!
Burning through the dark, I Am SELF's Path!" [4]

The Christ came to awaken humanity to love—unconditional love—as a tool, a bridge to higher awareness. Humanity, with its powerful mental capability, has repeatedly gotten stuck in "right-wrong"

---

4. Lee Warren, Sparrow Hawk Village, September 13, 2003.

judgments during its developmental process. Salvation, enlightenment, liberation all mean gaining freedom from restriction by becoming a conscious participant in God's plan.

The cosmic world is the home of the androgynous source—also known in Eastern philosophy as the Self—of all creation. Here rest the foundational universal principles that responded to the one who set all into motion. While the spirit rushed forth, the feminine principle received the seeds of spirit issued by the masculine principle, enfolding them in her ethers. Sophia participated equally in the process of creation by forming planes in which the fiery sparks, divine seeds, or the projected image and likeness of the divine could become embedded. The sparks descended into denser realms to gain experience and to mature under the watchful eye of the mother.

We can say that each spark leaving the Fiery World gathers to itself creative ethers, cloaking the descending essence in love-wisdom. Innumerable sparks clothe themselves as they enter the involutionary stream to return some later day when consciously aware of their own divine nature. For now, asleep to the divine within, they simply flow Earthward toward the physical world of matter, not knowing a tender mother travels with them to guard and guide. Each human soul (seed) will be projected into the physical world where a body will develop in which the psychological mechanism of personality will experience life, grow, and bloom. Once integrated and sufficiently mature, the return journey to the Godhead will begin.

While we are accustomed to thinking of ourselves as separate, in wisdom teachings there is but one—the collective soul of humanity—and each of us is a part of it. As scripture has always taught, *"We are one body."* We could say each individual is a "cell," a particle of the whole.

Indeed, we are one. In due time, we each will discover the quest for higher consciousness as our reason for being—we create our path of initiation by our choices and responses. Rarely do we realize we are attended by Mother Soul Sophia as we learn to blend loving kindness and intellectual integrity into unheralded triumphs that become our mystical lineage. It is through the wisdom of Sophia within us that the light of the Creator is born gently into the world.

> *Even in the Origin of the World document of the Alexandrian Gnostics, the 'first father', Yaldaboath, was brought forth from the depths by the Holy Spirit, who was called Sophia (from the Greek Sophia: wisdom). She was said (just as related in Genesis 1:2) to have 'moved upon the face of the waters' but, in this regard, the Semitic word ruah, which was translated in Genesis to 'spirit', actually meant 'wind'. Hence, Sophia was a wind-spirit. . . associated with the lily (or lotus flower) wisdom culture.*[5]

The spirit of prophecy and the living waters of spirit and truth associated with the Holy Spirit were forced into an underground stream where they became the esoteric underpinnings of civilization. Soul is the unseen life support of the individual personality in the same way that spirit invisibly supports evolving humanity.

Personality is *manas*,[6] the mind-being in which soul sleeps. Its proactive nature is motivated first by instinct and later by emotion and self-centered desires. Its goals may be quite worthy: to be good, successful, powerful, and beneficent. At the personality level such achievements are masculine whether activated by a man or woman seeking self-satisfaction, recognition, or ego gratification, or by a society responding to the power of the collective *maya*.[7]

Personality's task is to integrate the potentialities—energies of the soul nature—into each level of its expression: physically, emotionally, mentally, and spiritually. Simplified models see the physical, emotional, and mental natures as separate from the spiritual nature which makes up the fourth component. As the soul journeys through the dense world, the psychological (emotional plus mental) nature is integrated, fostering a

---

5. Laurence Gardner, *Realm of the Ring Lords* (Gloucester, MA: Fair Winds Press, 2003), 46.

6. Sanskrit, meaning "to think." Refers to the mind-principle becoming dual in the human condition—divided into higher manas (abstract mind) and lower manas (rational, concrete mind).—Parrish Harra, *Dictionary*, 165.

7. The agreed-upon collective hypnosis of a culture, religion, or society that seeks to regulate the guidelines of behavior for its people.—Parrish-Harra, *Dictionary*, 169.

91

new appreciation of the physical (physical plus *etheric* [8]) nature and the world of matter.

We can acquire deeper insight into this metaphoric description of soul as feminine and personality as masculine, if we compare it with the late nineteenth-century discoveries of right/left brain asymmetry and differences in the way males and females experience reality. In his book *The Alphabet Versus the Goddess: The Conflict Between Word and Image*, Leonard Shlain observes:

> *Because of their different roles, evolution, in time, equipped men and women emotionally to respond differently to the same stimuli. This resulted in men and women having different perceptions of the world, survival strategies, styles of commitment, and ultimately, different ways of knowing: . .In accommodating these differences, nature redesigned the human nervous system, radically breaking with all that had gone before.*
>
> *The left brain's primary functions are opposite and complementary to the right's. [Generally speaking] the right side is concerned with being, the left with doing. The left lobe controls the vital act of willing.*
>
> *The right hemisphere. . .contributes a field awareness to consciousness, synthesizing multiple converging determinants so that the mind can grasp the senses' input all-at-once. .*
>
> *[It] is also the portal leading to the world of the invisible. It is the realm of altered states of consciousness where faith and mystery rule over logic.* [9]

Dr. Shlain describes the various characteristics and skills inherent in each lobe and remarks that *"because of the constant feedback between the two lobes, hemispheric lateralization led to an almost infinite variety of*

---

8. The etheric body is about 1–1½ inches larger than the physical body and is often detected as a rather bluish white outline of the body. (This is not the aura.) It is the true substantial form, the framework, the 'scaffolding' to which the physical body necessarily conforms.—Parrish Harra, *Dictionary*, 86.

9. Leonard Shlain, *The Alphabet Versus the Goddess: The Conflict Between Word and Image* (New York: Viking, 1998), 16–24 passim.

responses, making our forebears supremely intelligent among animals. To many thoughtful people, it also seems to have created two subspecies of Homo sapiens—Woman and Man." [10]

The ideal partnership, be it marriage or any other, re-combines both sets of perception in the physical world. The imagery of the mystical marriage represents the desired relationship of the earthly human part of oneself (the masculine personality) with the divine feminine, (the *She who dwells within*) so little understood by humanity as of yet. Ready for true transformation, each of us must become a refined mind-being (manas) before we can surrender the conscious human self to the soul (the feminine presence). Every part of this journey is incredibly important in reaching the goal of becoming fully human and fully divine.

Truly here we find that hidden intelligence of Sophia hard at work out of sight, evolving humankind. Whether we seek Wisdom through religion, science, or art, She is always there fulfilling her vital service. In the book *The Earth Path: Grounding Our Spirits in the Rhythm of Nature*, Starhawk speaks eloquently of this ubiquitous and intentional creative life-force:

> *The Goddess is the presence of consciousness in all living beings; the Goddess is the great creative force that spun the universe out of coiled strings of probability and set the stars spinning and dancing in spirals that our entwining DNA echoes as it coils, uncoils, and evolves.* [11]

We are only now beginning to grasp the mystery of our DNA, vibrant with intent to nurture each and every one in order to develop whatever potential awaits. Dr. Jacqueline K. Barton, a professor of chemistry at the California Institute of Technology, and her colleagues are seeking to understand just how the double helix manages to function, heal

---

10 Ibid., 24.

11. Starhawk, *The Earth Path: Grounding Our Spirits in the Rhythm of Nature* (New York: HarperCollins, 2004).

itself, and split time and time again, *"spawning numberless generations of daughter DNA molecules in the course of cell division."* [12]

For centuries, Soul as the feminine creative influence (referred to by some as the Goddess) and nurturer of the awaiting potential was represented in icons as Sophia. She tends to be shown in robes of red—a sacred color of feminine power representing blood encoded with the DNA of human life. Such icons are usually mistaken for Mary, the mother of Jesus, until we are introduced to the mysteries. When we learn of Sophia's role as mother of the group soul known as humanity, a recognition of her place in history begins to dawn together with a revelation of her importance to the coming era.

In time we will discover she of the highest world is also embedded in the dense world with us. As we have journeyed, we have unknowingly carried her as an ember of sleeping fire cloaked within our very nature. Upon awakening, we become conscious of this inner self, called by whatever name.

While on the journey to spiritual maturity, this embodied ember will change its form—color, gender, nationality, and beliefs—in the world of personality like we change clothing in day-by-day human existence. Each change of outfits represents a lifetime through which greater experience is gained. Wedding its life-enriching energy to practical goals, this inner self refines its understanding amidst the challenges, thus bridging spirit and matter.

Now one is capable of awakening to a relationship to the greater Life. No longer believing we are separate from the One but knowing we are each direct representatives *"made in the image and likeness of the Creator,"* we remember we are divine, and the ascent back to the royal household begins. Father who is also Mother holds the light, love, and power for the sons and daughters, guiding them to a clearer expression of the divine nature. Once mature, each is deployed in service for the benefit of the whole, manifesting his or her part of the higher plan as prompted.

---

12. Natalie Angier, "Constantly in Motion, Like DNA Itself," *The New York Times*, "Scientist At Work," http://www.nytimes.com/2004/03/02/science/02PROF, quoting Dr. Jackqueline K. Barton.

12

$\mathcal{A}$ctivities

Let us continue to think of our human nature as containing four major components, or levels. From the least dense (having the most rapid rate of vibration) to the densest, they are the spiritual, mental, emotional, and physical. Each descending level has less capacity for consciousness than the preceding one. Sophia dances through these levels of reality. She stirs each with her presence and her nature.

These aspects express in the four worlds, or dimensions, as they are also known. Pure spirit, the fire, lives in the archetypal world; soul resides in the inner, or subtle world; the psychological nature dwells in the mental/emotional dimensions; and the physical, of course, occurs in the material physical world, the densest. Each houses Sophia, but so veiled is she, she remains unknown until we develop "eyes with which to see."

SPIRITUAL REALITIES
Guidance

MENTAL REALM
Aha's Inner Knowing

EMOTIONAL NATURE
Psyche

PHYSICAL/GAIA
Innate Intelligence
of Nature

The methods Sophia uses in each of the four worlds.

95

From Wakan Tanka, the Great Spirit, there came a great unifying life force that flowed in and through all things—the flowers of the plains, blowing winds, rocks, trees, birds, animals—and was the same force that had been breathed into the first man. Thus all things were kindred, and were brought together by the same Great Mystery.[1]

Our effort to discover Sophia intensifies as our conscious awareness expands from our dense reality into the subtler realms. To know Sophia more intimately, we must adjust to accommodate that which prompts us from within. Until we build a *witness consciousness,*[2] we usually miss such subtleties. Once we construct an objective platform from which to view our own life and develop an overview of outer life, we learn to sense her traces. Using her many disguises, she glides into the midst of our lives and touches us—sometimes gently, sometimes not. She often disappears just as we realize something extraordinary is occurring.

Wisdom becomes the guide to living skillfully

As we begin to notice in these more conscious "something-is-happening" moments, she is always close by. Meandering rivers illustrate how the feminine works within the physical realms. Her elusive message does not usually come directly to us, confront, or threaten. She bides her time, ponders, and like the river, finds those points of least resistance through which the living water of her Holy Spirit can flow. Little by little she creates a channel through which she can infuse the physical world with the consciousness of the higher.

A spiritual shift is brought about by this interaction. We are taught to regard spiritual law as best we can until the concepts become part of our nature. Then we can be so natural, relaxed, and open that spirit can play her tune through us. She inspires us to become a channel of her wisdom, even as the Christ enables us to embody love. In such a union, the heart

---

1. Chief Luther Standing Bear, SIOUX, from internet via Yahoo.

2. Witness consciousness is "an impersonal level of awareness created through objectivity and spiritual insight; a developed chosen perspective from which we observe life at work." —Parrish-Harra, *Dictionary,* 321.

can open. The lots of vital energy of divine love then moves with purifying effects through our being, bringing healing, will to good, and other creative energies from higher planes into lower frequencies. This impersonal, unconditional kind of love prepares us for the mystical insights that are to follow. The unique combination includes not only the "felt sense" of body and the related "inner knowing" of one's heart, but also other hard-to-describe experiential phenomena of a non-physical nature.

Physically. Sophia as Mother Nature is the innate intelligence of the natural world—the inborn patterns set in place that act themselves out in our physical body even without our comprehension. We have had little appreciation for cellular intelligence or the remarkable intelligence of an organ that knows how to perform its function. We are now learning our body has messages for us in its pain and functions. Some of us learn to ask for meanings, but many have not. We have long ignored the language of the body, but we are beginning to consider, "What is my body trying to tell me?" The intelligence within the physical dimension has long been split from our total awareness. Now we struggle to find an explanation of what has broken us into separate parts.

So now we are beginning to talk to our bodies, embrace their messages, and respect their signals. Our bodies cry out to be included, to be listened to and honored, not just endured as a necessary evil of the Earth plane which should be transcended. Just as Earth herself will no longer be silenced while pollution and environmental abuse builds, the body likewise seeks acknowledgment, care, and respect. The innate intelligence of the body and Earth desire also to share with us their own intrinsic love nature.

Emotionally. Sophia guides through our powerful emotional nature. We come to remember *"behind emotions are hidden feelings."* Abiding in our unconscious, suppressed and ignored, they have left us tired, drained, and damaged.

Fearful of our oft unstable temperament, we have struggled to control emotions and have often paralyzed or demeaned a part of the very wholeness designed to address our exile from the spirit within.

Now we are challenged to clear away the congestion of our emotional nature so we can discover a renewed sense of what we really feel about the issues of our lives. *"Feeling-states are* authentic," writes vascular surgeon and author Leonard Shlain. *"Feeling-states allow us to have faith in God, to grasp the essence of a joke, to experience patriotic fervor, or to be repulsed by a painting someone else finds beautiful."* [3]

As the emotional screen is cleared, feelings emerge to guide us to greater clarity. We discover the mind within the heart, and learn to use it for healing and revitalization. In time we learn to focus this emotion into devotion and dedication, gaining a power that keeps us moving in a desired direction.

With clarity achieved regarding feelings, we can begin to trust our newly discovered sensitivity. We note the prompting from within that registers as a feeling of "rightness." The feeling nature can now register the touch of the soul as it seeks to provide direction.

It takes time to recreate a functional harmony within this sensitive level of our nature that so easily bounces between pleasure and pain. With experience, it will develop into a means to assist us in our quest for wholeness, *"for wisdom will enter your heart and knowledge will fill you with joy* (Prov. 1.10).

Mentally. Co-opted by a power more popular but less balanced, we have believed intellectual vigor would restore harmony and provide peace for us and the world about. While we have struggled with rights and wrongs, denying ourselves in obedience to "law," the gentle nature of "inner knowing" has laid dormant and waiting.

Sophia's great task is to lead us to and through transformation

Each of us moves from gathering information by the power of the intellect to integrating it with intuitive experience as well. It is then that Sophia as the soul is grounded within. We learn that beyond intellect there is "knowing." Gradually soul's inner realizations make one wise. Wisdom becomes the guide to living skillfully, one day at a time, as a spiritual being in the material world. Physical pleasure, gentle feelings, and a mind prepared to function in a new way, give permission to connect

---

3. Shlain, *Alphabet Vs. Goddess,* 19.

with the presence within through joy and pain, passion and power. When we come to realize this, we truly begin dissolving the internal schisms that have diminished us; we can now rebuild the wholeness so necessary for healing and holiness.

A major difference Sophianic wisdom (inner knowing) brings is freedom from the confines of ego and its limited but dictatorial rational mind. Too often, inner guidance has been over-ridden for fear of repercussions: we might upset someone or be punished for following our personal perception and resisting outer authority. An internal struggle between our prized intellectual tool and the gentle but powerful inner prompter ensues repeatedly as the inner self battles to become integrated within our nature.

Hidden talents lie beneath the surface; new levels of being wait to contribute resources. If we can come to see our nature as fluid, free-flowing sparkles of life energy rather than rigid dense matter, we begin to hold a new perception of our being. We are more like a dancing waterfall than solid matter. Our mind holds us in restriction until the Self-within sets our true nature free to express.

In time we begin to dream, to recall the fairytales of our childhood, to wonder if indeed truth exists outside the box, and if so, can we discover it? Some say "no," but the poets and the song of the heart entice us to investigate. The wonder of new life and the sanctity of love strengthen us to dare to hear the wee small voice and to articulate the revelation from within.

The closer we get to genuine inner knowing, the fiercer becomes the ego, and the greater the tug of war within one's self until the choice is made. A commitment to the divine within breaks through the darkness and ego resigns, at least for the time being. A deep peace settles over and love-wisdom floods our nature for a time.

Eventually each will confront the limitations of the outer and find sanctuary within. Those who have found the "peace that passes understanding" gently encourage others, and the few become more. So it has been, but at this time the flow hastens as the divine feminine comes closer.

Spiritually. As we realize higher consciousness—called by whatever name—we come to know Sophia as *yin* the earthly representative of the feminine principle of Creation. She becomes our guide toward the Great Mystery. The wisdom aspect becomes increasingly strong as we tighten our relationship with the inner. Sophia's great task is to lead us to and through transformation, through challenges and reviews, to a new and higher plane of existence.

> *To speak of God as She in today's society is regarded as either brazen feminism or the deliberate reformation efforts of religious liberals. However, the tradition of the feminine aspect of divinity has a long history. From Ameratsu and Cannon in Japan, to Quanyin in China, to Tara in Tibet, to Shakti in India, to Akua'ba in Africa, to Isis in Egypt, to Ishtar and Astarte in the Middle East, to Demeter, Aphrodite and Venus in Greece and Rome, to the Great Goddess of Willendorf and Laussel, to Freya in Scandinavia, to Spider Woman and Ixchel the Weaver in North America, the Divine Mother has a long tradition in the history of the planet's consciousness. It appears that from approximately 40,000 BCE to approximately 5,000 BCE the Goddess was the primary deity figure. Over 90% of the figurines found from this period appear to be of a female goddess.*
>
> *Our planet has a need to reinstate a sense of the "Goddess" within its understanding of the divine; the nurturing principle of the female is needed to help guide our way through the maze of accelerated change which surrounds us.*[4]

She leads from darkness to light, making sacred the daily acts of living and dying, caring for others, nursing the infants and the ill. A motif of transformation begins to emerge in one's life. No longer is successful living equated with mere material productivity, but rather with a gracious and grace-filled interaction of unrestrained listening inward while nourishing everything touched—gardens, children, relationships, and projects—with the waters of one's spirit. One particular yogic prayer states *"she heals the fever of material life."* Bliss, the nature of the inner spirit, resonates at moments, bestowing its encouragement.

---

4. Gard Jameson, "The Goddess," received via email 11/13/03 from http://www.citynet.com/~arianna/search/.txt.html.

Some signal their readiness for her gifts. They ask questions great and small. What is my pain trying to tell me? Why does my psyche grieve? What is that wee small voice within? What overshadows my knowing? When I become quiet, what is that restlessness I detect? Dare I acknowledge subtle feelings I cannot explain, and accept intuition, as hard to grasp as it is?

Each query begets another, and soon we find we have unknowingly embarked upon a perpetual quest-without-borders. If we dare to push on, we may find ourselves venturing far from traditional safe harbors, but Sophia cares not. Once she gains our attention, she desires to draw us into her chambers. Sophia owns that proverbial field spoken of by Jesus, in which a treasure is buried. She invites us to take her shovel and dig (more and more of us are) so that we may share in her bounty—the discovery of Life behind life.

That part of Sophia we touch is like the tip of the iceberg. She observes our discontent and our apathy, tolerating our infancy. She warns, but we refuse to hear until resistance wanes and awakening cracks our protective armor. Sophia waits. Through the eyes of the Madonna, the expression of music, and myriad other creative forms, as well as through axioms of wise ones and words of wisdom long buried in traditions, she remains ever with us.

To discover Sophia we wander about collecting wisps of her presence, circling her territory, knowing we cannot truly capture her for rational analysis. The great Sophia is the fullness of soul, and the glimpses we catch are but traces of her presence registered by the inner nature on its own journey to maturity.

13

Power

*Desire, the secret fire of the heart, is a tricky thing, a lit match held to
the gas that ignites the transformations of our lives. Those who do not
realize the power of the heart literally play with fire.* [1]

—Normandi Ellis

To gain Sophia—inner wisdom—one builds the heart center, and learns to be merciful. She teaches what cannot be learned intellectually, privately guiding each, mentoring through painful avenues and dynamic adventures. *"Sages call it wisdom. Fools call it folly. Mortals call it suffering. Souls call it salvation".* [2] Sophia requires we face our fears, learn to love, and dare to be.

When we face major life lessons, we find ourselves at a testing point—the sephirah of Severity (Geburah) illustrates just such a point on the Kabalistic Tree. As we integrate what our challenges teach us, we move toward the center column of the Tree and gain the higher perspective of Mercy (Chesed).

Teachings tell us one cannot truly grant mercy to another in any situation until one has grasped what is to be learned through that particular lesson. Only someone who has had a given experience knows what powerful growth its specific challenge truly imparts. To relieve others of a test or trial does not permit the learning demanded by the circumstance.

If we "rescue" another, he or she will have to repeat the challenge in some other way in order to learn whatever that experience offered.

---

1. Normandi Ellis, "AB: The Intelligence of the Heart," *The Quest,* (Spring 1995): 30.

2. Aurora Terrenus, *The Shroud of Sophia* (Santa Cruz, CA: Publishing House of the Holy Order of Wisdom, 1988), xi.

Mercy acknowledges both the pain endured and the value of the happening. Knowledge thus gained enables one to respond wisely with compassion.

Whenever we are presented with a challenge, Sophia meets us at the edge of our mind. When we hesitate, she encourages with subtle nudges, prompting when we falter. She knows our nature even when we do not know ourselves. Even though we are unable to sense her, she works through our psyche to help keep us progressing.

As intuitive wisdom, Sophia dawns on us gradually. She breaks into our consciousness as we question or ponder. We might say she is an aha! She loves to destroy rigid crystallization and forces us to choose between the known and unknown, between the good and the good. Her touch can be a subtle force or an exciting breakthrough, but always there is a synchronistic goal, although we may see only a small part of it at any given time.

Sophia requires we face our fears, learn to love, and dare to be

Sophia manifests in each aspirant as the motivational drive spiritual ones must have. Biblical writings (Proverbs, Wisdom of Solomon, Song of Solomon, and Sirach) are resources to help us bring balance to what has been a heavily masculine portrayal of God.

Feminine attributes, both fierce and gentle, as well as the masculine, forceful and demanding, are to be perfected. In humanity, the attitude of following spiritual dogma has become so entrenched that separatism inevitably results. *"The truths contained in religious doctrines are after all so distorted and systematically disguised,"* wrote Sigmund Freud, *"that the mass of humanity cannot recognize them as truth."* [3]

Virtually exclusive identification with masculine values has skewed our foundation. The feminine nature that softens attitudes and serves through kindness and common sense can easily get lost unless Sophia, the inner knower, is consulted. When we lose our inner wisdom, we are truly lost.

---

3. Sigmund Freud, *The Future of an Illusion*, standard ed., XXI., trans James Strachey et al. (London: Hogarth Press, 1961 [orig. 1927]), 44–45.

Today we have an opportunity to uncover both old and new ways of recognizing the inner nature, learning to trust it, and restoring its value.

All life is driven by the desire to make, to do, to be. These are the secret powers of the God of Light. This is the pulse of the I AM. The secret of transformation is the secret of the heart, the nature of our passionate longing to create, to love, to express, to become one with, to be known.[4]

In wisdom teachings, each has the right to choose his or her personal path within the boundaries of civil law and social justice, but unconditional love is to be directed toward the personhood of every human being, whether or not they adhere to similar boundaries.

When in disagreement, one is not to cast another out of one's heart; rather, as spiritual maturity is attained, increased respect is demonstrated. We can dislike a personality, but we dare not deny divine love to another soul. Judgment is the trap of the intellectual mind which operates from less than soul awareness. We are not to close our heart. We may not like another, but we are charged to love each other—to keep the Lots Of Vital Energy moving through all humanity.

When we recognize Christ as love and Sophia as wisdom, ChristoSophia becomes the holy consciousness for which we quest. As we proceed to mature the Christ-within, the hope of glory, in order to be both loving and wise, we truly do begin to "think in the heart."

Such teachings underpin religious foundations as well as forming the basic psychological principles of healthy societies. Carl Jung used the kabalistic principles in formulating his perspectives of healthy functioning, as have many other modern wise men and women. Philosophers (like Pythagoras who was the first to call himself a lover [*philo*] of Sophia), prophets, seers, gurus, and shamans were the traditional wise counselors, comforters, confessors, and spiritual directors, who sought to anchor higher insights in the daily lives of their people.

---

4. Ellis, "AB: Intelligence of the Heart," 30.

We reclaim Sophia's importance as we reconnect with our sense of inner self. She remains with us even in our suffering. *"Tears, sorrow, and disappointment are bitter, but Wisdom is the comforter in all psychic suffering."* [5] Reiterating the words of feminine principles from the past, we realize these ideas are not new, but as we live with many new opportunities, we evolve to a higher turn on the spiral, allowing us to reintegrate them with new insights.

Those who actively serve humanity today follow in the footsteps of that small number in every age who become love-wisdom's fertile field. Responding to the stirring of that Divine-within, often in spite of staggering physical hardships and social rejection, these accepted their inner power, using it as best they knew how, to go about their Father/Mother's business.

> *The creative process has feminine quality, and the creative work arises from unconscious depths—we might say from the realm of the mothers.* [6]

It may come as a surprise to many in this twenty-first century to learn that Mother's Day, that billion-dollar seller of mandatory gratitude, *"began as a holiday that commemorated women's public activism,"* says Ruth Rosen in her article "Mother's Day for Peace."

> *The story begins in 1858 when Anna Reeves Jarvis organized Mothers' Works Days in West Virginia. Her immediate goal was to improve sanitation in Appalachian communities. During the Civil War, Jarvis pried women away from their families to care for the wounded on both sides. Afterward she convened meetings to persuade men to lay aside their hostilities.*
>
> *In 1872, Julia Ward Howe . . .proposed an annual Mother's Day for Peace. Committed to abolishing war, Howe wrote: "Our husbands shall not come to us reeking with carnage, for caresses and*

---

5. Carl Jung, attributed.

6. Carl Jung, *Modern Man in Search of a Soul* (1933) (tr. W. S. Bell and C. F .Payne), quoted in *Great Thoughts*, 217.

applause. Our sons shall not be taken from us to unlearn all that we have been able to teach them of charity, mercy, and patience. We women of one country will be too tender of those of another country to allow our sons to be trained to injure theirs."

For the next 30 years, Americans celebrated Mother's Day for Peace on June 2. . .In 1913, Congress declared the second Sunday in May to be Mother's Day. . .The new advertising industry quickly taught Americans how to honor their mothers—by buying flowers.

With a little imagination, we could restore Mother's Day as a holiday that celebrates women's political engagement. Imagine, an annual Million Mother March in the nation's capital with voices demanding social and economic justice and a sustainable future, rather than speeches studded with syrupy platitudes. Nineteenth century women dared to dream of a day that honored women's civil activism. We should honor their vision by rethinking the meaning of Love.[7]

The Mother of the World will not stand idly by, watching her home and family being destroyed. Her patience with patriarchal rule is spent. In hope that developing minds would choose intelligently, she held her influence in check. Now human recklessness demands her intervention; "The damage is too costly!" she cries. Too few are finding enlightenment, so for the sake of all, she intervenes.

Mother as protectress is not to be confused with Father as defender. Both are important, just different. The specific fierceness of mother bear when her cubs are threatened has long been noted. In some species, including the human, this role is often shared by males and females alike.

The defender "of the right," on the other hand, becomes politically active, striving on behalf of the collective entity or ideology of which she or he is a part: nation, faith, family, justice, and so forth. This focused power—when defensive—often accompanies duty in bold public dedication. In the heat of passion, however, it often becomes difficult to know where legitimate defense stops and unproductive counterattack begins.

---

7. Ruth Rosen, "Mother's Day for Peace," From an email, sender unknown, printed out on 5/7/03. Quotations of Julia Ward Howe from *Reminiscences* (Boston: Houghton, Mifflin, 1899), 327.

We have all witnessed political parties working harder at destroying one another than at constructive progress. Think how many atrocities have been visited on "unbelievers" by religious zealots in the name of defending the faith. The list goes on.

Have we not heard it said that "the best defense is a strong offense?" While that may be good strategy in sports, it is very destructive when used by human beings as an excuse to try to control one another. This is the force spoken of in the trite phrase "might makes right." Power, even if "altruistic," gained by use of such force can only breed ill-will and discontent in the long run, unlike the power of the soul, which abides deep within and works in subtle ways to keep us on track toward our true purpose.

Now Sophia's name is becoming evident in schools, programs, conferences, and titles. Her time has arrived. The long-patient divine feminine waits no longer. She rides the winds calling for assistance in restoring balance to the Earth, to humanity, and to the younger kingdoms.

Not only is Mother protectress, she is also prompter. She does not leave us alone—she will not leave us alone! Everywhere about us are her indicators, her guideposts. It is *our* nature that little understands what is going on, where the goal is, and what part is ours to play. To awaken us, to point direction, and to reveal level after level in which to quest, is hers to do. The returning Mother Wisdom pushes humanity to think beyond commonly held opinions, to seek a balance of justice and mercy during this opportunity for great change.

As we increase our awareness of Mother Wisdom/Sophia, we may be fearful of the power of the psyche with its enthusiasm, spontaneity, and impulsiveness. We have sought to dominate each area she rules by placing polite restraints around it.

Seeking to restrict her input to our conscious use, we deny the wholeness that will be ours if we decide to embrace life on her terms. Inevitably, we must confront the paradox of humanity and divinity that exists at the core of all religions, acknowledging the sheer power enfolded in each of us. As we come to know the truth of

Sophia does not leave us alone: she WILL NOT leave us alone

our nature, we remember Paul's admonition, *"Do you not know that you are God's Temple and that God's Spirit dwells within you?"* (1 Cor. 3.16). We are truly, "earthen vessels filled with God."[8] When we struggle to maintain tight intellectual control even as we seek freedom from our dominating personality nature, we are reminded of the often puzzling and confusing contradictions of life, such as the cryptic words of Jesus: *"Those who love their life lose it"* (John 12.25). As we accept the power of Sophia and her mysteries, we sail into the main artery of Life itself. We embrace grace, and go with the flow.

---

8. From a talk by Margaret Starbird in Salt Lake City, July 27, 2005, quoted by Elaine Jarvik, in "Mary Magdalene's Role Missing, Speaker Says," *Desert News*, July 30, 2005.

14
*L*ove

The body is an infinitely subtle, intimate and accurate mirror. It mirrors both the present and the past—in its movements and ever-changing expressions are reflected contemporary attitudes, ethics and conduct of the ever-present soul and of the Soul's (many lives) in the long-ago past.[1]

—from an Edgar Cayce reading

*L*ong before human beings evolved into the analytic, intellectual creatures of today, they were comfortable being a part of nature, and not necessarily the most superior part. Humans lived lives of instinctual awareness synchronized with natural rhythms amidst cycles of birth and death, feast and famine. As societies grew more urban, the natural arts were retained most easily by rural peoples to whom the modern word "pagan" originally referred. These continued to live attuned to nature, understanding their relationship to it.

People today who should know better believe that to be a Pagan is to be a godless heathen of some sort. . .many are startled when they hear or read the book title, The Pagan Christ. *Today, a Pagan is defined as anybody who doesn't agree with one of the major religions, particularly Christianity. But a* paganus *in Latin was [the same as] today's Italian* paesano, *a peasant from the countryside.[2]*

---

1. Edgar Cayce reading quoted by Douglas Baker, *Karmic Laws: The Esoteric Philosophy of Disease and Rebirth* (Wellingborough, Northampton, England: The Aquarian Press, 1977, rev. and reset 1982), 7.

2. Tom Harpur, "Christ-centred movements precede historical Christianity," *Toronto Star,* www.thestar.com, Apr. 18, 2004. 01:00 AM, accessed at http://thestar.com on 7/4/04.

Cloaked as Mother Nature, veiled as instinctive feelings or an innate sense of oneness, Sophia was always there, quietly guarding from out of sight until awakening came. Known as Mother of the World, the eternal companion to the Father has always played her part. Sustained animated life is created as Father breathes forth his vital spirit and Mother Matter accepts it to germinate a world of forms, human and otherwise. Together they energize their joint venture.

The combination of the two great principles grants us unfolding Life. We cannot escape their influence even if we hesitate to embrace them. Inner prompting reminds us of her life-giving mysteries whose manifold expression in human life can be arranged under six wide canopies: sexuality, birth, death, healing, intuition, and creative play. How tantalizing are her territories. Enticement is her nature; her mysteries are easily distorted to embody temptation, manipulation, and illusion—no wonder her knowledge was locked away.

Nevertheless, her mysteries remain sprinkled throughout the treasuries of both scripture and collective folk wisdom. Although often distorted into superstition, there is much awaiting our attention within formerly sealed archives of each expanding mind. Today, we are re-examining the areas Mother Wisdom rules with life-giving power that is so great we have been afraid to say her name: Sophia the Wise.

Her six major mysteries (sexuality, birth, death, healing, intuition, and creative play) are actually only mysterious when viewed from the lower mental, intellectual, and material perspective. We shall investigate each from a higher vantage point.

Sexuality—as holy sharing—blossoms with reverence, respect, and discretion. Much is to be learned from the mysteries of gender, eros, and sex in the journey to high consciousness. The importance of conscious sexual relations is stressed by some of the oldest traditions of both East and West—in Hinduism through Tantra, and within Judaism and Christianity by Kabalah, for example—which model a vast understanding of complimentary balance.

When is a man called complete in his resemblance to the Supernal?
When he couples with his spouse in oneness, joy, and pleasure, and a son

and a daughter issue from him and his female. This is the complete man resembling the Above: he is complete below after the pattern of the Supernal Holy Name, and the Supernal Holy Name is applied to him.[3]

Indigenous people likewise tend to recognize the correlation between the sheer power of sexuality—its push and how it is peppered through life—and how Mother Matter utilizes her ability to birth and renew, to destroy and cleanse. The wise know her to be a force with which to contend.

In the hands of the uninformed, this delicate area too often becomes a playground for lust, abuse, misuse, and/or control. Love and sex are different experiences. Ignorance abounds concerning the source, nature, purpose, and the appropriate means of expression of sexuality on all levels of being. Thus, unhelpful beliefs lead many to aspire to uncomfortable levels of asceticism, even as others try to satisfy inchoate urges with excessive hedonism. We come to learn as the Lord Buddha taught, the middle way is the safest for the majority of us.

Sacred sex can be used to aid those seeking to rebalance the tender nature and heal emotional wounds, as well as to ignite new life-forms for other souls. Life moves us through attraction to come together in order to empower each other, and to deepen love as souls reveal themselves in holy interaction. In addition, unfolding vistas beckon for two souls who comprehend the power gifted in reverent exchange of their essence with each other. Renewal occurs, as well as flashes of hidden awareness, as our nature experiences profound sensitivity and openness.

But sexual energy has many expressions in addition to physical sexual acts. It may be channeled into artistic creativity, or even held to rejuvenate the physical body itself. In time, through evolving awareness, we perceive sexuality as a permeating force of life, not just an action, but the underlying law of attraction that aligns all life toward wholeness, embracing dimension upon dimension. Transcending each individual's sexual preference—whether celibate, heterosexual, homosexual, or asexual—as we integrate the masculine and feminine contained in our psycho-

---

3. Zohar as quoted by Raphael Pataki, *The Hebrew Goddess* (Detroit: Wayne State University, 1967, 1978), 130.

logical nature, we achieve the mystical marriage within, the goal of the wise.

Just as each of us as an individual cannot achieve healing, wholeness, holiness, as long as we remain fragmented, so our society also needs to become aware of imbalances to be healed. Spiritual law teaches that whenever a society loses regard for gender, it disintegrates and, of course, to hold gender in high appreciation builds honor.

Both the social and personal implications of gender and polarity remain largely unknown in modern civilization. Physically, emotionally, and mentally modern humanity struggles to comprehend the significance of the law of gender. As the collective mind seeks both expansion and balance, public debate continues about whether gender-specific aptitudes and attitudes exist, and in what ways they attract, complement, or compete with one another. As we become more wise, a new respect for this mystery of Sophia will emerge and gender roles will again swing toward complimentarity.

The fall our world has experienced toward disregard of gender violates respect for the balancing principles of life. Disregard for the feminine handicaps the role of the masculine, even as it devalues nature and the environment.

In *The Divine Feminine: The Biblical Imagery of God as Female*, Virginia Mollenkott presents an interesting exegesis of the Hebrew words *ezer neged* which are translated "help meet" in the King James Bible story of the creation of Eve: "*but for Adam there was not found an help meet for him*" (Genesis 2:20). Note that the word "meet," is not, and does not mean "mate." Those who substitute the word "mate" for "meet" easily miss the point. There tends to be much confusion around this issue. This usuage of "meet" in the King James Bible is unfamiliar to us because it is most often used in a different way in modern English. The word "meet," in King-James English, as it is used in this passage, means "suitable" (i.e., "there was not found a help *suitable* for him"). Perhaps it will make it clearer if we notice that the word "helpmate," is a single word and as such cannot properly be switched to "matehelp." "Meet," however, is an adjective to the noun "help." Therefore, the sentence is just as correct written "there was not found a meet (suitable) help for him,"[4] as Mollenkott points out:

> *Many of us have heard patriarchal interpretations that reduce* ezer neged *to "helpmate," as if the female is mated to the male only in order to serve in a secondary and supportive role as man's helper. But* neged *does not emphasize matedness; rather, it emphasizes appropriateness or suitability, and thus implies equality. And the powerful associations of the word* ezer, *picked up from the way the word is utilized elsewhere, deny any subordinationistic intent . . .*
>
> Ezer *is used twenty-one times in the Hebrew Scriptures. Three times it refers to vital human assistance in moments of extreme need; sixteen times it speaks of God's direct assistance to human beings; and twice it is applied specifically to Eve, the human female. . . . [Of these] the Bible applies the word* ezer *to only two specifically named entities: God and Eve. . . . [This] creates an important analogy: Eve is to Adam as God is to humankind. Eve is Adam's* ezer; *God is humanity's* ezer.
>
> *In these. . . passages, the* ezer *is the one who is strong and autonomous, who willingly chooses to come to the aid of the one who is weak and in need. And of course that is exactly the concept of servanthood taught by Jesus and depicted in the Christian Scriptures. Power is not to be used to aggrandize the already powerful, but to empower others.* "Whosoever will be chief among you," *said Jesus,* "let [that one] be your servant" *(Matthew 20:27).*
>
> *Through Eve, women are identified as the* ezer *of the male half of the human race. Directly created by God who is our* ezer *both in huge public matters and in smaller internal crises, womankind is a unique channel of God's power to the world.*[5]

In our efforts to restore respect for the feminine we must not overreact in the opposite direction and cease to respect the masculine. This would handicap humanity as much as disregard of the feminine does. Division of the primal androgynous being described in the Adam and Eve

---

4. Definition 3 of "meet" in Merriam Webster's Collegiate Dictionary, tenth ed., says "precisely adapted to a particular situation, need, or circumstance: very proper syn see fit." The entry "fit" says "to be suitable for or to: harmonize with."

5. Virginia Ramy Mollenkott, *The Divine Feminine: The Biblical Imagery of God as Female* (New York: Crossroad, 1983), 74–78.

allegory was not intended to pit one half against the other half or to replace one with the other. The balance we seek today is not a simple adding back together of one half plus one half. Rather it is an opportunity for humankind to become more than the sum of its parts.

To find it significant to connect the linear/analytical mind of rational, logical (masculine) thinking to the associative/synthesizing mind of intuitive, inclusive (feminine) thinking seems at first glance to be a lot of unnecessary effort. However, as we begin to replace our old "either-or" attitudes with a desire for synthesis—a healthy whole—we come to realize that historically the world has always had two major cultures, work/reward and family/home, which have operated from entirely different values, but higher societies find ways to merge them into complimentary patterns.

The modern blurring of these milieus began in the United States during World War II when women's labor became necessary to the war effort. A few years earlier, the Soviet Union had declared women's equality and invited women to join the ranks of the revolutionaries. That period in the Western world saw the birth of the struggle between the "masculine" and the "feminine" paradigms; the inevitable had begun. As the impulse of a new era was beginning to be felt, the push for a "new and better model" of androgynous being was unwittingly set into motion. Freedom to become all one can be without gender restrictions began steadily increasing.

As the feminine mysteries continue to re-emerge in all their colorful variety, many are finding courage to look at themselves more deeply, and as they do, many also recognize facets of their inner nature that do not fit into the old patriarchal paradigm. But old power structures never succumb easily. A great deal of conflict and tension is still occurring in the human family as it continues to seek both expansion and balance.

Sophia reminds us it is often the part of wisdom to make haste gently, with great compassion both for our own inner journey, and for that of our brothers and sisters who live with us on Mother Earth. The divine feminine is midwifing this birth through all of its labor pains, and it is she who will welcome us into an expanded reality as we are born anew.

An eight pointed star of the Mother.

Be Thou My Vision

❋ *Close* your eyes and relax for a moment. Ask inwardly, *"What is the work of importance that my soul is to do?"* Wait: still yourself to become increasingly patient. Ask again of your inner nature, *"What is the work emerging through my soul, or spiritual consciousness, that is seeking to express in my life?"* Wait. Ask again, *"What is the reason for which I have come into the world of form?"* Wait in silence—patiently receptive—for an emerging sense of direction to come to mind.

❋ *Now shift* your attention to the bright light of the soul star over your head and observe from there your personality, body, mind, and style. See the personality: its own modes of operation. See your physical form: its strength and goodness. See your emotional patterns of love and maneuvering. See yourself giving and receiving: your sensitivity often so painful, your courage, and your struggle to respond clearly in those moments. Be aware of your mind asking, comprehending, and allowing change. See how your personality is becoming more and more attuned to its mother, your soul.

❋ *As you observe,* see the Christ-love active in your life, and see your wisdom aspect bringing a balance to the active force as you listen intuitively, waiting for the inner voice to prompt you.

❋ *Return now* to the thoughts with which we began. What is your point of focus, the true purpose of this life? What is the vision to which you can give allegiance? Are you moving toward it, comprehending ever more clearly a sense of direction?

❋ *Are you aware* of a deep-seated longing to do more, to be more? Where is the passion and fervor of your inner nature most active? With its help, can personality learn to better serve the vision for which you are striving?

✳ *Expand* the bright light of the soul star into a giant ball of beauty and color above you. As this luminous color slips over your head like a mist, allow your mind to bathe in that creative influence. Now invite the radiance of higher light to flow downward over you, to pulsate through your mental body, blessing and comforting, residing more completely within your inner nature.

✳ *Now focus* on the love-wisdom within your heart and bring to balance the active and passive parts of your being. Focus on the light of wisdom in the mind, and expand that center. Then focus on the light of love in the heart, and expand that center. Allow them to converge. As you are ready, call down the higher power of the soul star to cover and fill you with its great presence.

✳ *Rest* in this energy for a brief time. Do not examine your impressions and feelings (now is not the time), but recognize you have created an inner alignment for the expansion of consciousness within the personality, inviting the soul to guide and guard it in new ways.

✳ *We shall close* with these words: "Mother of my being, continue to work with me. Lead me to fuller expression of the part I am to play in the greater plan; continue to guide and direct me as I seek to fulfill my reason for being." So be it.

✳ *Take note* of impressions that come to you for at least the next 24 hours, as this exercise stimulates subtle responses within your nature. And it is so.

15

Lifecycle

The Goddess is the name we put on the great processes of birth, growth, death, and regeneration that underlie the living world.[1]

—Starhawk

Living as we do at the transition point between the birth of a new era and the death of the old, we can see the two streams conflicting daily. The old, crystallized and worn, struggles to hold on, afraid to give way for fear all it has built will be for naught. Yet the birth pangs persist, rhythmical and sure, one following another, each bringing the new a little closer. The unknown is dawning, birthing the cry of a new life soon to be embraced, while the old prepares to rest.

Part of this "new" information, was known to various cultures in the past, but was relegated to folk-lore and superstition as the age of reason superseded the older, wholistic lifestyles that had been centered around nature herself. Some aboriginal peoples, and a few others, retain this knowledge even now, but for most of the "civilized" population, what is really happening during Sophia's mysteries of birth, death, healing, and regeneration is indeed still mysterious.

Birth, the transfer of a soul from the unseen world into the material Earth plane, too often becomes the sterile property of the medical world, not truly comprehended as two realities overlapping.

While modern parents and attendants know that birth is never to be taken lightly, rarely do they realize how deeply these moments imprint

---

1. Starhawk, *The Earth Path: Grounding Our Spirits in the Rhythm of Nature* (New York: HarperCollins, 2004).

121

everyone involved. Early teachings suggest merely being present at a birth grants a mini-*initiation*,[2] as does presence at a death. Whenever the veils between the planes open, powerful interactions occur. Earth energies, and the greeting they implant in the basic nature of the infant, are not to be discounted. The qualities of the initial welcome affect the new individual for the duration of his or her physical life. Words, sounds, light, and emotions present embed themselves in the infant's psyche to restrict or empower the future that is offered. Awe imbues everyone there. The energy of the birthing room streams into the unconscious minds of all present, including the infant's, to ignite dormant seeds of karma and to set off resonances to which all will have to respond.

Birth and death are quite similar as each is the movement of an individual consciousness from one world to another. Both are significant doorways. The attendants at each are participants of great importance. Just as the quality of vibrations that greet and meet participants and child at birth have unseen effects, so do the vibrations affect the departing as well as those left behind, at death.

> *The breeze at dawn has secrets to tell you . . .*
> *Don't go back to sleep.*
> *You must ask for what you really want . . .*
> *Don't go back to sleep.*
> *People are moving back and forth across the*
> *doorsill where the two worlds touch.*
> *The door is round and open . . .*
> *Don't go back to sleep.*
>
> *—Rumi*

I recall a tender moment in India. One night in a small boat on the Ganges, we spoke of death, realizing with each passing moment, life is flowing toward its end. Placing tiny candles on blessed leaves to float upon the water about us, we contemplated the mystery of life and wondered what was dying in our lives at that very moment. Powerful thoughts formed as we sat gazing at the flames reflected in the sacred river.

---

2. In esoteric teaching, the word "initiation" refers to admission into sacred teachings or the spiritual life. Parrish-Harra, *Dictionary*, 132.

Candles floating on the water.
Tears flowing down our cheeks,
Hearts expanding, knowing, caring,
Personalities responding to Truth's touch.

"Truth is the highest peak of the mountain,"
so speaks our guide, Dawali.
Sincere, devout, a Hindu, educated and true
Knows action brings tension and response.

Life so strong, softens in the moonlight
We sit in the boat watching.
Fires burn bodies spent, life sweet
holds so much. Fingers of fire reach into the Ganges.

Each of us turn inward, each deepens
Pondering our lives, we review.
Asking questions of self in the city of death.
What is dying in your life and mine?

Breathe in and out, gently center.
Feel the rocking of the boat.
Each blesses self with the holy water
Knowing it to strengthen the power within Self

—Carol E. Parrish, at the Burning Ghats on the Ganges River, Oct. 7, 1996

Death—rebirth into the world from which we originally came— is not to be feared, but anticipated as freedom earned when the present quest is completed. Reverence for the dying process has faded, grief too often rules, and heartache dominates. Few can—as did shamans, priests, and priestesses of old—follow the beloved into the mists, relieved to see their safe return to whence they came.

Death is psychologically as important as birth. . . . Shrinking away from it is something unhealthy and abnormal which robs the second half of life of its purpose.[3]

---

3. Carl Jung, attributed.

The best most can do is to understand the process of dying, be supportive, listen, and respond as wisely as they can. We can engage in available training and see death as transition, understanding the powerful opportunity that so often calls as people and their loved ones move through the various stages. *The New Age Handbook on Death and Dying* [4] is one available reference giving this author's perspective. We can each continue to hold dear ones in prayer, surrounding the soul in light and love as it moves to its new home in the subtle world. Grief work is real work. Loving hearts are needed to give support to those who grieve. As we become increasingly wise, we learn this is one of the first kinds of service offered by awakened ones. Now we begin to know we are inhabitants of more than just the physical plane.

> *We do not become enlightened by imaging figures of light, but by making the darkness conscious.* [5]

One of the earliest records of death and dying ministry among Christians dates from AD 261. An outbreak of plague in the Egyptian city of Alexandria at that time was so severe, it is written, that every household was affected. The bodies of the dead and dying were cast into the streets. Christians of that era were still being forced to conduct meetings in secret. Nevertheless, at great risk of both arrest and infection, they emerged from hiding to nurse the sick, wash the bodies of the dead, and see to burials. Their bishop, St. Dionysius, recorded that *"many who healed others fell victim themselves."* Those who died were recognized by the church as martyrs of charity and were added to the Calendar of Saints. The entry may still be read today by turning to the date of February 28. [6]

---

4. Carol E. Parrish-Harra, *The New Age Handbook on Death and Dying* (Tahlequah, OK: Sparrow Hawk Press, 1982).

5. Carl Jung, attributed.

6. Robert Ellsberg, *All Saints: Daily Reflections on Saints, Prophets, and Witnesses for Our Time* (New York: Crossroad Publishing Co., 1999), 94.

Present even in suffering, Sophia shares grief. She embodies the elements of the Earth. Just as she graces moments of enthusiastic interaction with life forces at conception and birth, so is she present at death. When spirit withdraws and matter begins its return to its separate components, Sophia's sparks of consciousness continue to drive the process of each atom as it performs its encoded duty.

New awareness is now adapting our modern attitude, and rather than denying the significance of transitions, we are reinvesting them with new ways of acknowledgment. Even so, the idea of embracing death is more acceptable to some than to others.

The wise believe an approaching death is an important time for clearing unfinished business: healing of memories, releasing of regrets, and sharing of intimate feelings. Often this enables forgiveness and healing for entire families or communities and adds great value to this tender time. *The daily review* [7] becomes a life review. The inheritance—the gift of lessons learned—can now become a celebration of remembrance, with grace passing from generation to generation, blessing those who follow.

> *I am standing upon the seashore. A ship at my side raises her white sail to the morning breeze and starts to the blue ocean. She is an object of beauty and strength. I stand and watch her until she hangs like a speck of white cloud, just where the sea and sky come to mingle with each other. Then someone at my side said, "There she's gone."*
>
> *Gone where? Gone from my sight. That is all. She is just as large in mast and hull and spar as she was when she left my side. And she is just as able to bear her load of living freight to her destined port. Her diminished size is in me not in her.*
>
> *And just at the moment when someone at my side says, "There she's gone!" there are other eyes watching her coming and other voices ready to take up the glad shout, "Here she comes!" That is dying.* [8]

---

7. Also called the "Nightly review." In this exercise practiced before sleep, we review the day backward to capture situations needing repair or resolution. Considered an important discipline for serious students, this practice copes with mishandled situations daily rather than permitting an accumulation to be confronted after death. —Parrish-Harra, *Dictionary*, 194.

8. Author Unknown, loved by many.

Personal death is so unique we can't address it with many details, but no commentary on the subject can be touched upon at this time without a recognition of the death of an age. We watch an era of superb achievement turn into profound excess and over-indulgence at the cost of the disenfranchised. Glorious success has a sad death while from the same chaos new birth is emerging. We stand attentively in the midst of change, knowing birth and death are Life too.

Powerful survival keynotes have begun to sound and new paradigms are making themselves felt, just as they should. Another of Sophia's mysteries now gaining public acknowledgment and growing acceptance is the arena of healing.

Energy healing, having survived underground through shamans and mystics, emerges from shadows of disbelief and ridicule. It is available to anyone open to the esoteric approach to reality.

Today, with growing comprehension and glowing respect, the healer's hand more openly brings relief. New areas of discovery, expanded ideas, and energy yet to be put to use await the collective, as humanity's latent reserves are stimulated.

Always, some have accepted spiritual healing as a divine possibility while others could not. A number have struggled to find techniques as they marveled at healing tales found in both traditional and non-traditional literature.

Laying on of hands has held great mystique, as few practitioners could explain why or how it helped or healed. As more people follow spirit impressions and guidance, ancient techniques are rediscovered, new ones emerge, and higher regard for inner contact builds. Emerging new techniques await acceptance. Right now spirit-releasement and past-life therapies, while suspect to large numbers, are gaining favor. Results are encouraging. Participation increases and a new comprehension of the healing role of the Holy Spirit grows. The wisdom that "knows" guides the process. We find ourselves moving from observation and rationalism to participation and praise.

16

Intuition

The more the critical reason dominates, the more impoverished life becomes; but the more of the unconscious, and the more of myth we are capable of making conscious, the more of life we integrate. [1]

—Carl Jung

*O*f Sophia's six mysteries, perhaps Intuition and Creative Play are the least understood. They have much in common: intuition has been called "the play of consciousness." It is often confused with *psychism,* [2] which, though similar, is not the same thing. Intuition pours downward from the super-conscious, providing "knowings," while psychism's extra sensory perceptions perk upward from the individual or collective unconscious in a process quite similar to dreaming.

Both intuition and psychism, history records, often expand in fearful moments and trying times. The survival mechanism sends strong signals to support the well-being of humanity. Those most sensitive become restless when the collective psyche is so animated. Warnings of impending change, danger, and opportunity emerge here and there. Just as the infant prepares itself for birth, or the chick senses it is time to peck out of the shell, humanity senses change and is alerted from deep within that a new stage is arriving.

---

1. Carl Jung, *Memories, Dreams, Reflections* (1961) quoted in *The Great Thoughts,* 217.

2. Psychism. Extrasensory perception; sensitivity to nonphysical or unseen forces, allowing for heightened image and understanding. A capacity of the mind—or soul—to deliver impressions apart from an individual's physical and psychological aspects; a natural ability that allows conscious awareness of the realities and activities of subtler planes. This may be positive or negative, according to purpose and intent or level of consciousness. Ethical use of psychism does not intrude upon or violate the freedom or will of others.—Parrish-Harra, *Dictionary,* 228.

When unconscious, non-physical senses begin stirring with increased power to guide lives, we call this psychic awakening. Psyche—"of the soul"—rests in the basic nature and has counterparts to each of the five physical senses. Sight, hearing, touch, taste, and smell each have a non-physical extension which, when activated, can give rise to unique experiences. In time, this sensual knowing can be purified and harnessed to become a more direct and clearer intuition sense.

Simple exercises can awaken these extended senses and make them more readily available, but purification and preparation for greater service takes longer. Respected traditions encourage one to attain an evolving degree of spirituality while adhering to ethical guidelines whenever one seeks training in the arts of the world less visible. Inappropriate use of spiritual senses and skills can cause damage to both self and others, thus incurring karmic debts. We must remember, all spiritual people have ways of inner knowing, but not all psychics are spiritual.

Just as skill in the use of the five physical senses increases in predictable ways with specific training, so too does spiritual training enable the less-dense self to accomplish more specific tasks. As author, Shirley Nicholson has noted, *"intuition enlightens the mind, it does not eliminate the mind,"*[3] but data acquired through these more subtle senses can bypass the usual personality level of mind and pour down from more refined levels of existence. This, then, is harder to consciously recognize than input from the extended physical senses. With experience, however, we adjust our awareness to the soul's signals and come to better intuit our inborn connections. We listen inwardly and learn in the silence how to weave together a soul-infused life.

> *Psychic reality exists in its original oneness, and awaits man's advance to a level of consciousness where he no longer believes in the one part and denies the other, but recognizes both as constituent elements of one psyche.*[4]

---

3. Shirley J. Nicholson, "The Intuition: Knowledge by Fusion" *the Quest* 92, no. 2 (Mar–Apr 2004): 47.

4. Jung, *Modern Man in Search of a Soul* (1933) (tr. W.S. Bell and C.F. Payne), quoted in *Great Thoughts,* 218.

Phoebe D. Bendit, a clairvoyant, and Laurence Bendit, a British psychiatrist, studied the unfolding psychic senses and came to the conclusion that our psychic aptitudes correlate with our natural learning style. For example, if we tend to be a visual learner in our outer ways of gathering information, our inner visual sense will probably be the strongest. Should we be an auditory learner, inner hearing will probably become our most dependable sense. Likewise, if we are kinesthetic in our physical life, we shall find our psyche reflects this sense and "feeling about" something may be the strongest way we gather impressions.[5]

A word about this: my experience has been that work with healing has been the most helpful stimulus to the non-physical senses as one begins. As we learn to use our hands to feel energy, we also begin to find words for what we sense. As our interpretation of the sensations is confirmed, our trust factor provides increased confidence and we begin to note additional prompting. Soon we are more accepting of the messages we gather from others of our unfolding senses.

What we are really doing is teaching ourselves to accept non-physical sense information. When we dream, we feel, hear, think, see, and move while our body is at rest, so the non-physical sensory mechanism is already in place. Now we are consciously linking the physical we know with the non-physical of which we are becoming increasingly aware.

Accepted terms for the non-physical senses use the prefix "clear" or "*clair*" to distinguish them from the physical senses:

touch/feeling	clairsentience
hearing	clairaudience
seeing	clairvoyance
tasting	clear tasting
smelling	clear smelling

---

5. Pheobe D. Bendit and Laurence J. Bendit, *Our Psychic Sense: A Clairvoyant and a Psychiatrist Explain How It Develops* (Wheaton, IL and Adyar, India: Theosophical Publishing House, 1967).

Although the first three are most commonly addressed in Western thought, clear tasting and clear smelling are reported by yogis and others during states of spiritual ecstasy attained through meditation.

> *When the mind is turned upward into the* sahasrara [6] *and becomes stable in meditation there, the sound of thunder is heard and the tongue turns up against the soft palate. Then the aspirant starts to taste a divine savor. . .There can also be tastes of butter, milk, ghee, buttermilk, honey, and other things. . .When he meditates more and his* prana [7] *becomes stabilized in this place, the aspirant experiences divine fragrances. One can reach a very high state when one smells these.*[8]

Torkom Saraydarian[9] says we also have two additional senses to develop to become the completed human being. The first is "straight knowing," and the second is "common sense," which is not at all common. All our senses can become blocked at times by excess intellectualism, or by taking ourselves too seriously, but one of the hardest skills for many highly motivated aspirants to learn is how to relax and play.

What has happened to natural playfulness? Where has it gone? Perhaps we are afraid of being thought childish? Childlikeness is quite different from childishness. Childishness implies immaturity, pettiness, shallow thinking, lack of empathy, and greedy selfishness.

Childlikeness, on the other hand, has an open spontaneity, a quick response and playfulness. A light spirit and basic attitude of trust are some of the qualities Jesus referred to when he said "unless we become like a little child, we cannot enter the kingdom of heaven". To curb childlikeness is to lose the ability to feel awe and wonder, to learn, and to grow. It is to lose the strengthening quality of joy.

---

6. The topmost spiritual center . . . located in the crown of the head.

7. The cosmic life-force on all plains; the life-force within every human.

8. Swami Muktananda, *Play of Consciousness, A Spiritual Autobiography* (USA: SYDA Foundation, 1994), 195.

9. Consult bibliography for works by advanced spiritual teacher, Torkom Saraydarian.

How great is the play of the Mother of the World! She beckons to Her children from far-distant fields: "Hasten, children! I wish to teach you. I have keen eyes and alert ears ready for you. Sit ye down upon My garment. Let us learn to soar!" [10]

Creative play—perhaps only those who march to a different drummer truly remember how to play. To dedicate even a portion of one's life to joyful activity without a specific practical aim often invites guilt: "Oh, irresponsible one! How can tomfoolery exist among the dedicated? What will happen to the all-important work ethic? How can we perfect ourselves if we dare to play?"

Dare we not play? Our disciplined self has been made to feel we must conceal our creative urges somewhere deep within like an illegitimate child, too often excluded from the delight of daily life. Could we be rushing headlong into distress if we do not laugh, dance, sing, make love, or act foolish enough to find comfort in a few minutes of spontaneity?

How we play is related, in myriad ways, to our core sense of self. Play is an exercise in self-definition; it reveals what we choose to do, not what we have to do. We not only play because we are. We play the way we are. And the ways we could be. Play is our free connection to pure possibility.

[Play] may in fact be the highest expression of our humanity, both imitating and advancing the evolutionary process. Play appears to allow our brains to exercise their very flexibility, to maintain and even perhaps renew the neural connections that embody our human potential to adapt, to meet any possible set of environmental conditions. [11]

Little realizing the stranglehold of our Puritan heritage, we of the modern, goal oriented persuasion too often believe we must make our poor little self-within behave just so at all times. We must be *serious*, do an

---

10. *Agni Yoga* verse 20, in *Mother of the World: Selections from the books of the Agni Yoga Teachings for the New Era* (New York: Agni Yoga Society, 1956), 13.

11. Hara Estroff Marano, "The Power of Play," *Psychology Today*, July/August 1999, 37–40, 68–69.

exemplary job, achieve, and make obvious progress, even if we forfeit joy and lose our vitality in the effort. *What good does it do to gain the whole world and lose one's soul* begs the question. Sophia demands an answer. She insists we recognize our ill bodies and tempers, our discouraged minds and tiring spirits. As Mother Nature, she stirs our life currents to erupt through tantrums, illnesses, and discontent, demanding we change our neglect. She reminds us how we dishonor our bodies, our psyches, and our Earth, polluting them physically and emotionally.

We know diet affects our bodies but we must learn our thoughts and emotions do likewise. We come to realize a positive attitude, appreciation, and joyfulness lift the vibrations that tend to bind the body-form to heaviness. Slow to change, humanity resists new awareness even as it draws close.

Joy is the name given to the energy of the soul

We smile at gamboling calves or lambs; we laugh at kittens and puppies as they romp; we, however, frozen in place, resist being drawn into frolic. How do we allow the zest with which to do our transformation process to emerge , to become whole and holy? How brazen must one be to break free of restrictive patterns and a frozen heart? As we submerge ourselves in creative play, rigidity falls away.

Play can be the tones of gentle laughter or the sharing through twinkling eyes. Dear ones, we are to play or the spirit within cries. *"The opposite of play is not work. It's depression."* [12] Play breaks up the harsh formality of rationalism and creates cracks through which light enters. Play, laugh, smile a true smile, to lighten heavy burdens and brighten dark trials along the way.

Sophia understands rules, but her perception goes beyond them, often laughing at their rigidity. She appreciates humor and knows that being able to laugh at oneself is a good indicator of mental health. She is spontaneous; in looking after the well-being of her charges, she enables a new awareness of delight. Resisting excessive regulation and rational

---

12. Ibid.

thought, the heart—doorway to the soul—feels her rightness and rejoices. Mind dances as heart's truth leads the way. Like school children at recess, when we take time for relaxation, games, and laughter, we return to our daily routine refreshed and ready to begin again.

Joy is the name given to the energy of the soul. Children's voices, birds singing, bubbling brooks—such gifts play around the edges of our lives. Too long we have waited to embrace our inner nature, to playfully gain access to light-heartedness, and joyfully accept ourselves as what we are. Playfulness is a tool of balance and well-being. Creativity is to be enjoyed, encouraged, and enhanced in order for the rewards of Earth life to be realized. Thomas Moore writes:

> *The generic name for the group of singers gathered to chant the Mass or Divine Office was* **schola cantorum**, *a school of chanters. The Latin word* **schola** *referred to leisure and was related early in its history to* **ludus**, *game or play. Do you notice where the notion of school immediately leads us? Not into discipline, rules, burdens, and mental learning, but into the realms of music, game, ritual, and leisure.*[13]

There are several references to children in the Bible that speak esoterically of, among other things, the levels of self within each individual. Consider where this thought leads when you hear it as being addressed to your own internal critic and the inner child that is a permanent part of your being: Jesus said, *"Let the little children come to me, and do not stop them; for it is to such as these that the kingdom of heaven belongs"* (Matt 19.13–14). I would suggest that to stifle Sophia's spirit of creative play is to stop the child, thereby locking your adult self out of the kingdom.

Another esoteric interpretation is that we should be patient with anyone who is still immature. Jesus is saying, "don't try to keep those who are just beginning to listen to the teachings away from me. I am not just for those of you who are more advanced. Welcome the young, the inexperienced, the unlearned." We might say we are to welcome all Sophia's children including our own child within.

---

13. Thomas Moore, "Schooling Our Intelligence," *Parabola* (Spring 1997).

17

 **_Imageless_**

This unknown figure whom so many people encounter in their sleep speaks to the psyche and to the very cells of the body. She seems to push through from the very depths of the collective unconscious like a universal force that speaks individually and culturally.[1]*
—from* Dancing in the Flames

An unknown influence breaks through. It may be a thought unlike other thoughts; it may come as softly as a whisper, or like a bell demanding attention. In the manner most appropriate for each of us, Sophia steps out of the shadows and reveals herself, if only for a flash. We are fortunate if the call is loud, clear, and undeniable: usually it is not. Genereally a simple touch, a gentle reminder, a hunch, or a mysterious knowing makes a tentative impression. We sense something is happening, but have no explanation. Saying too much too openly, we are laughed at, so we become cautious. We begin to doubt. We fall back asleep, continuing our journey unaware until Sophia once again stirs us to awake.

Part of the challenge in introducing Sophia is that we have no mental image for her. *Clearly it is not enough to visualize sophianic power, but it is an important first step. . . Images do help.*[2] As we find ourselves rejecting the Sunday School picture of the stern grandfather figure with his long white beard, and the judgment this has come to signify, we stand

---

1. Marion Woodman and Elinor Dickson, *Dancing in the Flames: The Dark Goddess in the Transformation of Consciousness* (Boston and London: Shambhala, 1996), Introduction.

2. Dr. Susanne Schaup, "The Kairos of Spiritual Unity" paper given at The World Parliament of Religion, Chicago, 1993, and in Germany.

at a new beginning. With no image for an androgynous Father-Mother to turn to, we recall indigenous people utilized the concept of Father Sun and Mother Earth—in many ways the clearest symbols available both then and now.

For Christians it is interesting to recall that the late Pope John Paul II, who held the line against modernizing in so many ways,

> *publicly "... surprised both feminists and conservatives when he told a crowd of pilgrims in St. Peter's Square, in September 1999, that God has both a male and female nature and can be referred to as 'God the Mother'! A similar declaration had been made by his predecessor, Pope John Paul I, shortly before his death: 'God is both mother and father and is more mother than father.' Perhaps elderly men feel free at the end of life to kick over the patriarchal barricades in their spiritual lives."* [3]

Surprised as we may be at this admission, we know in our hearts this is so. A part of the anger many have felt at "the church" comes from its denial of that which we know to be so. When a truth is self-evident and yet persistently denied, we feel resistance, or resent the forms provided as substitutes for what we know in some deep level of ourselves. We can feel the pressure building to cry out. Made in the image of the feminine nature, women and sensitive men sense the unjustness of being denied expression—especially when the issue is not openly addressed. Even public acknowledgment of the oversight relieves some of the long-held hostility.

> *For nearly two millennia, the Christian Western Civilization has worshipped a celibate god stripped of his feminine partner. Spiritually bereaved, the lands and people now cry out for the return of the "Feminine" and the balance inherent in the "Sacred Union."* [4]

---

3. Charlene Spretnak, *Missing Mary: The Queen of Heaven and Her Emergence in the Modern Church* (Houndmills, Basingstoke, Hampshire, England: Palgrave Macmillan, 2004), 171; Ibid., quoting from Richard Owen, "Pope Praises 'God the Mother' to Pilgrims," *London Times*, 10 Sept. 1999.

4. Margaret Starbird from "Reclaiming the Sacred Union in Christianity" Workshop at Sancta Sophia Seminary, Tahlequah, OK, March 17-18, 2006.

Much fear exists around the word "goddess," so it is not a beneficial term to use today. The fury with which Judaism and Christianity opposed goddess traditions still lingers. For many, the word "God" likewise conjures up pictures of religious persecution and the ignorance of faith fighting against faith. "Mother" may be the best term we can adopt as Sophia becomes more acceptable.

We must realize we are not to return to the unconscious or instinctual way of life predominant during the ancient goddess era. Neither shall we resort to the abuse of power in which virtually every tradition has sought refuge as its peak passed. Humanity is a more conscious species now than it has ever been before, and we are developing new skills to blend with the innate as we go forward, in order to construct new lifestyles and greater perception. We are leaving behind the limited connotations traditionally attached both to the term "Father God" and to the term "goddess," and we are seeking a new vocabulary and a new identity for the Creator Almighty.

Spirit and matter are interpenetrated, not separate; they interact as yin and yang. Although the ratio of one to the other varies in different forms, all nature reflects the will of the initiator and the form of the responder. Creation is, therefore, of one essential nature: father and mother, masculine and feminine—not male and female as we know them in human form, but as impulse and reception. Neither the world nor humanity nor even the Creator can be whole without the marriage of the masculine and feminine natures.

As the representation of the feminine aspect of creation, Sophia partners with the impulse of the active masculine who set all into motion. The "he" part propels; the "she" part responds. Just as he needs her imaginative creativity to carry out his impulses, she needs the dynamic of his will to be complete. Her essence is never withdrawn but not always called into play. Tending to be passive in nature, form awaits the force of his will and her dynamic instruction.

This concept of linking partners or consorts (masculine and feminine) in spiritual consciousness is found throughout various beliefs. Pursuing the concept of mystical marriage, in Kabalah we have Shekinah and Tiphareth; in Hinduism, Shiva and Shakti; in Tibetan philosophy it is Method and Wisdom. Christ dwells in the inner world as the high consciousness which interacts with those personalities ready to be "Christed," or enlightened. This interaction is called "anointing" by some, and is done by the Holy Spirit—Sophia. It is the nature of Wisdom/Sophia to indwell every plane: physical, emotional, mental, and spiritual. Lower Sophia dwells within creation, awaiting activation so she can respond to the call of the higher. The partnership activates that which is innate to each plane as forms and personalities, in order to mature.

We are now awakening to concepts regarding Master Jesus and the possibility—many say probability—that he and Mary Magdalene were married. Increasingly, information is emerging to support such thought.

> *There were three who walked with the Lord: Mary his mother, and his mother's sister, and Miriam Magdalene, known as his companion. For him, Miriam is a sister, a mother, and a wife.*[5]

Highly respected religious scholar, Margaret Starbird, presents much credible, thought-provoking information concerning this idea in her books. From *Mary Magdalene, Bride in Exile*, we read of the customs of Jesus' time:

> *Theirs was a society where marriage was the accepted norm; it was the duty of a father to find a bride for his son soon after the boy reached puberty, and in any event before the young man celebrated his twentieth birthday . . .nowhere in scripture does anyone say that Jesus was not married. The obligation to marry and to have children was taken seriously. . . .While the anomalies [reputed celibates] we mention existed in Jesus' time, the norm in Judaism was marriage. Their language had no word for bachelor—the word used in modern Hebrew is ravak, which means "empty." Celibacy was not a desired state: "It is not good for the man to be alone. I will make him a partner like himself" (Genesis 2:18).*[6]

---

5. Margaret Starbird, *Mary Magdalene, Bride in Exile,* (Rochester, VT: Inner Traditions, 2004), 89; Jean-YvesLeLoup, *Gospel of Philip* (Rochester, VT: Inner Traditions, 2004), 65.
6. Starbird, *Bride in Exile,* 88-90.

In Gnostic writings "Divine Word" was paired with "Wisdom." Later in Greek, "Word" became "Logos" and "Wisdom" became "Sophia." A line of tension resulted as masculine power grew. Sophia then became increasingly linked with guardianship of the planet as Mother Earth, of the Hebrews as Shekinah, and later, of the Christians as the Holy Spirit. The Logos, or Christ, remains in the non-physical as the Holy Consciousness known as the Son—the SON (reflection of the divine) behind the SUN—while Sophia, the Holy Spirit, indwells and evolves each level of creation gradually back toward the Oneness.

Many new life-forms await discovery as other dimensions open before us

In the densest of matter she organizes cells and dwells therein. Hers is the sensitivity that expands and contracts in gems and rocks, the hidden vitality of the soil, and the crystalline design we now know exists in pure water. Thus she indwells all the matter of the dense world around us. Here, perhaps under duress, Mother Matter produces experiences through which she quickens the journey—both hers and ours—from the denser to the more subtle realms. She rides in the waves and churns in the wind. Her wisdom, innate and powerful, is there to prompt events that can propel us to higher awareness. Just as she can threaten, she likewise can create the beauty that uplifts.

Diverse is her work, for varied are the avenues of divine potentialities. *"Sophia gives the world qualities—she paints the Earth with color, sweetens it with aroma, and comes to us in the intimacy of touch."* [7] As the spark of consciousness in each inert particle, she is perpetually pushing to express, expand, reorganize, and unfold a higher form. The qualities of a dual active-passive creation have been long set into place. As his equal, she interprets his thought, shaping the rich design of each willed impulse. The ripple of Creator's force activates order as the masculine principle wills and feminine principle gathers quantities of responsive matter in every plane. Within these she organizes the fire of spirit into forms and shapes through which flow light, color, and vibration.

---

7. From the School of Spiritual Psychology 6th Annual Conference flyer entitled "Sacred Sensing."

In every plane exist points of consciousness to be cloaked in a variety of forms. Many new life-forms await discovery as other dimensions open before us. Similar to the rhythm of a poem seeking its poet or a celestial sound needing a vibrating instrument in order to be heard, she shapes matter in response to potentials desiring expression and lives within each form as the encoded patterns of nature, fulfilling the role of each until survival is threatened. Often external threats activate the will-to-live, Mother Nature's 9ll code, overriding the status quo. Eternally receptive, new crises within creation automatically invoke her to adapt old embedded codes to meet current challenges, stimulating evolution.

In our own species, Homo sapiens, Sophia's innate wisdom can be classified several ways. Mentally, we have levels of intelligence classified as instinctual, unconscious, conscious, and inspired. Within the folds of each level are dimensions easily overlooked and unrecognized in regard to wisdom.

Sophia leads us from believing we <u>are</u> a body to knowing we are an incarnated soul <u>in</u> a body

To those who ponder, Sophia becomes an illusive awareness at the edge of mind. Not fully amenable to conscious expression, we have not known how to relate to that which lives at the edge of mind, but intuitively we acknowledge "knowings" the instinctual nature provides.

Childbirth is a great example. Our head may not know how to produce that which is developing within, but at the appropriate time, inner systems shift as needed to bring forth the child. The libido that hides in the body has served the species by bringing forth new life. Not to be belittled, libido is one of the avenues of sensory perception placed in the human psyche by Sophia herself. *"When we turn away or neglect the sensory realm, we turn our backs on Sophia. Without depth of sensing there can be no possibility of experiencing soul or being receptive to spirit."* [8]

Powerful senses with which to explore the environment also exist in the subconscious realms in which innate Wisdom finds herself. Unconscious responses to subliminal organic molecules of smell, or pheromones, for instance, are an example of Wisdom's cellular intelligence

---

8. Ibid.

acting directly upon us. We often are not consciously aware of the reason we sometimes react to those about us with seemingly arbitrary and sometimes puzzling likes and dislikes. The perfume industry capitalizes on this, and advertising agencies address their messages to this subliminal level of mind to influence, affect, and sell.

Becoming more conscious is most often called "awakening" because the process is like waking from dreamless sleep. To become mindful of emerging opportunities for choice or expansion, our conscious self must become aware of the restrictive programming it has received subconsciously. As we evaluate this ongoing unconscious conditioning and understand its impact, we can make conscious decisions as to what we will keep or delete. It is no wonder we have been described as computers.

We have long given great regard to I.Q., the intelligence quotient. Measurement is determined by how effectively the mind can analyze, rationalize, and/or strategize. The term I.Q. recognizes the ability to retain information and process it in rational ways acceptable to certain systems. This level of mind is particularly useful to our outer activities.

More recently we have learned the importance of E.Q., emotional intelligence.[9] One indication of the presence of this highly valuable form of intelligence is an ability to "feel" with another, or have empathy. The skill of building rapport with others through developing genuine feeling requires it. Those adept at this are known as "people persons."

Yet a third type of intelligence is now emerging into public awareness. Identified by some as S.Q.[10], spiritual intelligence acknowledges that Earth and her kingdoms form an interactive system, affecting and being affected by one another. S.Q. works for the betterment of the whole, seeking to move the human kingdom into proper alignment of its members with each other, and with the other kingdoms of Earth to the benefit of planetary life. I would dub S.Q. as the Sophia Quotient. Working for the benefit of all is Mother Wisdom's role.

Sophia the Holy Spirit, as teacher and guide, leads us from believing we *are* a body to knowing we are an incarnated soul—a spiritual being

---

9. Daniel Goleman, *Emotional Intelligence* (New York: Bantam Books, 1995).

10. International Institute for Transformation—Live and Work with Meaning and Purpose, "Spiritual Intelligence Self-Test," http://www.iitransform.com/selftest.html.

experiencing a set of physical, emotional, and mental sensations in the dense physical world through life *in* a body. Additionally, we come to realize our individuated spiritual and physical selves are also components in even larger collective units, all part of humanity who is part of creation and Life, the One, the All—however we would say it.

The collective mind, like the personal mind, or psyche, consists of seemingly polarized characteristics in constant debate with each other. Not understanding the evolutionary role of such polarity-driven conflict, individuals and societies often believe balance is the ultimate achievement; however, the progress (evolution) of the whole is the most important goal.

Balance, in this sense, is actually a place of stasis, an inert point of reconciliation between two opposites. Since it is motionless, it can exist only briefly until the guiding consciousness of the moment tips the scale, allowing the innate urge toward maturity to resume its course. We pause at an eddy of life to catch our breath and rest, but to attempt to live in any resting place permanently is to atrophy and die. To live, we must sooner or later resume our journey.

The descended female element always abides within matter (mother is the form builder), while the incarnated masculine element's role is to initiate action. Another way to express this relationship is: personality recognizes a choice and makes a decision; this action ignites a chain of events through which personality learns lessons about cause and effect. In this manner personality draws upon the masculine principle to evaluate the choices and to make decisions, thus activating the "cause" to which the feminine principle innate within the material realm responds. Thus in each dimension we see Wisdom driving awareness (evolution) through her response to action.

18

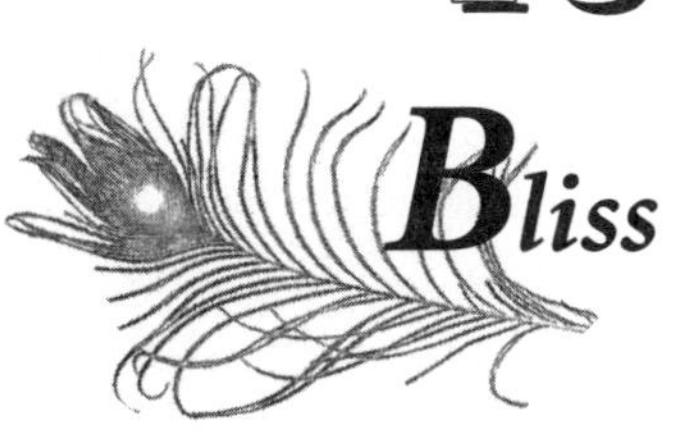

*B*liss

—Swami Muktananda

*I*n this critical new era we are advancing into a period of increased regard for the well-being of all, rich and poor, churched and unchurched. In order to properly acknowledge the progress achieved by the divine masculine, we must integrate its remarkable accomplishment with its necessary counterpart, the divine feminine—Sophia.

This balance checks the cruelty of rational power "over." It hastens soul-infusion which is the goal of a more enlightened collective wherein a co-working relationship between soul and personality is sought. When the perfected personality (the integrated three lower bodies: physical, emotional, mental) has achieved incorporation with the soul, this union empowers the personality to a new level of expression. We could say the task becomes to spiritualize the world of matter.

To spiritualize matter we draw the energy of higher consciousness into the denser outer life. This includes integrating each aspect of personality so that it can function as a healthy unit. It certainly includes bringing rational and inspired mind into a co-working relationship with our

---

1. Muktananda, *Play of Consciousness,* 230.

143

own personalities, as well as welcoming inner knowing within our mental processes.

Emotionally we check the quality of the surges this nature produces. Until we bring healing to our wounds and tame the anxious ego, we will most often deny our subtler feelings which live behind the veil of defense mechanisms. As ego learns to trust the inner knower, it can relax into safe participation with the tender feeling nature. We recall that behind intellect is inner knowing, and behind emotion is feeling.

Metamorphosis

Belief that difficult life experiences
teach more than easier ones
is not always correct.
Each experience offers infinite learning.
Ponder.
Be present.
Invite silent implosions of unfolding truth;
each holds infinite possibilities of joy
which abounds in the great Plan.
We discover it one jewel at a time.
> —Carol E. Parrish
> Meditation, 1978

The body also has to participate in this spiritualization process because cells themselves have recorded memory as well as the intelligence with which to do their function. So cells retain memories of the pain, the rejection, or the trauma experienced by the body. Healing or spiritualization of matter requires release of these tense imprints so revitalization can occur, whatever name we give it. Body, with its close relationship to heart and mind, requires love and appreciation long lacking.

The unawakened personality uses sexual climax as the unconscious way to rebalance this innate body consciousness; we know this as our animal nature. It tends to be demanding; yet, with gentle training, it becomes increasingly trustworthy and energetic. We need the "oomph" it provides for passion, drive, and daring. It transforms into the *basic self*[2] that can play, and be spontaneous and trusting.

In this study we seek a mystical comprehension of the veiled feminine nature hidden within the matter side of life. She, Mother Matter/Sophia, holds the space—the creative matrix, or womb—in which all things are made possible. From this space emerges a form through which the spark can come "to know" and to express. We call this the inner child, or the divine seed awaiting germination.

Long before humanity achieved its present mental prowess, it survived by the instinctual knowing within matter. Consciousness progressed—whether slowly, meandering aimlessly, or more quickly when threats to survival stimulated natural adaptations—in ways totally apart from the rational mind which had not yet coalesced.

In times of transition, such as the changing of the ages, during which the atmosphere and environment undergo chaos, life often becomes quite volatile as humanity itself transforms, striving toward a higher rung on the spiral of evolution.

Such times are always frightening for many while eagerly recognized as ripe opportunity by others. We can think "best of times, worst of times." Rapid changes destabilize society, upsetting the equilibrium of the status quo. Breakthroughs coming fast and furiously counteract the steady dynamics of traditional value systems. New concepts will become clearer as the future begins to take form. More and more leadership will gradually emerge to provide direction, and answers to crises will congeal into new systems.

One part of humanity sees only the despair and downward slope as another rises upward, affirming the new vision as transition reigns. In this shuffle, the collective of humanity develops a new center of gravity

---

2. (Also basic nature, lower self, or self with lower-case s). The personality we choose for this life, possessing certain characteristics, such as masculine and feminine traits. . .it includes our specific emotional and mental patterns, intuitive capacities, likes and dislikes, and so on.—Parrish-Harra, *Dictionary*, 33.

with new patterns, re-energized and more capable than before, even when it does not recognize what is occurring.

We could see this as masculine energy being invaded by feminine currents, diluting the world the masculine has built. In reality, this is a transformation. Since the Piscean era has been constructed of emotional-devotional drive, it has been quite forceful and often focused into narrow pursuits.

The incoming energy of the infant Aquarian Age-yet-to-be has a more thoughtful nature, more inclusive, more tolerant of diversity, and better fortified with a cosmic sense of beauty and orderliness. Its nature is humanitarian and universal with high sensitivity to resources, both human and environmental.

Currently, the energies of change swirl about in the group consciousness with little regard for personal goals and attitudes, permitting humanity to choose reconstruction or deconstruction through its collective will. Spiritual teachings say in this way humanity gets what it chooses.

Teachers call for the dedication of lesser will to higher will. Mystics promise the universe loves us and is committed to carrying us forward to enlightenment. By achieving soul-infusion (through transformation and the spiritualization of matter)[3] humanity advances itself on behalf of the collective and of the planet, moving all toward a closer relationship with the divine principles of love-wisdom.

Subtle senses often convey to our understanding a non-intellectual grasp of a situation. Some insights seem to just come into play, contributing to our role as a part of the whole. Generally our inner knower prompts us toward personal well-being, but not always. We may be playing a part in a collective drama of which we recognize little. Unexpected circumstances appear, as if from nowhere, to sweep us along. Coincidences and synchronicities abound.

It is the work of the world to pull us off our path; it is our work to keep ourselves on it

---

3. Think of this as increasing or expanding the light within each cell of matter.

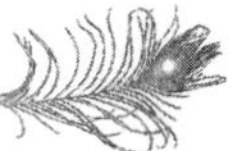

Moved at times to act in ways we cannot rationally explain, toward visions only partially formed, or goals so wispy we cannot yet articulate them, we surprise ourselves. This is particularly clear when we unknowingly participate in coincidences or synchronicities, and only later recognize their pattern. As we each own our personal transformation, we come to acknowledge those times of choice, desire, or inspiration that have guided us, even when we did not realize what was happening at the time.

In such a way all humanity builds the collective future, although most people see only the significance of the individual life he or she is experiencing. We mature gradually to emerge in due time like a butterfly leaving its cocoon. Within each, Sophia may stir as a hint, a dream, a vision, a perception, or a "just knowing"—all are applicable terms. She awaits an opening, then slides gently into place or leaps forth without warning. Both ways are rich with revelation and purposefulness. The feeling of rightness one senses demands an alignment with this "truth" of one's own nature.

We tend to think of the Holy Spirit, the Comforter, as pleasant like a nice picture of Mother Mary. Might she also be the temptress checking to see if we can stay true to our path, our higher nature, and our aspiration? She is also the trickster, the tester; each tradition acknowledges one. Temptation always comes to us in a beautiful package—desirable, lovely, and somehow particularly appealing.

Human life bounces between ecstasy and pain. Tender areas of challenge move us from perspective to perspective, maturing us as we go. As we progress, we usually meet a struggle between our earthly goals and our inner ones. The wiser we are, the more of "the big picture" we are able to see, so we are less prone to equate personal preference with good and personal distaste with bad. Increasingly we see our choices as being between good and the good.

The biblical book of The Acts of the Apostles might rather have been called The Acts of the Holy Spirit, as it recalls the marvels of Spirit at work in the lives of human beings, astonishing both those imbued with power and the incredulous witnesses.

Remember, it is the work of the world to pull us off our path; it is our work to keep ourselves on it. It is the work of the Holy Spirit to strengthen us in our inner knowing so that we can employ resolve and purpose. As we become more aligned to the higher will, we choose more easily between the various forms of "good" offered us, more ably discerning which is for our higher good or which is the best opportunity offered us at a given time.

Sophia, whether called Mother Wisdom, Gnosis, Holy Spirit, or one of the other names given her by different traditions, addresses that high point of consciousness recognized as the source of intuitive knowing. Jesus refers to this intuitive function of the Holy Spirit when he says, *"But the Advocate (or Helper), the Holy Spirit . . .will teach you everything, and remind you of all that I have said to you."* (John 14:26) This advocate is strong and transforming. Guided, we come into an ever closer relationship with the powerful feminine, as we are tended by her care.

> *[L]isting a few of the names Sophia goes by . . .is a lovely litany. Yes, she is Judaic, she is Christian, she is Buddhist, she is Moslem, she was and is and will be everywhere that anything is manifest in form.* [4]

Once recognized, her touch gains our allegiance, and with a bit more experience we respond more readily to the insights she brings as we become increasingly comfortable in her embrace. She inspires us as she lifts us above our usual level of comprehension, thrilling us with inexplicable realizations. As aha's abound we find ourselves within her bliss.

> *It is miraculous. . .If you do follow your bliss you put yourself on a kind of track that has been there all the while, waiting for you, and the life that you ought to be living is the one you are living. . . . If you are following your bliss, you are enjoying . . .that life within you, all the time.* [5]

---

4. Alice O. Howell, *The Dove in the Stone: Finding the Sacred in the Commonplace* (Wheaton, IL; Madras, India; London: The Theosophical Publishing House, 1988), 25, 26.

5. Joseph Campbell with Bill Moyers, *The Power of Myth* (New York: Doubleday, 1988), 120.

Dove of the Holy Spirit

A New Day Comes

"The oldest wisdom in the world tells us we can consciously unite with the divine while in the body: for this each is really born. If one misses his or her destiny, Nature is not in a hurry; she will catch up with that one someday and compel him or her to fulfill her secret purpose." —Rhada Krishnan

❁ Take a deep breath and begin to relax. Close your eyes. Now hear, sense, and feel a very light rain-like mist falling all around you. Take a breath, and smell the fresh sweetness of it.

❁ Become aware that this mist is the outpouring of an essence from the higher worlds, filling the atmosphere with a new vitality, quickening the spirits of all who can perceive its presence.

❁ Now let us seek to absorb this mist into ourselves, to capture its nourishment and bring refreshment to our personal nature. Quietness allows us to assimilate this essence that nourishes our true self. We know this is the Love of the Soul, the Mother watching over us, sending forth life-giving energy to work through us, her wonders to perform.

❁ A soft light grows within as we drink this love energy; the glow of inner wisdom blends with the mist of love, and they become one. We relax as we feel tender care surrounding us and we come to know our needs will be met.

❁ We are becoming stronger, clearer, and more vibrant day by day. This gentle outpouring provides all we need as we mature into our ever-wiser self—the mind in the heart and the heart in the mind are strengthened.

❀ Gently, the atmosphere returns to its usual state, but we know our inner nature has been revitalized. We feel new openness to the sensitive inner reality that provides the experiences and support we need in order to grow.

❀ We are grateful for our association with other dimensions, for the care we receive from them. We acknowledge our relationship to the divine by whatever term we may use.

❀ Now we return, embracing the body physical, respecting and caring for it as our personal vehicle of expression in this denser dimension. We understand we are spiritualizing matter by loving the body and engaging joyfully in the work of holding a high consciousness in the dense garden of creation.

❀ We sound the sacred OM gently and clearly three times, holding the thought, "Go and do a holy work." Daringly, we remember we have come into body to grow, to love, and to serve.

❀ We participate consciously now in the clearing of the miasma from the dense world around us. As world servers, we rejoice that we can participate in the transformation of our nature and our planet from the old to the new.

We give thanks. Amen.

19

Mystery

We shield ourselves from the mystery, for the mystery threatens and can even dissolve our egos. . .but the mystery will not let us alone, and there are always those disturbing moments when we stand face to face with the Unknown and Unknowable.[1]

—Jay Williams, M. Div. Ph.D.

*I*magine that each of us lives in a multi-story building but we have been restricted to the ground floor. We love our living space and enjoy it thoroughly. There is no sense of deprivation, all life is colorful and sensory, and we have no desire to travel elsewhere. We are comfortable in our ignorance that there are other floors besides the one with which we are familiar. This is basic human nature. Each of us has lived in such a way.

Then we begin to catch brief glimpses of clues that this building in which we live is larger than we thought. This is the beginning of our awakening to a larger reality. We awaken for brief periods of time—during pain-filled events, or when divine discontent penetrates, or in moments of ecstasy, or when we witness amazing "coincidences"—only to go back to sleep when life returns to "normal." So humanity travels forward in evolution asleep, occasionally awakening and then returning to sleep. The trick is to learn to stay awake.

---

1. Jay Williams, "Speechless Before the Mystery: Skepticism, Faith, and the World's Religions," a paper delivered at the 1993 Parliament of the World's Religions, Chicago, IL, and printed in *The Quest,* (Winter 1993): 29.

Before awakening, we drift unconsciously in our journey, with the basic goal of self-satisfaction as our prime mover. But as we come to realize our nature is soul, we can base more of our choices on inner knowing.

Teachings suggest we come to awakening through one of two significant means: 1) When the outer senses become saturated, desire lessens, so their hold over us diminishes; 2) Higher awareness arises from following the trail of subtle messages we have received, be they dreams, impressions, subconscious urges, or discovered synchronicities. Through these we begin to build a new perspective from which to view unfolding life. Even though veiled from humanity in general, this is Sophia, patiently guiding with her ever-present stimuli and unconditional compassion, and we begin to trust this "something more," this beneficent mystery.

Indeed, the *truth shall set you free* is a mystery, one never knows just how "truth" will work in one's life. As we come to recognize Sophia's presence, we can use her promptings and touches, coincidences and synchronicities, as aha's (like spiritual jolts) to keep us consciously aware of the help we are getting from our mother (Mother Wisdom). Then we do not neglect using our will to follow through on the flashes of direction we perceive. A Sophia-flavored life offers spice and dash. When we are stimulated, we taste her goodness and our expanded senses entice us to return time and time again to seek her presence.

Once our perception is acknowledged and our inner senses become more recognizable, she leads more clearly. Awakened ones demonstrate more perception, creativity, and inventiveness. Their spirit is freer to chart new pathways and to utilize her gifts. Certainly the paths to her are many, but rigidity often denies opportunity until a catalytic circumstance arises.

Until we discover we are one with the All, we suffer in separation. We have come from the Oneness; now we must return to the One—to knowing we are always enfolded in that all-encompassing essence we call Creator, Source, Father-Mother, Omnipotent, or Absolute. Lacking the extended-sense awareness with which to perceive that presence, the majority remain captive to the intellect.

Isolated within this ego-bound intellect, (the ground floor in our allegory) we have not known ourselves as a constituent part of the collective soul of humanity, much less as a member in the bodies of Earth, of the Solar System, the Galaxy—indeed, of the entire Cosmos. As awakening permits us to begin hearing the Mother of all these levels of creation, *Our* Mother, we are overwhelmed by the greatness of this extended kinship.

How do we preserve our individual integrity while we learn how all the discrete parts of this vast ocean of beingness fit together? Our quandary is eloquently stated in these questions posed by Sophiologist, Robert Powell: *"Poised between the inborn wisdom of the mineral, plant and animal kingdoms and the distant dance of the starry cosmos, modern human beings can feel lost. Where do we fit in? How can we come to a knowledge of ourselves that relates us responsibly to all the kingdoms of Nature?"* He follows these questions with information through which we may begin to seek our answers:

> *The path of Sophia, the Divine Wisdom, leads to such new star wisdom, as it opens an ever deepening knowledge of the mysteries of the human being: (1) the mystery of the body, connected with the four Elements, earth, air, fire, water; (2) the mystery of the soul and its interweaving with the seven planets; (3) the mystery of the spirit and its relationship to the twelve signs of the Zodiac. During the Middle Ages, at the School of Chartres in France, this path lived in the stream of Christianity that thrived there. The teachers and enlightened pupils at Chartres and elsewhere perceived Sophia in the Goddess Natura, as Rudolf Steiner describes:*
>
> *"The human being in his outer bodily nature partakes in the life and weaving movement of Earth, Water, Air, Fire which take on organic form in him. They who thus looked into the life and weaving movement of the Elements . . .did not see mere natural laws, but behind all this life and weaving movement they saw a great and living Being, the Goddess Natura . . .Then the teachers would lead the human being from a conception of his bodily life to an understanding of his life of soul. They made it clear to him: . .Your soul stands under the influence of the planetary world of Mercury, Jupiter and Venus, of Sun and Moon, Saturn and Mars. Thus, if psychology were to be studied, the*

> *human being's vision was directed upwards to the secrets of the plane-*
> *tary world . . .When it was a matter of considering the spiritual life,*
> *they turned their gaze upwards to the fixed stars and their configura-*
> *tion. They looked up above all to what is represented in the Zodiac.*[2]

All of these things have their impact within the collective cosmic system in which we live and move and have our being. We are not outside of it, we are immersed in it. But we entered life as spiritual infants. We only develop the ability to see beyond our crib little by little as we begin to grow up. Sophia knows that within each basic nature rests the seed of unlimited potential needing her care; it is we who may not know this.

Think of a seed planted within the earth: to germinate, it needs both light and water. The divine seed within our human nature likewise needs both. Tears provide the water. It matters not to the seed if these be tears of joy, delight, sadness, or rejection, they still provide the moisture needed. Tears are a part of the water mysteries of the divine way. Prayer and meditation invoke the needed light to arouse this seed, this quiescent self, deep within to begin the quest for conscious life. Stimulated by the light of the soul and the needed water, the consciousness enclosed within slowly puts forth its sprout.

At each stage, Sophia appears, advancing with us level by level

Consciousness advances as we progressively build an identity, one level after another within our unfolding nature. From conception, the individual cells and functions of the body are encoded in the DNA. Experiences encountered in turn stimulate the basic self which contains unfinished business left from previous incarnations. Though the entire physical is born, the true identity is yet to unfold. By age two, we begin to declare "no" and fight for personal boundaries. We claim our power and delight in expressing it independently of the will of others. Later we will learn how limited we are, but for now the exercise of personal power is progress.

---

2. Rudolph Steiner, *Karmic Relationships*, Vol. IV, Lecture 4, quoted by Robert Powell, *Star Wisdom and the Path of Sophia*, A workshop with Robert Powell, Portland, OR, July, 1994.

Yes, they are independent creatures, these godlings. They are hard to guide, to prompt, to nurture; but Sophia stays faithful to her task, awaiting the awakening of each. She cherishes and sustains every precious one, seeking to relate the embodied points of consciousness back to the One.

As youths, we gain greater stages of empowerment. First we know ourselves through the physical identity—name, size, and shape. Next we identify with our emotions. Like a drama queen or king, we journey through the world of desire, likes, and dislikes. As we unfold our mentality, we become increasingly comfortable, trusting the strengths of our personality, opinions, and personal knowledge.

At each stage, Sophia appears in her disguises, advancing with us level to level. Much as a child moves through school from grade to grade, our perception advances as does our focus of identity. A young child may be comfortable sharing inner awareness without inhibition. However, the more impacted we are by our society, the more resistant to, or cut off from, innate knowing we become. Fearing rejection if we appear to be different, we increasingly struggle for acceptance, to be of the same mind as our colleagues.

To be accepted is the main goal of group mind prior to individuating. In time this armor will crack as experience and pain, the great teachers, work on us. Personality will cry out—invoke, question, and demand—and the subtle nature held deep within will begin to stir. Mother Sophia, the Holy, is the answer to the homelessness of one lost in matter. She observes the ember within and patiently breathes upon it. Awakening begins. Sophia watches over the sons and daughters of the Most High, eternally ready to guide them home to the higher realms from which they descended.

In the beginning, Wisdom (Sophia), so the story goes, perceived the active will of Creator and rushed to fulfill his divine thoughtform. Thus she received the impressions and manifested them, filling plane after plane with life forms, each containing sparks of the divine. At the slowed frequency of the material plane, Sophia paused, to await the next impulse. Her spiritual nature was now imprinted upon all the worlds—spiritual, mental, emotional, and physical. Within her embrace each particle recorded her essence. Each minute atom and cell held as much of her wisdom as it could.

The imprint provided a specialized kind of intelligence, a subconscious instinct, specifically tailored to each unique life form. Mother Matter stretched herself to the very end of the frequency sent forth by the divine active impulse. Therefore she—the mother—indwells all matter, and her wisdom seeks to activate the potential held within every encoded part. Each awaits self-fulfillment so a response can be shaped to Higher Will, as best it can be perceived, in accordance with its divine design.

Mystery as Friend

There is That so far above we cannot fathom,
so far beyond we cannot comprehend.
Yet, from those outer reaches beyond measure
comes this strange speaker of our language
to sit with us, and share as friend with friend.

—Lee Warren
Sparrow Hawk Village, Winter 2005

20

*S*hekinah

When the thought arose in God of creating a world, He first created the Holy Spirit to be a sign of his divinity. . . And He created the image of the Throne of His Glory . . . which is a radiant brilliance and a great light that shines upon all His other creatures. And that great light is called the Glory of our God. . . And the Sages call this great light "Shekinah." [1]

—Judah ben Barzillai al-Bargeloni of Barcelona

Sophia, herself, may be called the greatest mystery of all: Queen Mother, Empress of Nature, Queen of Heaven, Mother Wisdom, Kundalini Shakti, Holy Spirit of Wisdom, Shekinah—her names are as myriad as her tasks. In every time, in every place her roles have been acknowledged even when she herself was not recognized. As Father God became identified within the Hebrew tradition, for example, Sophia did not fail to perform the role of Mother Goddess, Father's necessary counterpart for the function of creation.

Most of us think of Judaism as patriarchal without any concept that once upon a time a goddess was an important part of the tradition, and in some way continues to be. She is called Shekinah, *"She who dwells within."* This term comes from the Talmud and even though the Bible never mentions her name, most of us have heard it, linking it mostly with Kabalah.

---

1. John Nash, "The Shekinah in Esoteric Judaism," 3, quoting 11th-century Talmudic scholar, Judah ben Barzillai al-Bargeloni of Barcelona, quoted in Gershom Scholem, *On The Mystical Shape of the Godhead* (NY: Schocken Books, 1991), 21.

159

In the Kabbalistic doctrine of God, fully developed in the Zohar, the feminine element plays an extremely important role. As Gershom Scholem, the foremost authority on the subject, put it, the introduction of the idea that the Shekhina was the feminine element in God, "opposed to the Holy One, blessed be He", as the masculine element in Him, was one of the most important and lasting innovations of Kabbalism. [2]

The short story of the long history begins with the Biblical verb *shakan*, meaning "the act of dwelling" but taking the feminine form. The word "Shekinah" meant the aspect of God that dwelt among the people and could be detected by use of the senses. We may associate her with the glory of the Lord that filled the tabernacle in Exodus 40.35, "*Moses was not able to enter the tent of meeting because the cloud settled upon it, and the glory of the Lord filled the tabernacle.*"

From the Talmud we read, "*Let them make Me a sanctuary that I may dwell (**vd'shakhanti**) among them.*" Later translations said "*Let them make Me a Sanctuary so that My Shekinah will dwell among them.*" So here we see a separate entity being acknowledged. It is she, the feminine being, settling in to live intimately with her people.

Yahweh has been a demanding God for his people and while he worked forcefully and directly through his prophets, there was a need as well for a strong yet gentle feminine force to nurture and support.

during the 13th century, when Kabbalism invested Judaism with a new vitality, she emerged as a distinct female deity, possessing a will and desire of her own, acting independently of the traditional but somewhat shrunken masculine God, often confronting and occasionally opposing Him, and playing a greater role than He in the affairs of Her children, the people of Israel. Corresponding to this reassertion of her personality, she, although often still called by her old name Shekhina, summoned another name as well more fitting to her new and high status: Matronit, the Matron, Lady, or Queen. [3]

---

2. Raphael Pataki, *The Hebrew Goddess* (Detroit: Wayne State University Press, 1967, 1978), 32, 33.

3. Ibid., 32, 33.

Now the glorious mother figure returns. She is *Shabbat Hamalka*, Queen, Bride of God. She is celebrated around the world as the Sabbath candles are lit at dusk every Friday.[4] We must remember, the candles are lit by women only. Thus each woman is a priestess to the Divine Mother, and whether they know it or not, she knows.

Eastern teachings use the term *kundalini* for this inner presence. The word kundalini ("serpent" in Sanskrit) is often combined with the word *shakti* meaning "power." Thus *Kundalini Shakti* is often considered to mean "Serpent Power." In truth, however, it carries a connotation of "God Immanent," referencing the spiritual force or creativity awaiting within to be called forth.

In John 3.13 we read, *"No one hath ascended into heaven, but he that descended out of heaven."* This is summarized in an old teaching myth. The story tells us that the Kundalini Serpent (mobile life energy) was originally in Heaven, but one day she found a ladder that extended down to Earth. Being curious, she went down the ladder and enjoyed herself looking around. After awhile she tired of this and decided to return home, but although she searched everywhere, she was unable to find the ladder. This terrified the serpent, so she found a cave (the root chakra) in which to hide, coiled up three and a half times, and fell asleep.

When this power is awakened—generally through meditation—it moves up, and at each chakra meets separate energies flowing downward. This combination of energies activates, or opens, each center, affecting its psychology through higher states of consciousness. Upon kundalini's descent—usually at the end of meditation—each center retains a greater degree of balance and healthy power.

Egyptian writings traced back to about 3500 BCE say that during the deep darkness the Sun god enters the tail of the serpent. After passing through the body, the Sun god emerges through the mouth into the light of the new day.

The mystery of the Shekinah appears in various kabalistic writings concealed in symbolic terms. This conveys the idea of a feminine force

---

4. Ilil Arbel, Ph.D., "Shekinah," on-line article created 19 June 1999; last modified 27 April 2000, Encyclopedia Mythica, accessed 13 Sep. 2005.http://www.pantheon.org/articles/s/shekinah.html.

which is in exile in the world until it is redeemed, and as such, she remains with us, coiled at the base of the kabalistic Tree—the Judaic equivalent of the Hindu kundalini. Recall the directive, *". . . be wise as serpents and innocent as doves"* (Matt. 10.16).

It does not require much imagination to see the parallel between this and the passage of the kundalini from the darkness of the cave of the lowest chakra to its emergence into the light of the highest. Or, as understood in Kabalah, the emancipation of the Shekinah, who was trapped in the darkness of the world, is achieved. When the snake is coiled and motionless, she emulates the resting (sleeping) Godhead. She moves upward in response to the call from the higher. Awakened, she is now ready and able to express herself.

An interesting story tells how, as the Elohim were creating humanity in their image and likeness, they sought a place to hide the key to the god nature. The great ones debated hiding it high in the mountains or deep in the ocean. After lengthy discussion, they decided to hide it deep within the human being because that would be the last place humanity would tend to look.

So it is. We explore outer realities; we adventure and explore the world about us. Finally, when we think we have done it all, we ask, "Is there not more to life than this?" For most, only now does the quest for the real Self begin.

As each soul matures, capabilities known as Gifts of the Spirit are often activated

The Shekinah can easily be compared to the Holy Spirit. The Hebrews knew Shekinah as the guardian of their community, Israel, just as early Christians accepted the Holy Spirit as overseeing, protecting, guiding, and guarding their entire community, as well as being available to each individual. Invoked to overshadow the followers of Rabbi Jesus. She became Christianity's Paraclete (one who stands beside) and Advocate with the higher world.

Knowing his disciples would no longer have his physical presence, Jesus taught them to go within, to develop a relationship to the inner Kingdom through contact with *She who dwells within*. As the designated inner teacher of disciples, the Holy Spirit is to lead each in maturing the

Christ-within—the Self—so each can find her or his soul purpose and right expression as a part of the whole.

Therefore, Sophia/Wisdom untiringly accompanies each of us as our intuitive guide throughout our experiences. In her care, we are actively protected and nurtured—mothered. Just as Mother Nature herself cannot be seen, but her forms as rocks, trees, and animals can, so Mother Wisdom, the form builder, wraps the indwelling human spirit in bodies of grace, beauty, and purpose.

The maternal influence escorts humanity through individual and collective rites of passage. Many have sought and found their unique soul purpose, advancing level by level, discovering their own inner reality, as well as inner connections to others and to nature.

As each individuated soul matures, capabilities commonly known as Gifts of the Spirit are often activated. These gifts can also be thought of as "fruits." Here manifest certain abilities gifted by Spirit for transforming ones to use as they find their personal soul purpose. Always, the benefits—conveyed through the individual for the good of all—are somewhat awesome and inspirational.

> *To each is given the manifestation of the Spirit for the common good. To one is given through the Spirit the utterance of wisdom, and to another the utterance of knowledge according to the same Spirit, to another faith by the same Spirit, to another gifts of healing by the one Spirit, to another the working of miracles, to another prophecy, to another the discernment of spirits, to another various kinds of tongues, to another the interpretation of tongues. All these are activated by one and the same Spirit, who allots to each one individually just as the Spirit chooses.* 1 Corinthians 12.7–11.

Often sought, they have a timing and power of their own that defies rational analysis because they are rooted in the supra-rational, transcendent world of Spirit. In recalling Matthew 7.18, the Aramaic word translated as " ripe" reminds us we simply do not all get ripe at the same time.[5]

---

5. See footnote superscript 1.in Ch. 9 "Grace" for the passage that is referenced here. Neil Douglas-Klotz, "The Hidden Gospel of the Aramaic Jesus," *the Quest*, (Sept., Oct., 1999): 181.

Because various traditions have designated particular emotional patterns and/or behaviors as "how-it-ought (or ought-not)-to-be-done," there are divergent ideas regarding the significance, definition, and manifestation of the "baptism of the Holy Spirit." I would suggest the quiet wash of spirit that occurs in private prayer or meditation, wherein we are uplifted, centered, or inspired, is just as much the baptism of spirit as that which floods one in group settings and results in public phenomena.

Hidden in the darkness of the psyche, Sophia maintains vigil

One kind of experience impinges more on the emotional nature, while another is more akin to the abstract higher mental. The level of attainment of one's spiritual consciousness at the moment determines how the expression comes about. The emotional reaction may reflect the stimulation within the astral/feeling body, while the more subtle washing is sensed within the abstract mind/intuitive body. Both are profound for the receiver. The more subtle "wash" referenced is often related to unfolding sensitivity, to creativity, or to impressions not so widely recognized as Holy Spirit inspired.

The New Testament describes nine gifts granted by the Holy Spirit (1 Cor. 12.8–10). Since most of us are not familiar with the original meanings of the Old English biblical terms, we will examine each in the language of contemporary experience.

Wisdom is the gaining of new insights, aha's, or inner knowing. This is the "gnosis" gleaned in meditation and/or contemplation, wherein a particular new depth of meaning is realized by inner contact.

Knowledge is instruction received either from behind the veil of sleep, telepathically from a spirit being, or accessed through seed thought precipitation. Into the magnetized mind, one receives related thought, creative awareness, or problem solving as it pours forth from higher mind, granting new perspectives and/or information with which to work.

Faith is often defined as Finding Answers In The Heart. Experiences that reconcile and deepen both our inner and outer sense of trust create a deeper certainty—true faith. We build or discover within ourselves a point of consciousness that reconciles knowing and feeling, resulting in a sense of assurance from within that all is well; all is in God's hands. We now rest in the faithfulness of our contact with the inner.

Healing is truly the reconciliation of body, emotions, and mind. Addressing need wherever it exists, healing includes peace of mind as well as the healing of body, spiritual needs, and/or relationships. As healing occurs, correction of inequalities and disharmonies results in a renewed state of well-being. Even when life is difficult, we can receive this sense of inner well-being—the "peace that passes understanding"—to support us during the challenges that times of change bring.

The term, *working of miracles* affirms the use of natural laws existing beyond our present comprehension. What appears "miraculous" is in truth not a setting aside of physical laws but a discovery and use of rarely-appropriated universal laws to bring about that which does not seem possible. Many consider psychokinesis and telekinesis among such happenings.

Prophesy is the foretelling, in the awake state or in precognitive dreams, of unfolding events not yet obvious. It should be noted, often the purpose of this foretelling is to give individuals or groups a "heads-up," enabling them to adjust their actions in the present to assist, prevent, or modify the situation prophesied.

Discerning of spirits involves being able to identify sources, qualities, and/or values in spirit communication, or an ability to discriminate between astral and spiritual dimensions. Realization of what is accurate and what distorted is the true gift of discernment.

Various kinds of tongues is an old term for speaking from altered states in everyday language. *Glossolalia,* commonly called "speaking in tongues," is believed by many who practice it to have three basic functions: first it is felt that one's soul, bypassing the intellect and ego, is able to give pure expression to the great love and adoration it has for its creator; second, by inviting the Holy Spirit to pray through one in such a way, one is able to intercede effectively concerning things about which one has little or no personal knowledge; third, the Holy Spirit channels words of encouragement, inspiration, or instruction to others through a receptive speaker. Since the message is often transmitted in a language the speaker does not know, her/his own limitations of knowledge or biases cannot interfere with the transmission.

Interpretation of tongues refers to the intuitive, or Holy Spirit inspired, grasp of material which has been received via everyday language, in another common language, or in sounds, known as *glossolalia*, not common to an Earth language. The individual who receives the meaning shares it in such a manner that those present can glean true insights as to what spirit is attempting to convey.

While herein we identify the feminine as receptive, patient, and nurturing, she has an active side as well. Receptive to the higher world, she becomes active to the lower world as she triggers activity in the devotee (who in turn is receptive). Here then, manifest the gifts she activates.

The Holy Consciousness is androgynous in expression just as is all that is whole (holy). Both principles—masculine and feminine—abide here to be called forth as needed. Mother Wisdom can be tender or fierce; we have learned the Holy Spirit can be soothing or stimulating, according to need.

When one turns her or his attention away from dogma, doctrine, or a rigidly defined way, the protective presence that guides and stimulates becomes increasingly significant. Teachers through the ages, including Master Jesus, knew it is necessary for humanity to turn inward to find the "kingdom."

Awareness awaits each of us. Hidden in the darkness of the psyche, patiently watching, Sophia maintains vigil over the sleeping godling—the quiescent self—waiting for signals that awakening is nigh.

Like a mother hen sitting on her eggs awaiting an indication that her chicks are ready to peck their way out of restriction, in just such a manner does Mother Sophia wait and watch for the divine self to stir within her charges, so she can encourage maturation. Jesus himself once used this example. In Matthew 23.37 (KJV) he says, *"O Jerusalem, Jerusalem, thou that killest the prophets and stonest them which are sent unto thee, how often would I have gathered thy children together, even as a hen gathereth her chickens under her wings, and ye would not!"*

21

Synthesis

The intuition, . . does not work in a vacuum. It enlightens the mind; it does not eliminate the mind.[1]

—Shirley J. Nicholson

Nicholas Roerich, cultural leader and nominee for the 1929 Nobel Peace Prize, taught science, religion, and art.[2] Each of these, when followed as a discipline, takes its earnest students to the same source. Each is a map of how life functions according to a particular line of thought; each one can carry us to higher awareness. Each leads to inspiration and a new reality, freeing us to perceive beyond the limitations of the norms in which we live. Each uses symbology and methodology to explain its picture of the ascent toward the unknown.

As science expands, so does our vision of divine possibilities expressed within the framework of math and science. *"Slowly, even the most hardnosed scientists are coming to see that science is not detached but is always interactive. Scientists are part of the whole and therefore can never get outside to look at it."*[3] With our growing awareness of synergy, we expand our abilities to explore a mysterious multidimensional world. In our quest, consciousness gradually moves from fixed points of rationalism to the sacred within. Likewise, our religious rigidity relaxes, and we come to trust that with God, all things are possible.

---

1. Shirley J. Nicholson, "The Intuition: Knowledge By Fusion," *the Quest*, (March–April 2004): 47.

2. Ruth A. Drayer, *Wayfarers: The Spiritual Journeys of Nicholas and Helena Roerich* (Las Cruces, NM: Blue Waters Press, 2004).

3. Jay Williams, "Speechless Before the Mystery," *Quest*, (Winter: 1993): 27.

We are now discovering many similarities between the psychic, the physicist and the mystic. In his book, *The Medium, The Mystic, and The Physicist,* Lawrence LeShan shows that although they come from different points of view with different goals in mind, there is surprising continuity in the ideas of these three arenas. LeShan uses "clairvoyant" to describe the world of the "Medium" in the quotation below.

In the Clairvoyant Reality however, the best way is not the way of the senses. Since everything—including the observers (you and I)—is primarily and fundamentally related to and a part of everything else—then the best way of gaining information about something is to accept this "oneness," to accept that you and it are the same thing, and then you "know" about it in the same way you ordinarily know about yourself through self-observation."

The mystic says that to perceive reality we must go beyond the data of the senses. Our senses show us the world of multiplicity, which has reality and in which we must live. . . . Truth, however consists of more than the world of multiplicity, and for this we must go beyond the senses to view the other metaphysical possibility: the world in which everything flows into and is connected to and is a part of everything else.[4]

[Physicist] Max Planck wrote: In modern mechanics . . . it is impossible to obtain an adequate version of the laws for which we are looking, unless the physical system is regarded as a whole. According to modern mechanics [field theory], each individual particle of the system, in a certain sense, at any one time, exists simultaneously in every part of the space occupied by the system. This simultaneous existence applies not merely to the field of force with which it is surrounded, but also its mass and its charge."* [5]
[*Second brackets LaShan's,]

---

4. Lawrence LeShan, *The Medium, The Mystic, and the Physicist: Toward a General theory of the Paranormal* (New York: Ballentine Books, 1974), 38-39

5. Ibid., 65, quoting Max Planck, *Where is Science Going?* (London: G. Allen and Unwin, 1933), 24.

Knowing that the wisdom of the Source—that wisdom we call Sophia,—is everywhere present at all times, it is not difficult to see her being revealed in all these ways of thinking about the world. But even as we are beginning to know her oneness, we yet experience life at the personal level behind a veil of duality.

An illustration of the way our natures shift back and forth during the maturing process is shared by Helen M. Luke. as she recounts the following dream. Remember that allegorical dreams such as this are one of the tools inner Sophia (Psyche) uses to help us remember our source.

> *I dreamed that a child, my son, had a dream in which he was given a spade and told that his work was to dig the dust of earth and lift it to heaven. For every shovelful of earth he lifted up, he was to dig a shovelful of the dust of heaven and bring it down to earth. So it is in the life of time—every up followed by a down and every down by an up. In the life of time, the ascent and descent are known as a constant repetition, an alternation of this and that, but beyond time, in the totality, we shall know them as one. The above is as the below.*[6]

As spirit, we descended. The symbology of souls descending and ascending is helpful when linked to the collective prodigal son story—our story. In our journey through the human condition we gradually gather experiences, learning as we go. At some point, awakening occurs; we come to our higher senses. We determine we will arise and return to our father's (and mother's) home. As we advance on the ascending side, we progress to greater wisdom and higher awareness. Even though ascent progresses in smaller, slower increments than descent, humanity now matures step by step.

Long ago instinctual knowledge sank below the level of consciousness. It resides there as a good servant patiently doing its duty on the physical level, primarily as the maintainer of health and well-being. Sending messages through dreams and through signals such as pain, discomfort, urges, hunches, and so forth, Psyche often labors unrecognized until tension

---

6. Excerpt from Helen M. Luke, *"Such Stuff As Dreams Are Made On" the Autobiography and Journals of Helen M. Luke* (New York: Parabola Books, 2000), from "Footnotes," *Shared Vision Magazine* (March 2000).

mounts. Wear and tear increases as we experience human life, even for those who take exceptionally good care of themselves. The events of life add up and the inner nature becomes increasingly demanding. She wants to be heard. We may attempt to ignore her by denial, addictions, or other avoidance techniques.

We are only now recognizing matter is filled with cellular awareness. We have not always realized our bodies have intelligence, although we have often seen the survival instinct demonstrated in powerful ways within nature. Psyche, her supraconscious nature concealed, waits like a seed sleeping beneath the snow, anticipating the time to awaken. Body speaks an unknown innate language. Until now, few have asked, "What is my body trying to tell me?" Ask yourself, has your body whispered to you lately? Where is it asking for attention? Does it have to hurt or be hurt before it gets needed care?

Until our perspective becomes holistic, efforts to balance inner with outer will seem mysterious

Humans operating from self-centeredness have little sense of inner direction. The veil of rational mind hides the unconscious and maintains its separation from the supraconscious until some moment of deep awakening cuts through the ego, prodding, challenging the ego-centered personality to allow investigation of whatever changes such an arousal entails.

Our five physical senses (sight, hearing, feeling, smelling, and taste), belong to the basic animal nature from which humanity has emerged. Each physical sense has a corresponding psychic (i.e., of the soul) expression buried deep within: clear-seeing (clairvoyance), clear hearing (clairaudience), clear feeling (clairsentience), clear smelling, and clear tasting. These counterparts to our physical senses are alive and useable without physical awareness. They are stimulated by the instinctual nature and serve it well.

It is usually in dreaming that we discover this other set of senses—the non-physical—that appears to function in quite normal ways behind the veil of sleep. We know we experience physical, mental, and emotional sensations when dreaming. We may feel fright, experience pain or pleasure, taste, hear, converse, teach, learn, or solve problems, see color, feel warm or cold, and so forth—all through senses that seem just as real at the dream level as do our physical senses when we are awake.

170

These senses operating from deep out of sight provide certain distinct capabilities when called into action. This non-physical awareness can be cultivated to work for us while awake, as well. Using imagination, memory, and intuition, these senses gradually integrate with our outer physical ones in altered states of consciousness. We can achieve (generally with some effort and/or practice) what can be called "extended sense awareness." This psychic insightfulness is the result of an alignment of our conscious mind with the innate intelligence of Sophia existing within our basic nature. We then begin building a usable tool which can in time connect with our perception and guidance.

Once these inner senses are stimulated, people generally enjoy exploring new levels of inner competence. We discover by experimentation that we can intentionally harness these instinctual senses and learn to exercise them more consciously. Such training reminds us of other times we have had spontaneous feelings or flashes of "extrasensory" perception, but did not realize what was occurring.

Psychic development (as it is most often called) reveals our personal capability to sense and recognize whatever might benefit us, the strongest impulses generally appearing wherever we invest our time and attention. As a human being becomes increasingly self-aware, he or she reconnects to the innate sensing mechanism, replacing unconscious drives with informed, intentional choices. Now these extended senses are able to prompt personality through this mechanism in cooperation with the right hemisphere of the brain—"This I feel, sense, or fear."

Our right hemisphere keeps us in touch with the whole of life even while our left one rationalizes, categorizes, and divides. We learn not to discredit the role of either; the left hemisphere guides us through the dangers and opportunities of the outer physical realm. It assists us to make certain choices, to analyze situations, and to evaluate results.

With these skills, the personality learns the rules of the culture of which it is a part. It records its regrets and realizes its ignorance and at some future point will revisit these experiences to reappraise them, release them, and move forward. The restless scanning ego gains ground, building the confidence that will someday help to propel its inner seed (the quiescent self) toward maturity. However, until our perspective becomes more holistic—

which it will—efforts to balance the outer life with the inner world will seem mysterious.

The devotee discovers dreams and the insights they bring, then silence, and in listening intently to the stillness wherein it all exists (meditation), discovers a closer relationship to her or his inner nature. As this inner life expands and is increasingly valued, self-awareness continues to deepen. We remember, Jesus, as guru and esteemed Master, withdrew into quiet, honoring silence, creating time for beingness as well as for prayer and meditation, thus providing an active model for us. By following his example, we too learn to pray sincerely, to listen attentively, and to wait patiently. As our personal hope of glory (see Col. 1.27) matures, it is increasingly stimulated in ways unique to each of us and to the moment. This activated inner presence provides a sense of direction, increased knowing, and even if not too clear at first, fosters a new awareness. We learn to trust the inner presence, to call for her, to invoke her guardianship, requesting her to walk with us through our journey.

She reaches mightily from one end of the earth to the other, and she orders all things well. I loved her and sought her from my youth; I desired to take her for my bride, and became enamored of her beauty. She glorifies her noble birth by living with God, and the Lord of all loves her. For she is an initiate in the knowledge of God, and an associate of his works. The Wisdom of Solomon 8.1-4.

22

Veils

Within the analytical tradition of Carl Jung and the work of mythologists such as Joseph Campbell, there is much evidence to support the existence of the feminine principle (anima) within the human psyche alongside that of the male principle (animus). Jung's definition of spiritual growth within the individual in large part relates to the development and integration of those male and female components of the human psyche. [1]*

—Gard Jameson

*I*n Jungian terms Sophia is the universal feminine, the anima within. She guides us intuitively, most often communicating with us in her language of symbols. In such a way she shows us signs that restore us to life time and time again when we believe life has ended. She renews health and hope, providing direction for our journey uphill and down. Her contact becomes more and more an exchange through dreams and meditations as we accept the wisdom she offers in her own mysterious way.

Veiled as gifts of the spirit, symbolic icons, and in other acceptable guises, in the twinkle of an eye Sophia's presence may flicker or flash into our mind or lie dormant until called forth. When we see her symbols—perhaps a dove, or the moon, a spiral or a heart, to name just a few—we respond.

Working through the subconscious and superconscious levels of our being, symbols are often more meaningful to us than we realize.

---

1. Gard Jameson, "The Goddess," received via email 11/13/03 1:07 p.m., from http://www.city-net.com/~arianna/search/.txt.html.

Sophia uses a vast number in her expression, creating dreams, poetry, art, and music, as well as drama through which we derive vitality to keep on daring to live. The Greeks believed this was the true reason for theater and this made theater sacred.

From ancient times, symbols, mystery plays, and other renderings of the bards have conveyed hidden meaning and shared it. Never intended to be concrete or literal, they were meant to stimulate the subtle mind stuff, to stir the sediment, so to speak, freeing information embedded in the unconscious so that it would float to the surface for conscious use, prompting us to new awareness. In such a way we are invited to expand, to become more wise, to perceive what has evaded us before.

Many traditions have developed private systems of encoding layers of meaning for the chosen. Hieroglyphs were developed to preserve historical records as well as abstract ideas. Temple teachings used allegorical myths and metaphoric parables. Even today we often swap stories to make a point. Our relationship with others is affirmed through symbolic gifts we exchange, or through rituals with symbolic dress such as white worn at confirmations and weddings or black worn by many to indicate mourning.

Expanded insights are gleaned by those who ponder messages conveyed in symbolic language, allowing their own intuition to assist in establishing meanings. This is probably the way most of us interact with Sophia in our day to day life. A symbol stimulates a reaction and we seek to grasp a bit of its import. As the personality becomes clearer of emotional scars and false values, less distortion interferes with our perception. Overcoming obstacles of time, heritage, and societal norms, Sophia overshadows the whole collective, nurturing all of humanity. Some perceive the meaning of her touch more readily and more clearly than others, but all are being nurtured like seeds in the earth as each one experiences her presence in a unique way.

Sophia dawns gently on our minds, silently leading from one level to another

The most recognizable impacts of personal interaction with Sophia are insights resulting from her impressions. In other words, the

174

same message can be "broadcast" in symbols or language from the spiritual reality to many, but it registers as "truth" to some more than others. Personal beliefs color impressions in accord with each receiver's frame of reference, but "doses" or "drops" of truth will still be distributed to all. Such insights continually assist those who are ready to gradually dissolve personal distortion.

Many symbols carry a deep personal meaning—a valentine, wedding ring, school colors, special song, certain flower etc. Groups also respond collectively to such symbols as their country's flag or anthem, their company's logo, or their favorite team's mascot. Leaders of causes, religions, businesses, and other groups often use such symbols to encourage solidarity of support and cooperation from their followers. Information and sentiment attached to the symbol are well understood, consciously or unconsciously, without each individual having to clearly define the meaning in personal language. Modern symbols include the picture of Earth from space, helping hands, the smiley face, the sun and moon, music notes, mathematical notation, and so forth. Even commercial icons, such as McDonald's double arches for example, can take on a certain multiplicity of meaning: as when those golden arches suggest clean restrooms as well as food.

Good examples of universal symbolism are contained in creation stories from many traditions. Each tale includes a creator, seven days, the work of each day, a garden, the created human, and other common elements. Joseph Campbell opened the secrets of symbolism to thousands with his television series late in the twentieth century. In the privacy of their own homes, viewers could dare to ponder the treasury of symbols inherited as a part of the human story, whether learned through Christian, Jewish, Islamic, or other teaching myths.

The myth of the divine feminine is told over and over in various traditions, sometimes to venerate her (the Earth Mother, for example), and sometimes to incite fear of her, (as in tales of Lilith snatching babies). In recent decades many volumes have been written to remind us she has always been here, even though maligned and neglected often.

As rays of enlightenment spread across the sky of our awareness, Sophia dawns gently upon our minds, silently leading us from one level of comprehension to another. Most often we cannot easily say just when we shifted from frustration to hope, or when inner knowing stirred and perception became clearer. This is how the gentle side of the divine feminine works, unless a dynamic moment or specific need calls her into an individual's consciousness more abruptly.

The Eastern Orthodox Christian tradition (particularly the earlier Greek and Russian) retained numerous vestiges of a once beautiful grasp of Sophia that helps trace the fall (or what might be called the "push") of the feminine from grace. Their frameworks, though similar to the Western version of the Holy Spirit—once known as the Holy Spirit of Wisdom, or in older language as the Holy Ghost—see phenomena not as miracles but as natural signs of achieving attainment of the transcendent or super-personal levels of being. The mystical nature is an expected outcome of the wisdom we gather through living a life attuned to "righteousness," or "right action," a life of true spiritual maturity.

In Orthodoxy, Sophia is considered the gracious knower at the interface of spirit and mind, always prompting us to refine our relationship to the Higher.

The view of twentieth century Russian Sophiologists is that the father, son, and holy spirit have their being within Sophia. Sergei Bulgakov [author of Sophia: The Wisdom of God] claims that Sophia is the ousia or substance of the Godhead; she is "the divine essence." [2]

The feminine nature of wisdom is a strong theme in many of the Hebrew texts. Chapter 8 of Proverbs describes Sophia as the first creation of God, as co-creator of the world, and as the expression of joy and goodness in creation.

The Holy Ghost is one of the most complex images of Christian doctrine. Christ is himself the Holy Ghost; the man, Jesus, is engendered by and later infused with the divine Christ, and after the man has died,

---

2. Sergei Bulgakov, *Sophia: The Wisdom of God* (Hudson, NY: Lindisfarne Press, 1993), 66, cited by Cynthia Avens and Richard Zelley in "Walking the Path of Christ," *The Quest*, (Spring 1996): 68.

176

the Christ or Holy Ghost remains as comforter and redeemer, the invisible "breath" or "pneuma" which brings the experience of unity between God and man. Endless theological arguments on the nature of the Holy Ghost have been responsible for some terrible lesions in the body of Christianity over the centuries, no least the division between Western Catholicism and the Eastern Orthodox Church. . .Gnostic Christians interpreted the Holy Ghost as the spiritual Mother, and understood it as feminine. This is expressed in the idea of Sophia, the Greek word for "wisdom." [3]

Where judgments and flashes of insight are transmitted by unconscious activity, they are often attributed to an archetypal feminine figure, the anima or mother-beloved. . . . In view of this, the Holy Ghost would have a tendency to exchange his neuter designation for a feminine one. . . . Holy Ghost and Logos merge in the Gnostic idea of Sophia.[4]

What are we dealing with here? This invisible feminine "breath," which is an emanation of the divine, which has the male power to fertilize, yet which can be shared and experienced as comforter and unifier by human beings, . . . has a great deal in common with the Hindu Maya, which generates the cosmos and then is "left behind," incarnated in human beings. [5]

She is certainly acknowledged as more than "inspiration" and is credited as the motivator of poetry, music, and art particularly, although there also exists the concept of Sophia as inner teacher and divine prompter. She is recognized as guardian of the community (of believers) and stimulator of the faithful. Some even think of her as God's personal representative and regard her impressions upon them as most certainly a way God speaks directly to the devoted.

When Jesus, as the Christ, was no longer in physical presence as rabbi/guru/teacher, he left his disciples with ongoing protection and

---

3. Liz Greene, *The Astrological Neptune and the Quest for Redemption* (York Beach, ME: Samuel Weiser, Inc., first printing 1996, first paperback ed. 2000), 87, 88.
4. Ibid., citing Carl Jung, *Collected Works*, Vol. 11, 240.
5. Ibid., *Quest for Redemption*, 88.

guidance by placing them under the guardianship of the Holy Spirit of Wisdom. This representative of the Godhead, who nourishes all hidden potential, was specifically charged to hover over Jesus' followers just as the Shekinah had guarded the community of the Jews. In fact, since we don't know the exact words used in the Greek or Aramaic, they may have been referring to the Shekinah, because that was Jesus' tradition. At any rate we can see the similarity between the Shekinah and the Holy Spirit as mothers, each hovering over and protecting humanity as it moves toward the divine Oneness, the holy consciousness we call Christ.

Although a mighty church formed in response to the energy of love-wisdom that ushered forth at Pentecost, the practical application of her grace began to be lost in the years that followed. That which was empowering and inclusive—teaching and honoring each, separating none—was soon cloaked with the cultures and prejudices of the practitioners. Wondrously, Sophia remained faithfully at work, often veiled behind symbol and story whose true meanings were only recognized by mystics and those who would "listen in the heart," recognizing their connection to the inner source.

23

Symbology

Images do help. Symbols are powerful. They work on the subconscious and prepare the ground for the paradigm shift we need."[1]

—Susanne Schaup

Spiritual symbols usually hold a greater depth to be penetrated a bit at a time as our relationship with a specific tradition deepens. As it does so, the symbol reveals increased meaning to us. All of us have been touched by the manger scene, the most potent reminder of the Christmas season. The first crèche was designed and built by St. Francis of Assisi to make the symbolism real to the peasant people he was instructing.

Let's recall it as we give new meaning to the great truth held here for us. The Mother Mary represents the purified emotional aspect of our nature, while Joseph represents our refined intellect. The manger is the heart; the stable is our body. The star overhead represents our higher self, and the animals are the unawakened who are only aware of their own physical nature. Shepherds are those who are wisely watching over others, keeping harmony. The three kings are initiates who recognize the newborn Christ Consciousness as it is birthed in men and women, and present gifts of love, support, and assistance, welcoming each new disciple to the path.

As with all symbols and archetypes, the few presented here not only have definable meanings which can be written down in language, they also have effects within those unknown levels of being, the subconscious to which Susanne Schaup referred.

---

1. Dr. Susanne Schaup, "The Kairos of Spiritual Unity" paper given at The World Parliament of Religion, Chicago, 1993, and in Germany.

**YIN/YANG** The equilibrium of the elements is a foundation of Life, and the violation of this law leads to destruction.

DOVE A dove appeared at the baptism of Jesus as a meaningful symbol of the descent of the Christ, son of Sophia, the Holy Spirit. In contemporary Christianity it may simply mean the Holy Spirit. It is also used by other traditions to represent blessings from above or a sign of spirit presence. Today we are using it to signify peace, but it is also the symbol of Sophia, the divine.

**FISH** The outline of the fish became an underground symbol of identification for Christians during the early days of persecution. It continues to be used today. The fish is also the symbol of Pisces and of the Piscean Age. It is a symbol of equality as achieved by the use of the vesica piscis an integral shape used in sacred geometry.

CROSS IN CIRCLE The cross within the circle was known to the ancients long before Christianity. It indicated the dense world and the four directions existing within the boundary of the circle. In astrology this is the symbol of Planet Earth.

**CELTIC CROSS** The Celtic and other variations of the cross all affirm the challenge offered on this dense world of bringing spirit and matter (and heart and mind) together as a conscious being. In the Celtic, the "post" indicates the consciousness to be anchored on the Earth plane.

PENTACLE Pythagoreans considered its geometric qualities to be symbolic, both mathematically and metaphysically, of absolute perfection. To the Hebrews the five points are tied to the Pentateuch representing the concept of truth as a whole. In mystery teachings it symbolizes the human (whose nature is made of earth, air, fire, water, and ether)

being made ready for spiritual development by refining the physical, emotional, mental, spiritual, and social areas into which awakened ones are to shine their light.

STAR OF DAVID The sign of the disciple; also adopted as a symbol of Judaism. Composed of two triangles, it indicates an initiated one who has succeeded in aligning the physical, emotional, and mental aspects of personality toward the higher realities and in integration with the down-pouring trinity of spiritual energies bathing creation.

EIGHT POINTED STAR OF THE SUPERIOR MOTHER
Symbol of the Superior Mother of the higher world who watches over the dense mother's world of form—Earth and the many sparks of divinity trapped in the world of matter.

HOST & CHALICE Beautiful portrayal of host and chalice as used in Christian Eucharistic art, earlier esoteric symbol of soul (host) and personality made ready for soul infusion (chalice), the third initiation in Christianity.

OM The creative word deemed to be the original sound, the generative first tone that vibrated through the receptive void, shaping and continuing to maintain creation. It corresponds to the phrase in the Genesis account of creation "and God **said** . . . ." The root phonic of the *Amen* of Jews and Christians, the *Amin* of Muslims, the *Hum* of the Tibetans, as well as the *Aum* of Aramaic. It is a sacred syllable chanted by Hindus, Buddhists, and meditators from other traditions, including Christian. Spoken intentionally with reverence it aids one in aligning personality will with that of the One Creative Source.

Sanskrit OM

LOTUS The lotus stands for both beauty and achievement. Rooted in Earth (physical world), the lotus grows through water (the emotional/mental world), to blossom in air (the world of spirit). Opening to the light of the sun, it is a metaphor for the unfolding soul that now receives the radiant light of its Source. It is a sacred symbol of Hinduism and Buddhism, as well as a symbol for spiritual growth and is most often used to represent the chakras.

ROSE The rose is symbolic of great love, beauty, and perfection. Often placed upon a cross, the rose is a symbol of the soul in the West much as the lotus is in the East. In Western wisdom teachings it often represents prophecy and a being unfolding. The rose is considered a sign of Mother Mary and also of Master Morya of the spiritual Hierarchy. The scent of roses is experienced by many who consider it a sign of blessing from higher planes.

MADONNA & CHILD This familiar glyph represents mother and child and is usually thought of as Mother Mary and child Jesus. Esoterically, says Corinne Heline in *Mystery of the Christos,* it is said to be the "signature of our planet as seen from the higher planes."

THEOTOKOS A familiar image related to this work is one of a small human figure held over the heart of the universal mother. In Christianity this is usually thought of as Mary holding baby Jesus, but look again, for so often he shows a mature, rather than an infant face. A symbolic truth is preserved for us as we realize that, even yet, the mother (representing both the feminine principle and our personal soul) continues to watch over her child (each of us individually and collectively) as we develop our individual inner nature to greater maturity thereby maturing our collective soul.

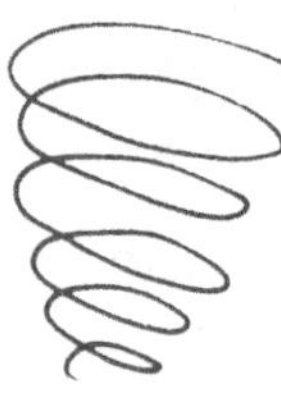

SPIRAL A symbol of the feminine principle, sexual energy, or the doorway to the sacred used by the ancients. It is most often used to symbolize the "doorway to the within" and is feminine in the same way that phallic shapes represent the masculine principle.

TOWER or A MARKER, STELE, OR STANDING STONE
A symbol of the masculine principle, sexual power. In Tarot it is representative of the ego, the ego having a masculine polarity in males and females alike. Most often used as a phallic symbol in most wisdom traditions.

LABYRINTH Unlike a maze which has false turns and dead ends, a labyrinth leads one unerringly from outer to inner and back to outer again. An imagined etheric temple that reflects onto the physical world a drawing of cosmic influences, the earliest archeological etchings revealed simple three circuit paths. Later they became seven (or more) as heavenly bodies became better known. The action of walking from left side to right in a particular pattern mimicked each human's journey from outer to inner, weaving together the left and right hemisphere of the brain until they reached the innermost heart (or the sun) within the labyrinth itself. Therefore keys to the inner nature are preserved symbolically in our Earth walk.

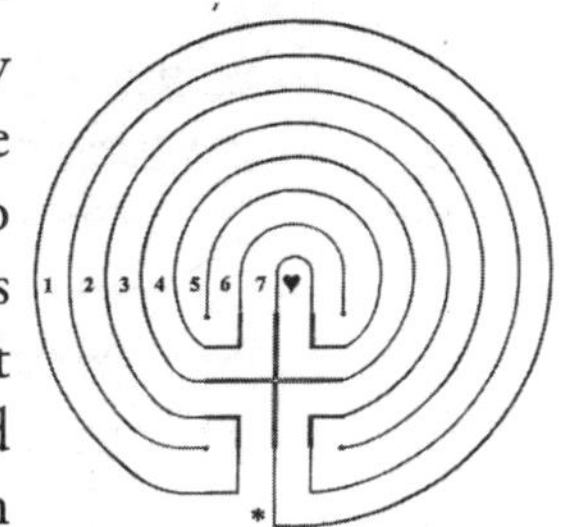

ZODIAC A band in the celestial sphere that represents the path of the principal planets, moon, and sun of our solar system, extending about eight degrees to either side of the ecliptic. According to the tropical zodiac, this band is divided into 12 parts, or "signs," each of which is 30 degrees wide and

From left center counter clockwise the signs are:
Aries, Taurus, Gemini, Cancer, Leo, Virgo, Libra, Scorpio, Sagitarius, Capricorn, Aquarius and Pices.

183

designated by the constellation for which it originally was named. The zodiac provides a systematic arrangement of the 12 astrological influences that affect all of evolving humanity. Thus personality types are determined by birth (sun) sign. In esoteric philosophy planetary position provides insights to the rhythms, strengths, and weaknesses of the inner and outer nature.

ZODIACAL SIGNS The signs of the zodiac convey the name and identify the resources of a particular influence. The oldest psychological system, it is still in use by many. The three most important signs influencing each persons nature are represented by the individual's sun sign, moon sign, and ascendant. The ascendant, also called the "rising sign" is found on the horizon at the time of birth. The sun, or birth, sign is the constellation in which the sun is located at the time of birth, and the moon sign is the constellation in which the moon is located at the time of birth.

COLORS Colors are not only wonderful phenomena in their own right, they are also symbolic of powers, attributes, and energies. In *Bridge to Superconsciousness* Rick Prater elaborates:

> *Energies can manifest on various levels as color, taste, feel, smell, states of consciousness, and so on, from the lowest physical to the highest spiritual. By linking with the soul and invoking various colors, we can visualize, imagine, and actually see these colors as they flow down the central channel [the spiritual parallel to the spinal cord] and radiate into the energy field. . . . . We can invoke colors anytime, such as in personal relationships and social situations to heal, uplift, balance, and energize. For example, we might help someone overcome negativity by invoking pink, the energy of love and goodwill. Or we might help someone to think more clearly by invoking blue, a stabilizing and calming energy.*[2]

And, of course, we are all familiar with the universal application of red to mean stop, green for go, and yellow for caution, to name but one of many ways individual colors function as a kind of shorthand, symbolic of whole complexes of behavior and meaning within human cultures.

---

2. Rick Prater, *Bridge to Superconsciousness* (Mariposa, CA: Source Publications, 1999), 74.

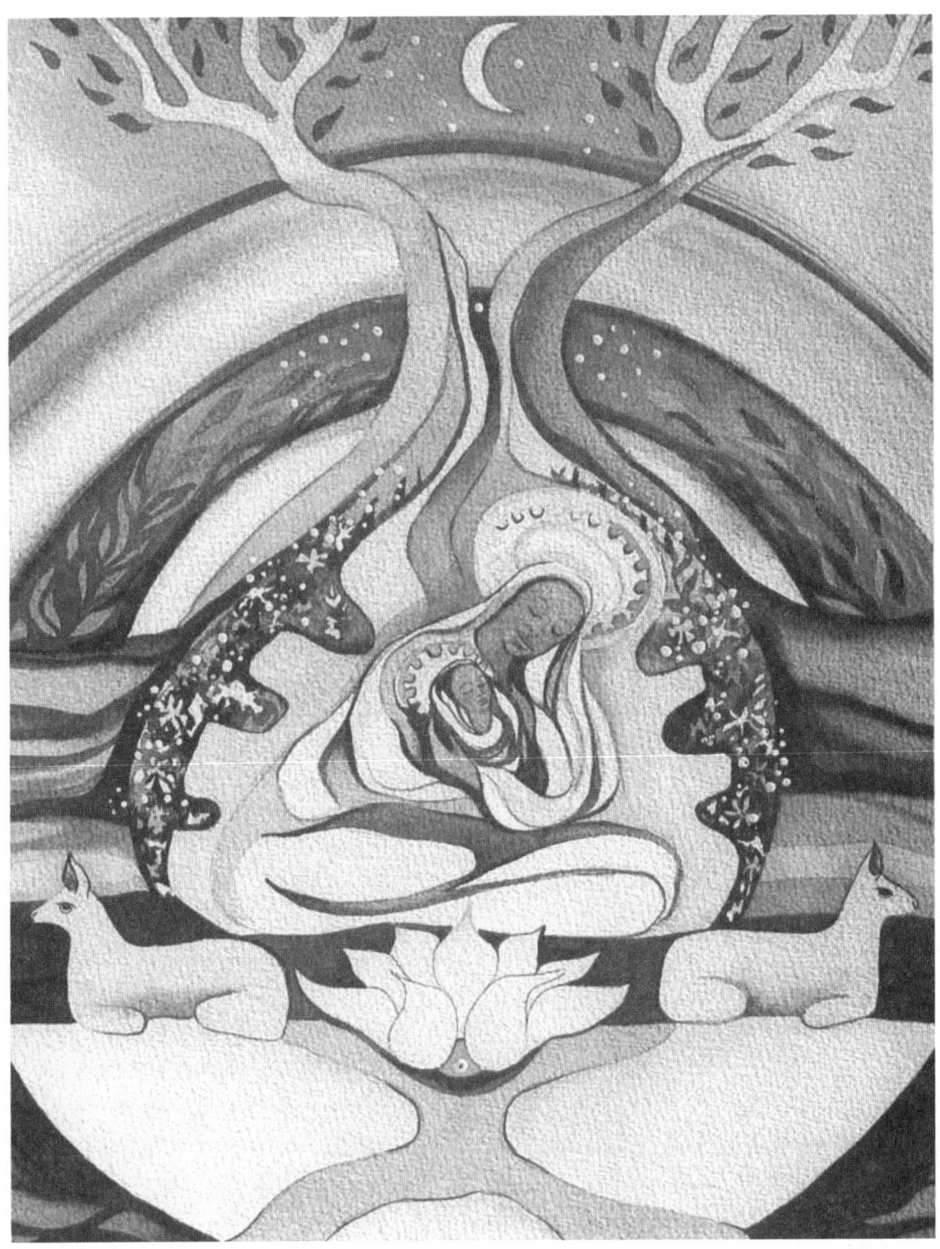

"Rainbow Birth" is the work of Kansas artist Ann Nunley.
Her visionary watercolors explore the rhythmic harmony of natural forms,
while her use of vivid esoteric symbols reflects a deep universal wisdom.

Allowing Love to Flow

❖ Become quiet and turn your attention inward. Rest in the silence, allowing it to bring comfort and peace. Take a few minutes to allow this peace to calm any sense of restlessness. Bring a deeper awareness of the inner nature to the mind as it is centered and at rest. Now take several gentle breaths and allow yourself to go deeper and deeper within. A deep sense of peace abides within and gradually fills your being.

❖ Now in your mind's eye, pick another individual and hold that one in your consciousness. See the inner presence of that one at work within his or her life. Do not direct, just observe. See and acknowledge the higher working in some manner within the other.

❖ Send support, love, or encouragement to this other. Direct a joyful thought of well-being to her or him. Share the positive energy of your nature with this one, then thank the person for letting you touch into his or her private space. Bless this one and now release this effort.

❖ Now pick an individual you do not care for or do not understand, and make a clear attempt to see the inner presence of this one who likewise seeks unique expression.

❖ Do not judge or analyze; do not resist; just relax and observe to see if an awareness of the wisdom aspect at work in this other life can be noted. Bless that inner presence knowing it is the same wisdom that works through you in your own life and experiences. We remember there is one human soul, and an aspect of it works within each of us and through the instinctual consciousness of all creation.

❖ Now we release these thoughts and return to our outer awareness. Let us rejoice and invoke joy—the energy of the soul—to assist us as we grow in appreciation of those we know and love, as well as those we do not understand. We acknowledge the importance of what we have gained by closing our meditation with the time honored blessing, *Namasté.*

Namasté

I honor the place within you
where the entire universe resides.

I honor the place within you
of love and light, of peace and truth.

I honor the place within you
where,
when you are in that place in you,
and I am in that place in me,
there is only one of us.

This translation of the Sanskrit word *namasté*
is from the 4th anniversary issue of the magazine *Avatar.*

24

Darkness

[Black] is the color of night and the shade of soil. It cloaks midnight and blankets the depths of caves and grottos. In previous cultures, the most popular totem for a chief male divinity was the sun and, by extension, light; goddesses have been associated with the moon and, by extension, night.[1]

—Leonard Shlain

No writing on Sophia would be complete without a mention of the Dark Sophia. Around the world there persists a great devotion to the Black Madonna or Dark Mother, she whom I call Black Sophia. *"Many medieval churches, extending in a wide arc from Russia across Europe to Spain, had as their most sacred object a statue of a black Mary."*[2] Some say she, as Creatrix of and dweller within the material world, appears dark because she is of the dark earth. *"Like the black, abiding earth, her simple being is so vastly present that we have not noticed it."*[3]

> *In ancient Egypt, Isis personified the black loam lining the banks of the Nile Delta; . . The earthly incarnation of Cybele, the great Roman Tellus Mater, was a huge black stone. The statue of Artemis at Ephesus, the most famous shrine of a goddess outside of Egypt, was also black.*[4]

---

1. Shlain, *The Alphabet vs. the Goddess,* 267.
2. Ibid.
3. Caitlín Matthews, "Sophia: Goddess of Wisdom," *Gnosis Magazine,* No. 13, (Fall 1989): 26.
4. Shlain, 268.

She reminds us of the veiled, hidden, out-of-sight women whose suffering has no voice—lost, disrespected, regarded as being of no value. In our modern world we deal with the dominant power of the light skinned, though ironically, many of the "white" race paint themselves to add more color and tan their skin to be darker. Do we know why?

As a form of Lower Sophia, to most she has been lost. Nevertheless, various people, especially the indigenous, do remember her. The love of the mother carries many through their struggles. *"The influence of Sophia is characterized by a will imbued with eternal faithfulness to the Spirit, an endurance that remains steadfast even when confronted with awful ordeals and terrible burdens."* [5] The welcome receptivity given to dreams and shamanic practices still exists here because she continues to visit her own, and her guidance remains of value.

Common sense often dwells amidst the disadvantaged. Here, in the thick of painful daily struggles to meet even the most basic needs, the Black Madonna is still beloved. Regardless of nationality or race, she remains with her people. A variety of statues, large and small, include remnants of old, odd-shaped, faceless stones, darkened with smoke from sacred fires and primitive rituals still performed where her memory remains. Chants linger in strange places as medicine men and midwives invoke the assistance of spirits and/or the Mother with new births or with taking the dead across to the faraway home.

> *The blackened old stones once venerated as goddesses and the crystalline virgins of esoteric spirituality are not so dissimilar, for they both represent Sophia at the archetypal extremities of her appearance. Neither image is better or more achieved than the other; Sophia is not interested in qualitative judgments, but in what works. Accordingly, she adopts the form most near to our heart.* [6]

In a quest for a mother who will accept us when we can't quite make peace with our errors, it is easier to turn to a simple mother

---

5. Robert Powell, *The Most Holy Trinosophia and the New Revelations of the Divine Feminine* (New York: Steiner Books, 2000), 134.

6. Matthews, "Goddess of Wisdom", 22.

acquainted with misery than to the lovely Virgin, perfectly obedient and always clean. In the heart of our dark mother, love for us endures without judgment or pretense. She helps us deal with the undeniable fact that we live in a world we can neither control nor comprehend, a world with which we often cannot cope—in which we can only endure.

> *"She is the silent companion who stands at our elbows as we toil. . . daily grappling with humanity's problems, . . striving to reflect the light of the spirit in our world."* [7]

Our dark Mother Sophia abides with us in our own darkness, but her efforts do not go unrecognized in the higher realm. As the spark of Divine Mind, or *Epinoia,* she has indwelled the human race—Adam—from the moment Spirit began its involution into the dense, dark material world. An unknown scribe wrote of the Gnostic myth of Sophia in one of the scrolls found at Nag Hammadi:

the blessed One, the Mother-Father, the beneficent and merciful One, had mercy on the power of the mother. . . And he sent, through his beneficent Spirit and his great mercy, a helper to Adam, luminous Epinoia which comes out of him, who is called Life. And she assists the whole creature, by toiling with him and by restoring him to his fullness...and by teaching him about the way of ascent. [8]

In the early church, titles given Mother Mary included Seat of Wisdom, Mirror of Justice, and Gate of Heaven. Most of these were ancient titles ascribed to other feminine deities long before, but they help us trace the lineage of Sophia in such a way as to know she has always been with us.

As we long for love, we may seek it in all areas, and if fortunate we will finally find it, most often in service. Made in "the image and likeness

---

7. Ibid., 26.

8. *The Apocryphon of John* in, *The Nag Hammadi Library,* James M. Robinson, ed. (San Francisco: Harper & Row, 1988), 116.

of the divine" she is our feminine role model. To give ourselves to a work or a cause so totally that our heart opens to the Great Heart is at last our reward. There is no way to tell this to another, it can only be learned by doing. But we can fulfill our own need and in so doing, others, if they have "eyes with which to see," can observe that it is so.

> *She cannot be comprehended. Her blackness is the blackness of incomprehensibility; of night, of the shadows that fall across the day; the blackness of Africa; of the other side of the moon. It is precisely that darkness that allows the imagination, the unconscious, to fill her with qualities that are indefinable, mysterious. . . .*
>
> *She is the Mother of the mysteries, of arcane knowledge, secret intuitions, . . her blackness is a black hole, pulling in everyone who contemplates her, sucking our consciousness into her mystery. . .*
>
> *She can be fierce, gaunt, . .lush, bejeweled as at Guadalupe; or dressed in kitsch wedding dresses. The kitsch is indeed essential—it connects her with the hopes, dreams, the groans and laments of the ordinary people. Thus the Black Mary is a people's Mary. . .*
>
> *Thus the Black Virgin takes into herself those aspects of the feminine, the Goddess, suppressed in the White Virgin. What are they? Sexuality, power, ferocity, cruelty, rage, fear, rebellion, warlikeness, envy—these are qualities that would not normally be associated with the conventional Virgin Mary.*[9]

Likewise we need to ponder the dark Madonna within ourselves—the unknown who springs into action during an emergency, or who rises to the occasion as need be without thought or hesitation. We also have the queen within who wants everything perfect, and who, when not treated just so, can take offense unnecessarily. Disciple, "know thyself." We are she. The beautiful writer on Sophia, Caitlín Matthews, says it so well:

> *These polarized appearances—as Hag or Queen of Heaven— are the two sides of the coin, one archetypal power. Just as coal and dia-*

---

9. Roger Horrocks, "The Divine Woman In Christianity", in *The Absent Mother*, Alix Pirani, ed. (London, UK: Mandala, 1991),124, 125.

*mond are both carbon—that basic substance of life—so does the
Goddess of Wisdom manifest her power through seemingly opposing
appearances. The Goddess of Wisdom is seeded within us all.*[10]

*While having dual form, Sophia does not naturally lend her-
self to dualism—in the sense of a polarization of good and evil. Yet in
the text "Thunder—Perfect Mind," Sophia speaks of herself in an
extensive list of antithetic epithets which take into account the misun-
derstandings that may arise in the person of dualistic mind:*

> *It is I who have been hated everywhere*
> *And who have been loved everywhere.*
> *It is I who am called life:*
> *And whom you have called death.*
> *It is I who am called law:*
> *And whom you have called lawlessness.*
> *It is I whom you have chased:*
> *And it is I whom you have restrained.*[11]

It is fitting that Dark Sophia should speak to us by night, behind the
veil of sleep. In dreams like the following from Helen Luke's book, *Such Stuff
As Dreams Are Made On*, Sophia grants us a higher view of all the failures and
disappointments we have experienced. In her hands, we find our life takes on
a golden shine.

*I remember a dream that came to me about 15 years ago. In
it, I held in my hands a rare piece of midnight-blue material of heavy
silk, about ten inches by ten inches. Fine gold threads were woven into
the dark background in what seemed an entirely haphazardly way,
making no coherent pattern and having, it appeared, no meaning. Yet,
I knew in my dream that a woman had written here, in gold thread,
the story of her life.*

*I interrupt the dream to explain that in actuality this woman
was an old friend of mine. She was older than myself and had meant a*

---

10. Matthews, "Sophia: Goddess of Wisdom," 22.

11. Ibid., quoting from "The Thunder-Perfect Intellect" 16:9–17 in *The Gnostic Scriptures: a
New Translation with Annotations and Introduction by Bentley Layton* (London: S.C.M. Press,
1987), 82.

great deal to me since my youth. Yet, outwardly, her life appeared a complete failure. None of her great artistic goals had matured, she was crippled by illness, her husband was dead, and she had barely enough to live on. A few days before my dream, I had a letter from her expressing her sense of ultimate and irremediable failure. I remembered her indomitable courage in the face of every kind of suffering and how my every contact with her as a girl and all through the years had jerked me out of triviality and subservience to collective opinion. She reconnected me with a sense of the meaning and dignity of life.

In the dream, as I tried to decipher the jumble of threads, I suddenly knew that I was looking at it from the wrong angle and I gave the cloth in my hand a quarter-turn clockwise. Immediately, I saw a beautiful and coherent golden pattern, and in the centre, exquisitely embroidered, was the figure of a woman holding a child and her robe flowed out from her shoulders like a river of gold. In wonder, I questioned in the dream how my friend could possibly have created this lovely, intricate thing. The answer came to me clearly. She had done nothing but choose a direction for each line of stitching with all the consciousness and integrity possible to her, and the pattern had emerged and the picture had been woven to be seen in all its beauty by those who would learn to make the quarter-turn.

This isn't the only dream in which the quarter turn image has appeared. Imagine the psyche as a circle. If a line is drawn bisecting the circle horizontally, the half-circle below the line is the unconscious, instinctive and dark, while the half-circle above is the clear light of consciousness. One may see in this image the collective attitude of most people. If people can make the quarter-turn, if they can bring up the dark things and give them equal status with the light, while at the same time the light descends into the dark, then earth is raised to heaven, and heaven descends to earth.[12]

12. Excerpt from Helen M. Luke, *Such Stuff As Dreams Are Made On* (Parabola Books), from "Footnotes," *Shared Vision Magazine* (March 2000).

194

25

Archetypes

There are as many archetypes as there are typical situations in life. Endless repetition has engraved these experiences into our psychic constitution, not in the forms of images filled with content, but at first only as forms without content, representing merely the possibility of a certain type of perception and action.[1]

—Carl Jung

Ancient wisdom of all traditions records the interaction of the Creator with humanity, filling pages with, *"God said . . . ."* Dreams, rescue stories, dramas, teaching myths, and parables witness to the importance of our primary relationship with the Creator. An archetype is a living thought pattern that occupies the unconscious mind of humanity. It may express itself through dreams, symbols, myths, and/or emotions.

Although a given archetype may be generally the same over much of the world, its particular form may vary from culture to culture and age to age. It is for this reason scripture often needs to be interpreted symbolically to stay true to its spiritual content. A literal, concrete, or sectarian interpretation may miss the universal content altogether.

When humanity entered the age of reason—a period of rapid development of the masculine expression—Sophia rapidly went underground, appearing primarily in subjective flashes. In the Christian

---

1. Carl Jung, *Collected Works,* Vol. 9, as quoted by Seldes, in *The Great Thoughts,* 218-219.

tradition, Our Lady, Mother of Jesus, became the remaining archetype of the divine feminine. Just as the Orthodox, Catholic, and other branches of Christianity minimized the divine feminine—at the same time continuing to honor her in various degrees—many non-Christian traditions viewed the feminine through their own narrowing archetypes as well.

Such transcendent feminine archetypes as Isis, Athena, Aphrodite, Blindfolded Lady Justice and the Statue of Liberty, though still acknowledged by some, have lost most of their power and, for the most part, evoke only a ho-hum attitude.

Indigenous people continue to honor her archetypes in their relationship with Mother Earth or Mother Nature. The Maya, for example, retain many of their native beliefs by covering them with a thin veneer of Catholicism. At the same time, however, their thinking process is becoming increasingly rational in a natural response to the masculine influence in which they find themselves.

For roughly the past 5,000 years, we have been increasingly building our mental body, emphasizing the more rational capabilities. The separation of science and religion during the age of reason hastened the building of the rational mind for most Western cultures. We surrendered our intuitive global sense of meaning and sought to nail down more specific linear concepts. We became increasingly analytical and judgmental, reducing everything to two rigidly defined categories—right and wrong.

Now living in an exciting period of rediscovery, we advance toward a needed balance, integrating the progress made under the tutelage of the empowered masculine impulse. While the intellect was being so stimulated, the rational mind rapidly developed, and the mystery of the mother was increasingly masked. As Sophia re-emerges, some are frightened by what they regard today as heresy, not realizing she has been with us always, even when veiled.

As we move from one level of collective maturity to the next, learning from each experience, religion serves many in a manner similar to that of a handrail. Some progress up the staircase step by step, lesson by lesson, without grasping the banister; but for others it provides much-needed assistance in stabilizing their ascent toward the greater goal of spirituality. A challenging thought I would present is that religions always

points toward the past; and spirituality always points toward the future.

Religions are based on the achievements of founders—saints, sages, holy ones—so followers attempt to reach the same level of grace or enlightenment by concretizing the founder's teachings. It is such rigid emulation of past achievement that is referenced as a backward look.

Spirituality, however, always has a goal for practitioners to become more than they are—indeed, to eventually surpass their former role models. So spirituality looks to the future. There is a powerful Eastern concept called "spiritual cannibalism." It teaches that the student is to devour all the teacher has to offer. Having done so, the student adds the mentor's teachings to his or her own spiritual wisdom, and thus becomes greater! This is the concept expressed by Master Jesus when he said *"Very truly, I tell you, the one who believes in me will also do the works that I do and, in fact, will do greater works than these"* (John 14.12).

To gain this awareness, it is necessary to move from religion (from *religio* meaning "supernatural constraint," designating obedience to a system of dogma and creeds) to spirituality, living in the light of our inner spirit. The true purpose of religion is to carry us to spirituality—illumination/enlightenment. As we become increasingly alive in the spirit, the inner nature guides us, expressing its wisdom both to and through us.

This recent historical cycle has seen humanity challenged to develop its mental nature and the wonderful tools that resulted to facilitate life in the world of duality. The rational mind had to be built, and to some degree integrated, before we could advance to higher awareness or come to "know" in more subtle ways. The requirements for "knowing" are shifting because a new era is to emerge wherein a more direct relationship to the soul is to occur.

Even as humanity came into its adolescent stage with the inevitable "I-can-do-it-myself" illusion of autonomy, the divine feminine was not absent. The inner presence prompted humanity by "conscience" programmed into individuals—at first by culture, education, religion, or experience, and later by the soul, as the true inner spirit began to make its

197

impact. Sophia offers her guidance through the physical body by sensation (pain, pleasure, weakness, fatigue, etc.), through the psyche by feelings and knowings, (ESP, excitement, hunches, sorrow, apprehension), and through the soul as intuition and straight knowing (assurance, "I don't know how I know, I just know,") according to the inner age (i.e., spiritual maturity) of her charge.

While long ago *logos, agape,* and *koinonia*—all Greek words of theology—became part of the Christian vernacular; *Sophia* did not. She is currently appearing because only now are we ready to perceive differently. Trapped in judgment of one another, adhering to the letter (but not the spirit) of the law with one ego trying to trump another, we have magnified our separations. When we are in pain or see the damage we have done and/or catch a glimpse of a higher way, we rethink values. In the Christ nature (love) we are made one; in Sophia we experience the wisdom-consciousness love brings, and thus seek to become fully human and fully divine.

Reread Proverbs to see how Wisdom is praised. Ancient chapters sing of Sophia. Every time you see the English word "Wisdom," read it in your mind as "Sophia" and you will discover her—Sophia, the wise mother. For those longing to know the Christ in a more holistic manner, Sophia re-introduces the feminine insightfulness to partner with the picture we have of Jesus as the Christ. Remember, Jesus showed great regard for women and feminine energies while embracing all. His way of acceptance and his teachings of love pointed to the path of the heart—humanity's next great goal.

In another verse, Jesus speaks of himself as a child of Sophia. At the end of a passage that reports criticisms directed against Jesus and John the Baptizer, Jesus says:

"John the Baptist has come eating no bread and drinking no wine; and you say, 'He has a demon.' The Son of man [a reference to Jesus himself] has come eating and drinking; and you say, 'Behold, a glutton and a wino, a friend of tax collectors and sinners [outcasts]!' Yet Sophia

is vindicated by her children." [Brackets and emphasis supplied by Borg.]

Here Jesus speaks of himself . . . as a child of Sophia. Taken together, these two passages [Luke 11.49-50, Luke 7.33-35] imply that the early Christian movement saw Jesus as both the spokesperson and the child of Sophia, and that Jesus himself may have spoken of himself in these terms. [2]

As change manifests, requirements shift and new influences are called into play. The resulting evolution of the human condition benefits through these shifts and changes. As noted by Helena Roerich, through whom the Agni Yoga wisdom teachings were given, *"There is a rule in the foundation of the Teaching (or rather a law) that 'all must be performed by human hands and feet.'"* [3] Creation (planetary consciousness) advances through degree upon degree of refinement in the quest for high consciousness as well. Respect for our environment, which includes all the various kingdoms of nature, is a sign of human advancement.

Today, a number of well-defined philosophies and religions are adjusting as we move into an interfaith era wherein the emphasis will be to find commonality and a new acceptance of one another in spite of differing concepts important to each path. *"One may climb a mountain from the north or from the south—the result is still the same,"* [4] Agni Yoga reminds us. Or said another way,

One plays on twelve strings, another produces the same tune on four, and a third limits himself to two, creating just as many harmonies on them. Does it matter how many strings one requires for harmony? The essential thing is that it be created. Let us not wonder at or criticize variety, for we shall not find even two grains of sand alike. [5]

---

2. Borg, *Meeting Jesus Again,* 102-103.

3. Agni Yoga Society, Inc., *Letters Of Helena Roerich I,* 24 June 1935 (Agni Yoga Society, Inc.), http://www.agniyoga.org, (accessed June 29, 2004).

4. Agni Yoga Society, Inc., *Agni Yoga,* 32.

5. Ibid., 612.

The Creator (also called the "No-Thing" in mystical Kabalah) loves variety. We witness this as we observe so many species and types of animals, plants, and minerals, not to mention the myriad personalities and physiologies of human beings.

In wisdom teachings, all the majesty of the unknown that exists in the rich dynamism of creation is united inseparably as paternal and maternal principles. *"That About Which Naught Can Be Said"* produces a reflection in each successive plane and in each unit of consciousness which dwells therein.

Think of creation as a hologram. Every person is immersed in the larger hologram and can observe it only from his or her position. We each see the same whole but from an individually unique perspective. At the same time, we each are miniaturized versions of the whole, having the same qualities it has, whether we recognize them or not. Becoming able to see this imagery of the divine—this love-wisdom or ChristoSophia—in the human kingdom is a necessary step toward "enlightenment," the goal of the mystic.

The term ChristoSophia might seem to be a combination of the Christian Messiah and a mythical Goddess, some sort of holy androgyne. It is not. It refers not to an entity or being, but to a state of consciousness achieved by a blending of heart and mind inspired by a partnership of love and wisdom.[6] David R. Hawkins says that ChristoSophia is holy consciousness, the "Eye of the I," the perspective of God pointing us toward wholistic (holy) awareness. [7]

---

6. ChristoSophia. In Esoteric Christianity the holy consciousness of one in whom a state of balance, the love of the Christ and the wisdom of Sophia, expresses through the human nature. This term acknowledges the Christ (love) born within as it evolves to reveal an inner wisdom (Sophia), thus blending heart and mind becomes the Christ Consciousness. —Parrish-Harra, *Dictionary*, 52-53.

7. David R. Hawkins, *The Eye of the I From Which Nothing is Hidden* (Sedona, AZ: Veritas Publishing, 2001).

26

Reformation

It is not possible for the bird of humanity to fly on only one wing,[1]
—Helena Roerich

At some future point, historians will note this particular modern period as the Second Reformation of Christianity. During the closing decades of the twentieth century and early years of the twenty-first century, significant numbers—both churched and unchurched—are approaching spiritual maturity. Much ancient wisdom and arcane research, previously held in trust by a select few, is becoming more readily available.

Heretofore "Mother Church" has served as guardian of her infant sons and daughters. She continues to preserve the purity of the immature body of believers until they are able to fulfill their role as the "Bride of Christ"—which is Sophia alive and well within humanity in a conscious way. Other traditions similarly guard the "innocence" of their faithful masses by "pre-digesting" core ideas into codes of conduct and simplified beliefs. These they teach, asking for a commitment based on blind faith, not on true "knowing."

Christianity with its passionate devotional nature has developed high idealism and respect for duty. It has etched for disciples a well-defined path supposedly modeled on the life of Master Jesus. The authority of the church, governing with a masculine style, utilizes the powerful influences of its birth era. Rules of the faith have been delineated into

---

1. The Agni Yoga Society, Inc., *Letters Of Helena Roerich II,* 23 April 1938 (n. p. Agni Yoga Society), http://agniyoga.org (accessed June 29, 2004).

201

straight forward do's and do not's (based on the Ten Commandments) to which church-decreed laws have been added.

One's acceptance within the community of believers (and usually within the culture in which one finds oneself) is based on compliance. In this system, obedience is the work of the "child," and evaluation is reserved for the "parent." Power exists in the hands of the authority. Organized faith meets the need of "sons and daughters" who willingly conform. Like all healthy infants, however, these grow up to require more personal freedom and richer food.

Unlike the paternal authoritarian model which required universal blind obedience, this new epoch requires personal spiritual cognition from each *willing* participant, granting to every one unconditional value no matter what their choices. Only by re-establishing respect for the feminine element will humanity be able to accomplish this.

Agni writings emphasize the neglect of the feminine principle. Today's still imbalanced world does not yet willingly give full rights to all. Opposition, however, only intensifies the forces. Woman, demanding her cosmic rights, is acquiring an appreciation of her power—a power that enables each of us, whether male or female, to uncover *all* of our talents and gifts. We will now be able to balance our inner sense and our outer intelligence in order to find our true reason for being and bring it into appropriate expression.

Naturally, as with each new skill, we express ourselves less well in the beginning, but with continued practice, we improve our skills and develop a new way to be. The more inclusive qualities of Sophia can now teach us how to rectify past abuses of power and how to use mind with more intuitional skill. Judgment based merely on rational or linear thinking, limited as it is by its "either-or," two-dimensional nature, is dehumanizing to the soul of both the one expressing and the one toward whom judgment is directed. Again we note the Agni teachings, reminding ourselves the heart of hearts never chooses to be destructive as it moves us through chaos toward order.

Now all the great teachers will affirm the rights of women.
Therefore the coming era will be not only one of great cooperation, it

will also be the age of woman. Woman will have to be armed with courage, and first of all, she will have to restrain her heart from unwise giving, for there must be a golden balance in everything." [2]

Each sensitive person has to learn to refrain from "unwise giving" (women particularly, due to centuries of being subservient to masculine authority, being fearful of loss to other women, and having to maneuver for protection from the powerful men to whom they were attached). Even today this is not easy because a residue of distrust lingers in the basic feminine collective, as well as in individual basic selves, to be overcome. Manipulation of others to protect one's personal power is a natural outcome. The sensitive self wants to be loved; we all do. Yet sensitives must learn appropriate boundaries and be wise in facing challenges. Courage is needed to follow our "heart" (meaning our soul prompting), rather than our emotionally based desires. We learn the difference between personality's "wants" and the goal of the soul. Soul purpose becomes a priority as we gain more spiritual maturity.

Living a life of service dedicated to anchoring love in the human nature helps each aspirant advance from operating under the letter of the law of his/her tradition, to cooperating with the spirit of the law. After the astral nature is purified of its glamours and illusions, we discover within ourselves the wise heart center that enables us to anchor love in the face of the just and the unjust. The purified heart center receives the promptings of the soul, and even when our mind does not understand, our heart perceives right action.

'You shall love the Lord your God with all your heart and with all your soul and with all your mind.' This is the greatest and first commandment. And a second is like it: 'You shall love your neighbor as yourself.' On these two commandments hang all the law and the prophets.
Matthew 22.37-40.

---

2. As quoted in *Mother of Agni Yoga,* (New York: Agni Yoga Society, 1956), from *Letters of Helena Roerich.*

The Great Commandment elucidates our goal. Additionally, we recall, *"love is the fulfilling of the law."* (Rom. 13.10) With these directives etched into our spiritual nature, we set out to bring ourselves to maturity under the direction of Mother Wisdom. We begin to know how to translate the lessons of the past into harmonious daily actions within the culture of which we are a part. In The Wisdom of Solomon (8.3-4) we find the great teacher who can resolve the mysteries of God's knowledge. She reflects these greater truths into hearts that love and care. We then can begin to live them as our own.

As one's personality (the "he" part) acknowledges one's soul nature (the "she" part), one begins to move toward a higher comprehension of life itself. Now the conjoined masculine and feminine—the yin-yang of human life—begins to interact as a "soul-infused" personality. Likewise, Sophia is God's change agent, her pure spirit permeating those inner places within us which call out for healing and transformation. *"Herself unchanging, she can change all things; she makes all things new."* (The Wisdom of Solomon 7.27, 28).

The first work is to open the heart center to birth the love consciousness. Once this is achieved, we are ready to seek the wisdom that awaits. The emerging combination acts in a transforming manner upon those dedicated to building a new kind of awareness, also known as Christ Consciousness. The soul infused self—Christ-within, the hope of glory, as this divinity within is known in Christianity—is a miniature of the Christ (son) of the higher world. Just so, the *She who dwells within* Sophia is a miniature of the divine Sophia of the Higher World. Herein exists an infant self with its yin-yang qualities of love-wisdom ready to shine in its own right, to become a blessed one.

Among such buried treasures is the concept of the Second Person of the Trinity as Mother. Throughout the Byzantine East, churches were built in honor of Christ as "Holy Wisdom"—Hagia Sophia. Christ, in the East, has always been identified with Wisdom in the Jewish Scriptures, and Wisdom is exclusively a female figure. If the Byzantine East made the fertile connection between Christ and Sophia, it failed, however, to follow this connection to its ultimate conclusions. In the Latin West, mystics spoke from time to time of Christ as Mother. Most eloquent among these was Julian of Norwich in the 14th century. She, too, connected Christ with Wisdom and called Christ "our true mother Jesus." [3] [Robert Lentz's lifework is painting icons of contemporary and forgotten saints].

Knowing Christ as love and Sophia as wisdom, we call the name ChristoSophia, not limited to a conjunction of two beings called Christ and Sophia, but a rebirth of consciousness beyond duality (remember the "eye of the I") with no sense of subject-object awareness. It in itself acknowledges the mystery of holy androgyny.

Speaking of Christ as Sophia means that he can also be properly referred to as she. "She is a reflection of the eternal light, untarnished mirror of God's active power, image of his goodness" (Wisdom 7:26). It is Wisdom who creates and orders the world, making manifest the divine will. And it is Wisdom who delights to be among the human race, teaching us her ways. Historical and cultural circumstances led her to become a male human being at the Incarnation. A female in first century Palestine would not have been allowed to do what a male could do. As the Incarnation continues to unfold in the Mystical Body after Christ's resurrection and ascension, however, it is again the female Sophia who best expresses the mystery of the Second Person of the Trinity.

Russian icons have depicted Sophia/Christ as an androgynous figure with wings and bright red skin, wearing imperial Byzantine robes. Androgyny was as close as my predecessors dared go. [4]

This is not an entity or being, but a holy consciousness birthed within; an accomplishment achieved by the blending of heart and mind energies; an awakening of the Christ-within so long asleep. Hard to describe and difficult to define, it can only be comprehended by

---

3. Robert Lentz, "Christ Sophia," *Creation,* (July/August 1990): page 30.
4. Ibid.

experiencing it. It is unitary consciousness, not intellectualized, but made known by gnosis.

> *By so tying she/he together in my heart, I recovered my balance and got used to the light. Christ Sophia is a very dangerous memory for Christian people, one which many—perhaps leaders especially—will continue to try to bury. She accuses us of our many sins against women, gays, and the earth itself. She demolishes our theological excuses against the ordination of women. But she brings us a blessed freedom that comes with every expression of the truth. She is an earthy, playful expression of our God. By welcoming her back into the heart of our faith we can regain a catholicity—a wholeness—we have lacked so long.* [5]

A returning matriarchy cannot resolve the challenges of our time, but the return of the divine feminine brings a movement to restore balance, thus assisting the creation of a complementary capability within humanity. The collective can then begin the effort needed to establish an unprecedented co-working between the sexes. Such an achievement can begin to usher in a new order of creation, an era that will resolve alternating strife and maximize human potential—fully human, fully divine—more than merely seeking higher states of consciousness. A new kind of being will begin the quest toward the goal that has long been held within humanity. "Made in the image and likeness," humanity is charged to become wise in the right use of its potential, existing in the "I AM" as it comes to *know* the Creator. This is the promise of the "I AM THAT I AM," the enlightened truly realize the healing of the nations and the greater meaning of salvation.

At this future yet-to-be-realized royal moment of the human journey, we shall see the demise of both the matriarchy and patriarchy as we understand them now. In their place we shall see an integration and appreciation for both masculine and feminine principles. The alchemy of the

---

5. Ibid., 39.

mystical marriage will be for all people, and thus a new and complementary state of existence will be created that can fulfill higher potential within a humanity balanced and whole. Love-wisdom, ChristoSophia, is to be known for ourselves, as well as to benefit all humanity.

On a transcendental level, there is already only one world religion. The word "religion" is from Latin *re, "back" or "again,"* and *ligare,* "to bind," or "to tie." Its purpose, in other words, is to tie back together, to reconnect humanity to the source from which it has come. Alice Bailey writes, *"Religion is the name, surely, which we give to the invocative appeal of humanity which leads to the evocative response of the Spirit of God."* [6] To evoke a response from the higher worlds to the cry of humankind is significant. It honors the bond between the inner and outer and encourages humanity to invoke the energies of above so inner and outer realities construct together. We do not always grasp that humanity itself calls forth the power, action, and/or events from the higher planes; nevertheless, it is so.

---

6. Alice A. Bailey, *The Externalization of the Hierarchy* (NY, NY: Lucis Publishing Co., 1982), 596–597.

27

Creativity

I hold a vision of the feminine principle being honored. I can see it in my own dreams, in my friends dreams, and in the dreams that people write down and send to my office. It's clear to me that the feminine is pushing through and trying to be known. She wants us to bring her to full consciousness[1]

—Marion Woodman

A new kind of spirituality is being fueled by the "disciplined creativity" born in our modern society through our personal desire for self-realization. Aware that a life well lived is an art, we are now resurrecting, often through meditation, the desperately needed creative impulses that facilitate self-guided spirituality. We are learning to trust instinctual knowing and to put it to conscious use step by step.

Great restlessness emerges whenever individuals and/or collectives allow themselves a greater freedom of expression. When no one knows quite where the boundaries are, a time of experimental activity sets in. In everyday life cycles this occurs as teenagers move toward adulthood. In a similar manner, a certain percentage of humanity is currently moving toward spiritual maturity as it gains access to the personal freedom our modern society has permitted. Recognition of creativity grants confidence and thus encourages expression. Thus we find ourselves living in a time of exploration and self-discovery.

---

1. Tami Simon, "Femininity and the Wisdom of the Body," an interview with Marion Woodman, *Magical Blend*, Issue 33 (Jan. 1992), *Magical Blend's* website is www.magicalblend.com.

Sophia must laugh at the stir she causes. She picks up her skirts and dances with delight as her intuitive wisdom drops in to take us by surprise. She helps us see the many options life has to offer, inviting us to become the heretics of our day, those able to choose, by daring to listen to her whispers. Each of us in our own way must learn to pick our steps while embracing inner guidance if we would allow silence to lead us. An exciting trial and error period is necessary to establish a comfort zone of personal beliefs, inner awareness, and self-imposed boundaries.

Now, when we listen inwardly we begin to hear *She who dwells within.* As we gradually learn her language we traverse a confusing time, similar to adolescence, of not knowing just what to believe or how to respond. Herein we must each struggle to find our way. Each awakened one establishes his or her own field of experience from which to draw conclusions. The resulting personal references will then serve us in our next stage of development.

Our perspective shifts from the busyness of outer life, comparable to seeing the world from a fast moving train, to that of a walk in the woods. We shift to being a respectful participant of the evolving life, not just a swiftly passing observer. As we learn to view life from centeredness, we find both our service and our growth pattern.

Rationalism locks humanity into a destructive dead end

In order to transit from a broken world to a unified one, each human being has to discover a part to play. Knowingly, or unknowingly, each one of us contributes either to the problem or to the solution. Rapid changes are occurring as the new incoming vibrations bombard the planet bringing new influences and shifting demands. As these influences nurture each of us, independence and individuality increase. Wiser ones are to inspire self-knowledge, encourage divine insights, and promote higher values for group life, in order to offset humanity's current extremes of self-centeredness.

Right relationship—human to human and kingdom to kingdom—must assume importance, whether within the world of nature or with others, at work or at play. High consciousness treasures the religions of the world and can never condone their being reduced to mere rational concepts, as feared by many. The plan of the subtle world is to awaken us to mysteries long preserved in myths, legends, and dreams. We are to grasp the message held in literature, in art, and in nature.

Gradually we will come to realize rationalism locks humanity into a destructive dead end, a maze without an exit. Mystery teachings reveal to humanity its own sacred nature—sensitive and creative—where fresh insights wait to enrich a world within worlds, a never-ending spiral of guided possibilities.

The Western world in particular is ready for a contemporary, contemplative spirituality that is interfaith wherein each collective honors the holy within every other body as well as its own—aware that each one approaches spiritual maturity according to its own inner pattern and timing.

A percentage of every organized religious body as well as vast numbers of unaffiliated individuals have matured sufficiently to be questioning and demanding. Indeed, by our free use of modern tools of communication, much that certain ones would like to keep quiet is quickly known. Each part of the world discovers rapidly what is happening in countries at a distance. We have international friends and contacts that keep us "in the loop" as we live in the "end times."

Such technology has radically challenged the ignorance of humanity in regard to its relationship to the world in which we live. The re-emerging regard for our relationship to Earth, and the realization that all life upon her is a global community, expands as feminine principles become accepted.

As our insight deepens, so will our grasp of the essence of the myths, archetypes, and parables that have for so long guided humanity. Two equally strong pictures of the future currently vie for power in the group mind. They have developed around the word "apocalypse" from *apokalyptein*, meaning "to uncover" or "to reveal".

Literalistic reading of the wholly symbolic biblical book of Revelation has stimulated great fear. The struggles that lie before, as well as within, us will create either "the final great catastrophe" or will become the ultimate "birth pains" as the divine feminine brings forth the new heaven and the new earth.

> *A great portent appeared in heaven: a woman clothed with the sun, with the moon under her feet, and on her head a crown of twelve stars. She was pregnant and was crying out in birth pangs, in the agony of giving birth.* Revelations 12.1,2.

Jungian psychologist Dr. Edward Edinger (as cited by Clonts and Demetry in *Apocalypse of Peace*), explains that *"the 'sun-moon' woman of Revelation takes these heavenly bodies as pre-existent male-female energies, then gives birth to a child who unifies both in a single being."* [2] We need to remember the pre-existent male-female energies within us now are seeking to unite in a single being, our personal ChristoSophia.

As Drs. Clonts and Demetry elaborate on Edinger's theme, we discover our planet likewise is birthing a next stage:

> *This child of wholeness is none other than that part of humanity now being reborn as a single planetary being to take conscious charge of its affairs. The light and love of the Father, God's masculine face, is coming into alignment with Mother Earth at both the physical level and the soul level of the Mother Presence. Our own souls, as well, are being drawn rapidly into alignment with these great cosmic forces in process. This is the process for which the many world prophecies have attempted to prepare us.* [3]

Sophia, the Wise Mother, is advancing in her role as Mother Earth and awakening her children to be better participants in the role they play in Earth's journey. With the expansion of the heart-mind in humanity, we can undergo a more gentle birth and experience a collective "apocalypse of peace" by deliberate co-creation with the intensifying spiritual powers, or new energies as they are more frequently called, presently bombarding the planet.

Dedication to dogma will diminish over time. It is a cover for fear—fear of change, fear of the unknown, fear of not being in control.

---

2. Demetry and Clonts, in Ch. 2, "Creating from Stillness," *Apocalypse of Peace*, quoting from Edward F. Edinger, *Archetype of the Apocalypse: A Jungian Study of the Book of Revelation* ed George R. Elder (Chicago: Open Court, 1999), 98-101.

3. Demetry & Clonts, in Ch. 2 "Creating from Stillness," *Apocalypse of Peace*.

Dogma is not just a religious phenomenon, but a defining factor of many secular vocations, as well. It can as easily call for an unbending allegiance to the blinkered god of reason as for unreasoning, blind faith in outer religious or political authorities.

Dogmatism insists on accepting something as absolutely true, even when there may be cause for reasonable doubt. The problem with dogmatism lies not in the concern over whether or not something is true, but in the refusal to think in the light of higher mind.

There is some variation among those who seek refuge in unquestioning dogma. Among these mostly law-abiding fundamentalists (some of whom can be found within any religious, political, and scientific, camp) are also found those who:

> *"are driven by fanatical resentment and possessed by the dark face or shadow side of collective archetypal forces," explains Edinger. "These zealots [terrorists also come from this ilk] are willing to sacrifice their lives for a perceived collective gain and often have expectations of personal reward in heaven as well. They have convinced themselves that they are agents of divine justice and punishment, and they believe they are bringing in a new and better world order."* [4]

The Revelation of Saint John: The Path to Soul Initiation by Zachary Landsdowne, presents a timely explanation of this much-maligned book of the Bible. By allowing us to view these words of mystery from another perspective, Lansdowne's book creates hope and understanding, refuting the fear-and-anxiety-producing "left behind" series. His wise way of presenting this clarification allows verse-by-verse access to both the English text and its psychological meaning. It is also rich with references to enhance our grasp of initiation, if we so desire. [5]

Wise ones are desperately needed as current events demand justice and respect for all plus freedom from want and fear. High principles

---

4. From a letter to the editor written by Edinger to his local paper in 1995 following the tragedy that befell the David Koresh cult in Waco, Texas. George R. Elder, editor's preface to *Archetype of the Apocalypse,* xvii, quoted by Clonts and Demetry in Ch. 1, "Approaching a New Heaven and New Earth," *Apocalypse of Peace.*

5. Zachary Landsdowne, *The Revelation of Saint John: The Path to Soul Initiation.* (York Beach, ME: Red Wheel/Weiser, 2006).

impress upon all an entitlement to freedom of expression coupled with a responsibility for right use of resources. Great and small interfaith ministries within all traditions are needed. Each tradition needs some sensitive ones to respond to spirit so that the processes used to guide advancement for the whole can be enriched.

Certain individuals are to consciously lead by connecting their inner efforts with outer lifestyles in order to deliver their part of the vision for the new world. As more witness these efforts, more will join the process. Robert Powell of Germany, writes in *Divine Sophia, Holy Wisdom*:

> *The working of the Holy Soul is bound up with the mystery of love. This comes to manifestation as the impulse toward community between spiritually striving human beings. In Old Testament times the activity of the Shekinah (Holy Soul) was especially focused upon the community of Israel, to prepare for the First Coming. Now, in our time, it is a matter of the [spiritual] community whose task it is to prepare and bring to realization the Second Coming. This is a pure love impulse directed to the heart which entails not only devotion, but also knowledge.*[6]

While Sophia is divine wisdom, it is true she is hard to comprehend. If wisdom were either easy to come by or easily grasped, there would be many more wise ones. She is, however, the essence of nature—natural to each, the knowable essence. Innately in alignment, she holds the knowledge until ready and receptive ones form, and all creation blooms.

---

6. Robert A. Powell, *Divine Sophia, Holy Wisdom*, 2nd ed. rev. (Nicasio, CA: The Sophia Foundation of North America, 1997), 14.

28

Blooming

*T*oday, large numbers of individuals recognize there are several consciousness levels within each human being. Many spiritual and psychological traditions acknowledge such, although each, naturally, defines them through the semantics of its own system. Think again of these levels of consciousness as a multistory building. Some persons think the bottom floor is all there is. Others know of only the first two, the physical and emotional levels. Actually, there is emerging a fairly clear delineation of seven levels. Our degree of awareness varies, as do our interests, concerns, and the activities of our internal and external states as we travel through the levels in much the same way as one utilizes an elevator to move from floor to floor.

From a spiritual perspective, each level is regulated through a non-physical energy center which, in Eastern thought, is called a chakra. Most often symbolically portrayed as a lotus, each center lies waiting, folded

---

1. Carol Morrell, "Bloom Where You Are Planted," song lyrics written for Rev. Carol E. Parrish after a retreat some years ago.

into itself like a bud, until the movement of spiritual energy causes its petals to unfold into a beautiful flower open to the light of high consciousness.

Each of the seven major chakras corresponds to a specific physical anatomical point. At each ascending center, the quality of consciousness is refined and expanded to include a greater awareness of all that exists around us physically, emotionally, mentally, and spiritually.

The lowest center is located in the etheric body near the base of the physical spine. At this level the union of spirit and matter is maintained as the basis for physical life, so issues of basic survival emerge here.

At the next level, centered in the lower abdomen, a healthy respect for sexuality, sensation, gender, and sensitivity to one's surroundings gradually develop. The expression moderated through this center seeks interaction wherein we hold each other in high regard without pursuing self-serving purposes or mere sexual gratification. Either with tender guidance or through hard lessons, sensation and sexuality gradually are refined to become a part of spirituality. Appropriate integration occurs as we learn reverence for gender and the natural processes of life.

Moving our attention to the solar plexus center, we come to recognize our skills and capabilities in the roles we play as participants in the drama of daily life. Empowerment gives us confidence to use our talents and gifts for the benefit of ourselves and others. Appreciation arises for the will within our nature; as we progress, it is built, tempered, and honed to comply with our developing grasp of what is appropriate in the light of higher will.

Maturing through our own life experiences together with assistance from mentors, we are now better able to align with an inner sense that transforms our coarser personal will (developed by the activity of centers one and two) to a more harmonious will. Our daily practice facilitates the process. We make a choice to become a more refined individual with an ever greater service to render. As we continue to blend ego and higher awareness, this

Hidden in the cave of the heart is the godling who is to emerge eventually as our personal Christo-Sophia

"center of will" becomes a radiant lamp for the personality, shining light on all issues of personal life and upon the processes of the rational mind.

The next step in our ongoing evolution of consciousness is of primary importance, as it presents the task of "opening the heart." This fourth level—vital to planetary life at this critical time—serves as a bridge between the inner and outer life. Generally, personality relates to the outer physical reality, while the non-physical, or inner nature, reflects the soul and its vast experiences that we do not always recognize. The open heart allows the faculties of the higher self, or true Self, to begin adapting the ego to purposes seldom acknowledged at the personality level. Here, hidden in the cave of the heart, is the godling who is to emerge eventually as our personal Christo-Sophia. Inner ponderings stimulate the spiritual seed to germinate and gradually develop the wisdom needed to forge a relationship between the inner and outer natures.

Remember, a seed has two requirements: water and light. Thus water (tears [2]) and light (the *soulstar* [3]) are necessary for this quiescent self to sprout. The invoking of light from the higher world activates Sophia to come to our aid as teacher. *"The Helper, the Holy Spirit. . .will teach you everything"* (John 14.26). When the Holy Spirit blows on the spark deep within, the inner fire begins to blaze. Energized by the activity of higher centers, the heart is no longer merely a base for emotion, but through persistent devotion, becomes a sensitive touchstone of the Soul—Mother Wisdom.

The fifth level begins the higher development of the inner nature in its quest for Oneness with the All. This throat center, once energized, is further amplified by the magnetism, charisma, and sensorial awareness of the sensual second center, and is sometimes referred to as a higher octave of the second. Active in nature, it blooms with latent creativity as we give voice to our revelations. An authentic style develops that is uniquely our own in method and/or mannerism. Such people are often

---

2. Tears are a natural response whether they come from sorrow or joy.

3. Soulstar. A symbol of a bright star over the head represents the presence of the soul from which the personality has descended, and continues to be overlighted—an archetype to constantly remind personality of its source of power and true nature. —Parrish-Harra, *Dictionary*, 279.

called "his or her own person," may have strong charisma, and exhibit a unique flair.

The sixth level, the brow center corresponding to the "third eye," observes the process of inner and outer life unfolding. Hugh of St. Victor, a Saxon Christian mystic (c. 1078–1111), taught that each person has three eyes: the physical eye with which to see the material world, the mental eye with which to perceive ideas and concepts, and the spiritual eye with which to see the plan or will of God at work. The mental eye seeks truths and glimpses of reality to which it can relate, and the spiritual eye unites with the soul in transcendent insight as revealed by contemplation—we "see" with the eye of the soul.[4]

As our lesser will harmonizes with higher will, a strengthening of the sense of how to fulfill one's own part in a higher plan develops, and with it the necessary drive to set this into action. Here we connect with the sense of what is "ours to do," generally with a stirring passion that refuses to be denied.

The highest level, the crown center on top of the head (the thousand petalled lotus), receives the outpouring of energies the soul delivers to the inner presence so that the personality can be increasingly adapted for soul purposes. *"Remember, ye are gods,"* soul whispers. Her echoing words of wisdom encourage her charge as does the energy of higher contact—lots of vital energy. Love is stepped down center by center, octave by octave, guiding us in transformation.

As an ongoing practice of wisdom ways persists, personality draws more and more of the fiery substance—higher frequencies—through the soul star into the earthy nature. More and more, aspiration ignites and sustains personality as it is being remodeled from within. While the head center becomes increasingly sensitized to receive impressions and transmissions, the brow center observes and quickens, making one more aware of a higher plan. It gradually comes to carry the flame in the heart, emitting love-wisdom. Through experience, the heart learns to recognize the

---

4. Hugh of St. Victor cited by Ken Wilber, *Eye to Eye* (Garden City, NY: Anchor Books, 1983), 3, quoted by Parrish-Harra, *Dictionary*, 125.

difference between emotion and the touch of the soul, between personal and unconditional love.

Increased creativity results as Wisdom refines her instrument. No longer quiescent within, she is now more readily noted. Felt as a flow alternating between expressing and resting, she stirs within the body. Think of this as a gentle but persistent geyser, rising and falling, developing a smooth rhythm for her greater and greater expression. Resting in the physical world of matter until the Godhead calls, she responds, arising to prepare us, one by one, for the next great evolutionary shift.

Said another way, the Christ-within is love-wisdom indwelling as the true spiritual nature of each individual. As dedicated daughters and sons, disciples are taught to grasp their truth and to withstand the consequences of it. Without preparation, exposure to higher truths and energies tends to confuse. In John 16.12, Jesus said to his disciples, *"I still have many things to say to you but you cannot bear them now."*

Also in the New Testament speaking to those who prepare themselves for initiation is the following: *"God is faithful, and he will not let you be tested beyond your strength, but with the testing he will also provide the way out so that you may be able to endure it"* (1 Cor. 10.13).

When energy ignites in an unprepared life, the delicate psyche is shaken, but when prepared, it can remain steady in poised self examination and make empowered choices. Too much effort too fast "burns" the mechanism, doing damage that may require healing before more progress can be made.

For this reason, mentors, spiritual directors, and gurus guide others carefully along paths they themselves have traveled. Each helps the next, and together the safety net is woven to sustain larger and larger numbers as humanity advances.

World servers, a modern term for disciples, prepare themselves for contact with the higher realm. Discipleship demands as exacting a train ing as any other specialty. Successful candidates envision excellence, always striving to be as clear as possible about events going on around them, utilizing careful discrimination in their responses.

When we think of biblical disciples, we recognize the Master gave them attitudinal guidelines and many mysteries to ponder as well as commissioning them to serve. We are to acknowledge the world servers in every country, race, religion, and ideology. Remember also, John the Baptist who was contemporary with, but never a disciple of, Jesus, was true to his own calling. He too gave his life to fulfill his mission as God's prophet and was recognized by his own followers. Jesus expressed strong support of John's position.

Jesus began to speak to the crowds about John: "What did you go out into the wilderness to look at? . . A prophet? Yes, I tell you, and more than a prophet. . .Truly I tell you, among those born of women no one has arisen greater than John the Baptist. Matthew 11.7–11.

Likewise, the Bhagavad Gita offers comforting words when we find our path is different than that of our friends or family.

Better to follow one's own svadharma, however humble, than to follow another's, though great. By engaging in the work prescribed by one's own "inner calling," one does not miss the mark. Bhagavad Gita 18.47.

Modern disciples open themselves to the freeing grace of the higher world and to the inner direction their sensitive natures perceive. Enabled primarily by the sincere efforts they make, devotion moves through them, sensitizing them to spirit's touch, as well as to impressions from higher realms—to guidance from the soul, and in time, from the Spirit.

Jerry N. Uelsmann (b. 1934). Untitled, 1994.
Gelatin Silver print. Collection of the artist.
"The Spirit of the Goddess in Modern Art"

A Beautiful Personal Garden

✱ We pause and turn our attention inward. In the inner eye, see the pleasant early morning light shining upon you.

✱ See yourself as a bud full of tightly folded potential.

✱ Feel yourself responding to the warmth of the sun; feel it stimulating you, awakening creative juices within, and calling you to greater life.

✱ Breathe now, and stretch into that light, realizing you are stretching into the fullness of your being.

✱ In your mind's eye see your bud-self unfolding—opening to the light—gaining color, fragrance, and beauty.

✱ As you stretch out your petals, you realize you are but one flower in the garden of Sophia. Other unique blossoms are around you: some tall and stately, some diminutive; some are bolder while others are more delicate and hidden.

✱ Each of us is a flower, each a part the whole, in this sacred place where seeds grow into their fullness.

✱ Now raise your awareness into the light above your head and look down into the center of the flower that is your tool of expression, your own unique personality. Look for a symbol, color, or form that builds there. Ask for a symbol and wait. When a symbol or impression appears, accept it and contemplate the meaning or guidance given.

✳ Hold the quiet. Breathe easily. Recall and contemplate "the answer lies within." Here within your own centered-ness you are always connected with Sophia, the Wise One.

✳ Affirm allegiance to your personal reason for being. Enjoy being a flower in the garden of Sophia and a spark of wisdom in the collective consciousness of humanity. Gradually see the garden in your mind transform into a picture of the sea of humanity. See people: males and females of every age, rank, race, and lifestyle; busy or at rest; with plenty or with little—every single one a cherished member in the human family of which you too are a vital part.

✳ Personal spiritual growth is achieved through a balance of law and love, through strength and tenderness, through aligning our lesser will with higher will. As Sophia heals our ambivalence and duality, the bud that is our own nature unfolds its petals to reveal the fullness of its bounty.

✳ Speak the OM now, gently and easily. Allow the sacred sound to flow from deep within your hidden nature, joyfully rising to give itself to the outer. Allow a sense of the real YOU to send outward your prayer and love for Life itself. Just as the fragrance of the flower wafts on a breeze, so too, your vibration blends into the atmosphere to bless all it touches.

— Shanti.

29

Progeny

We recall the words of St. Paul, *"And now abideth faith, hope,
charity, these three; but the greatest of these is charity"* (1Cor.
13.13). As one would expect of daughters of Sophia, each has her own
special characteristics. In the Orthodox tradition, a beautiful icon symbolizes a particular meaningful teaching concerning Sophia. It is taught that
when one awakens to Sophia—Mother Wisdom—her developing nature
gives birth to three daughters: Faith, Hope, and Charity. Spiritual aspirants sing their praises.

> *Faith is the bird that feels the light when the dawn is still dark.*
> —Sir Rabindranath Tagore

Faith, the lovely one who finds answers in the heart, links heart,
mind, and soul to bring knowing from within. The Masters say the faithful approach infinity through the heart. Knowing humanity has lagged for
centuries, here is a key to how the few find their way to higher consciousness: The heart is the bridge over which devotees progress from personality to higher centers of consciousness.

Faith lives in the heart as an assurance of inner connectedness to
life (whether known as our Soul, God, or Wisdom)—an awareness that,

225

once it comes to life, gifts us with an inner sense of connection to the essential goodness of life itself. We "know" with our "knower" that we are connected to the Universal Consciousness and that it cares for us, even when we do not always have "proof": this felt assurance strengthens us as we find our way through the muddle of the moment.

Take hope from the heart of man, and you have left a beast of prey.[1]
—Ouida

Hope sees the positive in the midst of challenge. Here, one is able to hold on to the goal, concept, or understanding, staying on course regardless of conditions. Hope sustains us when we are the unfortunates in a situation, or when we are facing overwhelming adversity, helping us to believe life will once more become manageable.

To remain positive presents another kind of challenge. As one faces the half full/half empty glass, one must train one's own nature to see the importance of even the half-filled glass. Hope expectantly awaits the opportunities that will come, knowing if she persists victory will be hers. Hold on, persist; perspective counts.

Charity doth not behave itself unseemly, seeketh not her own, is not easily provoked, thinketh no evil. 1 Corinthians 13.5 (King James Version).

Charity, often inappropriately translated as "love," (a better translation would be "will-to-good") gives others the benefit of the doubt. She chooses not to judge but to believe in the goodness carried within others, not just within herself. She can say, "the other is also a soul in their experience," or, "I can see the light in him or her even though I don't enjoy the personality." Because Charity finds trust more pleasant than judgment or suspicion, she is willing to vie with malevolence again and again, calling upon courage as needed. She is well attuned to God, the Good.

The symbolism is unquestionable. The Wisdom abiding in Sophia births faith, hope, and charity within our willing nature, transforming us.

---

1. Ouida (Marie Louise de la Ramée) [(1838-1908) British writer], *Wisdom, Wit and Pathos,* (1870) quoted by Seldes in *Great Thoughts,* 317.

We then serve as a light on the path, for ourselves as well as for others. Dedicated pursuit of the qualities inherent in Wisdom quickens the true Self to bring forth its gifts. The lots of vital energy birthed within one's heart brings Christ-like love—the goal of the people of Christ. Thus, mind and heart are joined in the quest for spiritual maturity. This union of love and wisdom, or ChristoSophia, is only now coming to the fore.

Historically, Christians have been taught their work was to revere God and be obedient to His will, or to the will of Christ Jesus, as God's only divine offspring. Until now, many have acknowledged themselves as daughters and sons (holy heirs) of the Most High, believing this was accomplished through Jesus in some way, though exactly how varies from sect to sect. Nevertheless, learning to live honorably, to regret errors, to make amends, and to be as "Jesus-like" as possible is a common ideal throughout Christendom. Some denominations and traditions have had more exposure to the "Mary Model" than others. This model also offers obedience and humility as defined for us by whatever spiritual approach we have learned.

Nurturing energies of the higher planes are bringing a new consciousness

Our present effort, however, is not just to continue as the "good child" but to mature into the Christ Sophia as did Jesus, the way-shower and masculine model of combined boldness and sensitivity. Mother Mary likewise models both feminine qualities of endurance and the masculine trait of courage. We often fail to think of the courage Jesus' mother displayed in staying with him to the end. We need to remember, the disciples, for the most part, fled, leaving the holy women at the foot of the cross. Both Mary and Jesus are models of harmony and balance, courage and endurance, within the role and age in which they lived, as was Mary Magdalene. Little acknowledged by tradition, now her role, resolute and steadfast, gains greater significance. These well-represent enlightened lives for us to model in our time and in our path.

As the infant Christ-within matures to become ChristoSophia within our lives, we strive for a consciousness that is stable, balanced, and whole. We welcome the divine influence which seeks to reveal and mature both the masculine and feminine in every individual, as each principle is to be equally honored.

The term ChristoSophia is modern and primarily used within the esoteric Christian tradition. Other traditions have their own names for the balanced whole (holy) within. We find the term "Atman" in the Hindu religion, "Buddhahood" in the Buddhist philosophy, and "Horus" within the Egyptian mysteries, to name but a few.

All religions of the world—when not fanaticized—carry humanity toward spiritual maturity. What we call "Christhood" in Christianity denotes a particular level of spiritual maturity to which we aspire. The fulfillment of hope-filled prophecies concerning the future of humanity and planet Earth depends upon the transformational energies of love-wisdom expressing through modern disciples to actuate our part of the solution and to restore harmony. Each tradition acknowledges in its own way the existence of the inner presence and has recorded practices for its adherents in order to help bring about individual transformation and, as enough individuals are awakened, planetary restoration.

She who dwells within, Sophia, nurtures the infant consciousness as it wakens, strives, and matures. Knowing our potential, the holy feminine is not content to sit idly by but calls the Higher Self to activity. Our nature softens as heart and mind become betrothed; this inner harmonization is called the Mystical Marriage.

The imagery of the mystical marriage describes the union of the earthly human soul with the heavenly bridegroom we know as the Christ. Holy Consciousness in its active love role dispenses lots of vital energy to all planetary life. The two aspects of humanity are mirrored in the biblical imagery of the "kings of the earth" and the "bride of Christ."

> *To become a conscious* I-being *on the earth, every human must become a 'king' [strong, self-loving, confident, masculine in nature], a* man *who can rule [be under his own direction]. Yet, to move beyond the stage of the lower self, however well perfected, the human being must go on to purify his soul in the selfless pursuit of knowledge and in*

selfless deeds of love so that he can also become the 'Bride of Christ,' a woman who can give birth to a child [the spiritual self within]. [2]

The Way of the Heart leads one to the ultimate goal of Christian life—spiritual union with the eternal bridegroom—the Christ Consciousness. We must ask, "what part does the feminine nature of the divine play in this quest?" J. J. VanDerLeeuw, author of *Fire of Creation,* writes, *"no conception of the Holy Ghost is complete which does not also consider the doctrine of the Motherhood of God."* [3] Understanding this will lead the world directly to a Motherhood of God awareness and a new comradeship of the sexes. In a lecture, Rudolf Steiner once said:

> *We can represent what lives in the soul under two aspects: the aspect of sensation, the great impulse giver. . .then there is what illuminates the soul as ideation and mental pictures; this is the part of the soul at rest which receives its content from outside. The soul at rest which allows itself to be fructified by impressions from the world, is the Mother. The sum of sensations through the universe is the masculine of the soul, is Father. That which allows itself to be fructified is the feminine in the soul, the Mother in the soul, the eternal feminine. That through which the human being becomes conscious of oneself is called by the mystic, the Son.* [4]

An important realization of modern spirituality, more important presently than in the past, is that we must accomplish our individuation before we can receive much heavenly help. A healthy, balanced, mature ego is necessary to fulfill the "fully human" segment of the journey. Once this is achieved, we can choose to turn our attention to inner life, with the goal of becoming "fully divine."

---

2. James H. Hindes, *Renewing Christianity* (Floris Books, 1995, Hudson, NY: Anthroposophic Press, 1996), 100.

3. VanDerLeeuw, *Fire of Creation*, 113.

4. Hindes quoting from a Rudolph Steiner lecture held in Berlin, 29 Oct. 1904, printed in *Uber Philosophie, geschichte and Literatur,* Vol. 51, collected works (Verlag, Dornach, 1983), 203, Hindes' translation.

Nurturing energies of the higher planes flooding the Earth at this time are bringing a new consciousness to both humanity and planetary life. The vibrational resonance is being speeded up as the dense material plane is being made to vibrate at a new frequency. A wide band of frequencies has always existed, but the material plane, accustomed to functioning in very few, has had to be adjusted extremely slowly.

Although humanity has had eons to mature, it has progressed far too slowly (we have been called "the laggards of the solar system"). We are quickening now, though, and this is creating a lot of chaos and crises on the planet. Through meditation, opening heart and mind, efforts of kindness, honoring and respecting other pathways, and practicing the Golden Rule, humanity can raise its vibrations to a healthy frequency, and as it does, we shall see the violence and chaos cease. A part of this is natural for the closing of an age, but we can hasten the shift to better conditions by consciously participating in establishing new and higher vibrations. This work begins by understanding "all is vibration" and there is a healthy resonance toward which we need to be moving.

The use of beauty is a major tool for the years ahead and vitally significant. Color and sound vibrations affect all of us. We need quality music from masters of the past (who were ahead of their times), as well as new music being gifted now from higher planes. As well, we need colors compatible with the sky, water, mountains, and greenery. Trees and flowers contribute to our well-being. We must renew our appreciation for the life giving vitality of the Mother, both as Mother Matter and as Mother Wisdom, Sophia.

As we raise our vibration, it will emanate outwardly, affecting our surroundings, encouraging the individuals with whom we live and work. This is reflected in the things we wear, the jewelry we use, our home and office décor, and even the automobiles we drive. Denser energies are on the downward curve; lighter energies are the fresh and vital ones. As we travel within ourselves and with others on the upward-bound path, we are performing our task of uplifting the world about us. We can do it. This is the shift for which we have been waiting.

To be tested, not denied; to be loved, not rejected—here is the dilemma. The path of initiation is a spiritual journey that sequentially begins anew moving us rapidly through *recapitulation.*[5] The development of one virtue assists with the development of every other virtue. Laughingly, initiation has been described as a 25-watt bulb becoming a 50-watt, then a 75-watt, and in time a 100-watt bulb. This is an accurate analogy. One might say all initiates are born again and again to increasingly expanded awareness, learning new lessons, continually working to become all they can be. The ideal is to be a wise one, utilizing love-wisdom in all we say and do. Our goal is to mature spiritually so each can gratefully utter, "The Father-Mother and I are one."

---

5. Recapitulation. To recall, repeat, or re-experience. . .In spiritual thought we recapitulate our experiences of previous incarnations to reach a level of knowing more quickly so that we can again advance on a path of new learning. Recapitulation moves rapidly compared to new growth, which proceeds more deliberately. —Parrish-Harra, *Dictionary*, 235.

30

*H*erself

Wisdom is no longer for me a white-bearded old man, but an elusive flirtation, and merry Holy Spirit...hiding in all creation, waiting for us to discover her through consciousness. We need only a consciousness developed enough to find her, hidden all about, by looking with a loving eye. An early myth speaks of her hiding playfully in "drops of light" in every atom and within us in every flash of insight. Love and wisdom are one, not opposites.[1]

—Alice O. Howell,

The life-giving energy traveling from the Superior Mother reflects the higher principles with decreasing clarity as it is stepped down plane to plane. It registers on every level in some manner; however, it becomes less and less conscious as it descends into denser realms. Thus the reflection called the Inferior Mother, responding to that higher impulse through her many latent patterns, seeks to fulfill higher will as well as possible.

In this light, the symbology of the "Veiled Mother" becomes meaningful. Now we understand the struggle of spirit to work through the garb of matter. Tiny points of instinctual consciousness respond innately as best they can to the guiding principle. The great archetype of feminine consciousness, Mother Wisdom in her Queen of Heaven role, arcs her energy Earthward. Although rich with potential, the sparks in the world

---

1. Alice O. Howell, *The Web in the Sea: Jung, Sophia, and the Geometry of the Soul,* (Wheaton, IL: Madras, India: London: Theosophical Publishing House, 1993), 48.

233

psyche are for the most part unconscious and subject to easily distorted programming.

Women, sin, and sex have been overly identified with one another because as the masculine initiation path secured itself, resistance to the feminine approach was strong. She represented that which was to be resisted. Her mysteries were seen as traps, temptations to avoid; her attributes were seen as having little value. They awakened the very feelings and urges the rational mind was resisting. In masculine style, to do one's duty—to define the goal and go for it regardless of the price—became increasingly significant. That which could not be logically analyzed and evaluated or forcefully controlled lost value.

For many women, qualities that were no longer acceptable atrophied into the negative traits of the feminine: universality became aimlessness; patience gave way to stagnation; adaptability became carelessness; spiritual stillness turned into inertia; and receptivity became unresponsiveness. As they had served their purpose, they now became seeds of disgrace. The masculine had come to the foreground, power shifted, and a new era was begun.

No matter what we have done, such does not, indeed cannot, separate us from divine love

On the masculine path of initiation different ways were offered to prove one's worth; obstacles were to be overcome and strategies for competition developed. One-upmanship assured superiority. As individuals excelled, it appeared progress was being made, so how progress was measured became increasingly important. Ownership and aggressiveness became major markers of success. Physical prowess and mental acuity determined who earned recognition. The goal was to explore and map the outer world to understand physical reality and discover its laws. Reward strengthened motivation and bolstered concrete values. The spoils of the conquest were distributed by winners, those who became champions, kings, and rulers.

The gentler side of human life was left in the hands of those measured as less capable: women, children, the elderly, and the ill. To gain honor and demonstrate valor, the courageous and physically strong came to the defense of the weak, giving added significance to the role of the masculine.

In the just completed masculine cycle, humanity developed the analytical and calculating capabilities of the rational mind. As this strong masculine influence gained power, linear thinking veiled the feminine. She sought ways and means to protect her values, ensuring their survival out of sight until the masculine power was spent. Mother and her daughters had to wait. Her patience persisted.

The journey to ego strength is a risky one, for when achieved we must then resist capture by the world with which we have been involved. We must win our strength and must have gained enough self-esteem that we are ready for the "what's next" that life holds. But if we become addicted to the ego rewards of the outer world, we can go no further. We "lose our soul" in love of the outer, and the sensory world takes over. We will then spend our physical life seeking personality satisfaction.

In both Eastern and Western teachings we are warned we can lose our way on the path. By unwise choices we often involve ourselves in lessons and struggles which are not necessarily a part of our own plan. Even as we gain insights from such experiences, we may continue to disappoint ourselves and not achieve the inner peace we seek. Though we shift attitudes, face much pain, or gain compassion, if it is not our path, we have missed our mark. We can lose track of our soul purpose in this life and make our life (or journey) more difficult than it has to be.

The Greek word translated into English as "sin," is *amartia*, meaning "to miss the mark," referring to an archer failing to hit the target. The word "sin" used in religious teachings means a breach of prescribed moral codes, dogmas, or specific doctrines. Violating (or failing to live up to) a teaching is "missing the mark."

Should we aim at perceived perfection, we will find it an impossible target to hit. Often our failure produces guilt and/or resentment: we feel pain and anxiety as we undergo trial (quite literally we try ourselves in our own mental court). We may have set too grand a goal for ourselves, or an incorrect one. No matter what we have done "wrong" or failed to do "right," it is most important that we know such ***does not and cannot*** separate us from divine love.

In time we will recognize our error, seeing it for what it is, cease our allegiance to it, and move on more knowledgeably. As we gain deeper insights we can obtain a better sense of flowing with destiny. The next step is an initiating step toward divine purposes—our soul quest. The challenge, then, becomes to be "in the world but not of it," because we have learned there is a better way. *"This could mean, for example, not always reaching out to change the world immediately when suffering comes to us, but living with the pain long enough to hear what it has to teach us before acting."*[2] Now the divine feminine takes hold of her son, personality (in either woman or man) and begins to be Mother Wisdom in all this implies.

Sophia wears many crowns in the most silent of roles. She has authority over the young incarnated personalities embodied in matter, yet goes unrecognized, having to prompt from behind the scenery of outer life; however, as individuals discover inner realities, she readily serves those willing to evolve in her care.

Undergirding the love energy of the soul is Wisdom, who will birth her daughters— Faith, Hope, and Charity—within each willing psyche

When we begin to think in such a way, we uncover old terms such as "Superior Mother" and "Inferior Mother" referring to different aspects of the divine feminine. She is called Superior Mother in her function as the Mother Wisdom aspect of God and the producer of all seeds—every possible expression—that dwell within life's great reservoir. Here she is the mother known as unlimited potential, Higher Wisdom, Sophia.

Inferior Mother is the name erroneously given to Mother Earth wherein the seeds of densified physical life abide. Here sparks of consciousness live in restriction, embedded in the minerals, plants, and animals, as well as humanity. Each contains potential. Each spark awaits animation in order to unfold the beauty, talents, and gifts of the Sophia within the world of matter. Each seed will, in time, evolve from old embedded patterns into the individual uniqueness of its spark. This consciousness embodied becomes "Lower Sophia." Immanent within each psyche she

---

2. Hinds, *Renewing Christianity,* 103.

faithfully abides, awaiting liberation. She is both the inner knower of God's psyche and the witness of God-self in each individual.

We remind ourselves there is but one Source and we would be one with it, knowing humanity and the dense world are but rough reflections of potential as yet unpolished. The task of humanity is to expand consciousness—to remember *"ye are gods"*—one by one, until a sufficient number of striving ones impact the larger collective of humankind. Humanity will then learn to care for planetary life and to "keep the garden" (Genesis 2.15) for lesser life, for one another, and for the whole of creation.

To do this we must open the collective heart and mind, then share whatever resources we have—talents, money, abundances. These are not for any one alone, but are to move through hands of stewardship for the well-being of all. This responsibility of humanity remains largely unrecognized at this time.

Humanity is the major player in this critical time for both itself and for planetary life. Today's world servers are, for the most part, the disciples of the past—chelas, as they are known in Eastern approaches. A recently coined term is "cultural creatives."

We must thank Drs. Paul H. Ray and Sherry Ruth Anderson for their efforts in defining this emerging sub-culture. Ray and Anderson use the term "cultural creatives" to designate individuals who envision a new way of being-in-relationship to one another and to creation, in response to an impulse they may or may not totally comprehend. Those who recognize this impulse are said to have progressed to "responsible awareness."[3]

Wisdom teachings say each child of God is invested with power (her/his creativity) which can be used for either enlightenment or destruction. As maturing children of the Most High, we have been preparing from ancient times for the birth of Self by way of religions, traditions, and transformational processes. Spirituality is the natural result of this maturing process. The primary purpose of religion is to point us toward our

---

3. Paul H. Ray, Ph.D., and Sherry Ruth Anderson, Ph.D., *The Cultural Creatives* (New York: Harmony Books, 2000).

inner nature which can then be awakened by the inner presence who guides the maturation of the Self-within.

When the outer form of a tradition fails to satisfy any longer, the inner essence takes over, and the individual disciple and/or the collective begins to stir in discontent. The *law of chaos* [4] comes into action. As a few people birth the needed "next-step" awareness; it is immediately acknowledged by a few more. Then, more and more individuals become magnetized to the new vision and more changes begin to emerge, often in several places at the same time.

Whether we call ourselves "awakened ones," "disciples," "world servers," or "cultural creatives," it means we see a new possibility. We envision a new manner of life—a higher curve of the spiral—with more to offer for the well-being both of the individual and of the whole. Currently a shift in perspective has begun; a new momentum is growing.

The emerging vision of potentials provides upgrades to life in a variety of ways, but the ultimate result is a natural falling away, like baby-teeth, of the old social, mental, and emotional structures. Even though they served us well, they are no longer adequate to our needs. Just as Mother Nature has programmed new teeth to appear at the proper time, so has Mother Wisdom implanted in us the necessary drives for the building of a new way. We can already see evidence of the new consciousness in the increasing blending of races, more acceptance of a variety of perspectives, an interaction of the various religions, and a growing appreciation of styles, foods, architecture, and other ethnic-specific elements from different cultures.

Such aware ones are now actively accepting the role of guardians and caretakers of the future. As these continue to be receptive to impression, Sophia—the World Soul—increases her guidance and prompting for the benefit of all while planetary life enters the next stage of maturation.

From Eastern thought, we discover *Tara*, (the Cosmic Mother from whom all potential flows) bringing wise, true spirituality that sets

---

4. Manifestation disintegrating back to the elements of creation. We live in a time of rediscovering certain laws of operation that apply at times of dissolution. These patterns presently are defined by physics, as well as by metaphysics and quantum physics, as the "laws of chaos."—Parrish-Harra, *Dictionary*, 48.

238

one free. We have no name for this awakened, purified, and prepared sensitivity to higher consciousness in Christianity unless we remember Sophia like the ancients did as the part that "knows." Steiner says, *"when the astral body has been completely purified it is called in esoteric language 'the Virgin Sophia.'"*[5] This part embraces the love of Christ to birth the Christ-within. Loving and wise, Sophia undergirds us in our endeavors. Remember, *"Let the same mind be in you that was in Christ Jesus"* (Philippians 2.5). This mind is the wise mind.

A stimulated inner life gives birth to the infant divine that is to mature and then guide the evolving life. Undergirding the lots of vital energy of the soul is Wisdom, who will birth her daughters—Faith, Hope, and Charity—within each willing psyche. Sophia multiplies herself in each human as the inner presence expresses. She then guides each Christ-within, sustaining it as it strives on the path of initiation.

There is no end in sight. Once we dedicate ourselves to our quest for enlightenment we dare not abandon it; if we should, ego will take up the slack while our inner contact and sense of direction will diminish to wait for a future opportunity. At the end of each Earth life, the progress we have attained remains, enfolded within the permanent atom of the soul. This inner record re-awakens when it once again is given the freedom to flower by our glad response to the sensitive stirrings of soul.

---

5. Hines, *Renewing Christianity*, 103.

31

Kairos

Kairos is a moment in history when God's time is fulfilled. It is not perceived by objective observation, but only by "existential participation" in the words of Paul Tillich.[1]

—Susanne Schaup

We are already participating in the changing of the world as we have known it: Nothing will ever be the same. It can be better or worse—it will be better only if we make it better—so this is a perfect time to hope, dream, and image our "what-if's." Energy and effort have cracked old thought patterns just enough for new thoughts to be wedged into the collective armor of "that's the way we have always done it," allowing us to begin anew. As we struggle with new ideas and budding feelings we cannot yet identify, we begin to wonder, "Are the thoughts passing through my mind mine or yours, Oh mother of us all? Whisper louder. Don't make me wonder: shake me, wake me, and make me heed your tender wispy caress. Don't let go—I am lost enough already!"

The work is done by open hearts and open minds. Growing awareness has sharpened our understanding of the validity and sacredness of other traditions, not just the one into which we were born. In fact, it is much easier for the average Christian to study another religion than to trace down the complete unvarnished history of her or his own.

Susanne Schaup, a wise German woman with a strong vision and much wisdom, has graciously agreed to share her analysis of Sophianic

---

1. Susanne Schaup, "The Kairos of Spiritual Unity," speech at the Parliament of World Religions, Chicago, 1993.

spirituality—especially as it relates to the Christian tradition—based on her own careful, extensive research. The following words are from "The Kairos of Spiritual Unity," her presentation to the 1993 Parliament of the World's Religions in Chicago.

I intend to speak about spiritual, not religious unity. The focus is on spirituality, which is a broader term. It derives from spirit, the Spirit "which bloweth where it listeth," and is not the exclusive property of any particular religion. It is that inner drive which makes us reach out for each other, which led some of us to search for the roots of our tradition, to understand how it became what it is; why this religion of love has been so ineffective in the face of human aggression; why women have been degraded; why the churches bowed to patriarchal rule. Some of us are driven by the spirit to investigate the contradictions inherent in our religion, and some took a close look at its entanglement with the powers that be. Power is a crucial concept, and we shall come back to it later.

The pioneers of feminist theology—some of the best come from America—scrutinized the Bible in search of feminine aspects in our traditional image of God. They found a wonderful, sublime and mysterious figure—Sophia in Greek, Chokmah in Hebrew—Divine Wisdom, perceived as feminine, and so intimate with God that she is called his "darling and delight," his workmate and sharer of His throne. She is concerned with the earth and delights in human beings. Sophia reveals herself in those parts of scripture which are called the wisdom tradition of the Old Testament and the Apocrypha. She is a most charming and benign figure. Her femininity softens the image of the angry and jealous God. If we listen closely to her pronouncements, we perceive astonishing parallels between the old Goddess and Sophia.

Indeed, the ancient Hebrews were surrounded by cultures which still worshipped the Egyptian Isis, the Babylonian Ishtar, the Phoenician Astarte, or the Phrygian Kybele, and Jahwe is seen to lash out ferociously at the cult of the goddess. As the ancient goddess was put down in a process that took thousands of years, so women were put down and subjected to patriarchal law.

There is a flood of literature about all of this. Sophia is well-documented today. Her complex journey from a concept of Greek philosophy, the Platonic ideal of wisdom, to that divine personage in the Old

Testament, her subsequent cooption by *logos*, and her final projection onto Jesus Christ, partly also on the Virgin Mary, has been well researched. Sophia—although she has no part in the Holy Trinity nor the stature of a real goddess—could not be subdued forever. In the course of 2000 years of Christian history she emerged time and again. She turned up in visions of certain religious minds as late as the end of the nineteenth century, when the great Russian philosopher and poet Vladimir Solovev stumbled out into the desert near Cairo by an inner command, to search for Sophia. On the second day she appeared to him radiant, full of love and promise, and utterly changed his life. It seems that she particularly chooses times of crisis and spiritual decline to manifest through inspired minds, to restore the balance lost by the dominance of a patriarchal God.

Early in the Middle Ages, when religious life deteriorated in Germany, a nun rose up, Hildegard of Bingen, and in her many visions she gave testimony to the reality of the Divine and the living God in a constantly evolving universe. Hildegard perceived Sophia, the feminine wisdom of God, clearly. Some of the visual images carried out in shape and color according to her instructions show an interpenetration of the male and the female within the essence of God. Curiously, she has no comment on this striking sexual symbolism. In her teaching she followed orthodox Christian doctrine. Sometimes she saw more than she knew how or dared to explain.

When Lutheran theology, in the wake of the Reformation, degenerated into a lifeless, abstract rationalism of incredible intolerance, Jakob Boehme stood up, the untutored Silesian cobbler, and his insights into the polar nature of God influenced religious thinkers and poets in Germany and abroad for centuries. He too saw Sophia and dedicated to her one of his works.

All the Russian Sophianic thinkers knew their Boehme: Solovev; Pavel Florensky, the allround genius who died in a Stalinist death camp in 1937; Sergej Bulgakov, to name just a few.

When in the late twenties of this century Germany was preparing to enter the darkest period of her history, a terrible form of perverted patriarchy, a man had just published three articles which were later issued as a book: *The Rise and Fall of the Masculine Age.* The author was Otfried Eberz, a classical scholar and universal historian. He traced Sophia in the mythology and religious traditions of all ages and cultures. He reconstructed the gradual usurpation of matriarchal values by the emerging patriarchy, and linked the succession of social systems and mainstream culture of all peoples to this gigantic paradigm shift in prehistory. Like below, so above; like above, so below. As radically as any feminist Eberz analyzed the cause of our modern crisis. There was no doubt in his mind that the rape of the Goddess and her violent overthrow sanctioned any other rape and act of violence. Patriarchy is clearly based on the power of the stronger over the weaker—"might makes right"—whereas matriarchy was based on the principle of relationship and love. Eberz draws on many sources of antiquity, going back as far as the myths and sacred books of India and the wisdom of ancient China.

For him, the only ontologically valid philosophy is that idea which is inherent in the matriarchal system of values: androgyny, as the eternal desire of polar opposites to unite. There is no dualism, no dichotomy, no hostile opposition, but the desire to unite, to suspend Otherness in the creation of a Third, which then gives rise to the "ten thousand things," all the complexity of the world. This, according to Eberz, is the eternal philosophy, the *philosophia perennis*. Hence his invocation of Sophia, his passionate appeal that the world return to the Sophianic principle. This does not at all mean the rule of women, but a system of life-enhancing values based on the principle of love.

There are two points I am trying to make in this presentation: first of all, that the concept of Sophia as the feminine Divine responds to a deep need of the human soul for wholeness and the integration of polarities. In our Judaeo-Christian tradition no female was allowed to trespass on the all-male Trinity. In other words, the great archetype of the Divine Mother was suppressed with disastrous consequences for our religion, our social and family life, the relation between sexes and human relations in general, the destruction of our environment. But Sophia will not stay down. She cannot be suppressed forever. According to the Scriptures, Sophia withdraws when she is rejected. But she will reappear with stunning force if a crucial minority, or even one inspired person, will bear witness to her. We have a rich sophianic heritage, although it never was allowed to enter mainstream culture. Let us bear witness to it now. This is the *kairos*, the moment in history when a step has to be taken, a quantum leap in our perception of God and Mankind.

244

My second point is more difficult to make. It is more a question than a statement. It concerns the future, but a future so rooted in the present and therefore in the past I cannot think of it in terms of time, but rather as an existential category of burning immediacy. To bring this down to earth: what is to be done? Where to start? How to bring about this change of consciousness that will reconcile male and female in our own minds and thus transform our image of God? Basically we know what needs to be done; but we don't do it. There is the immense staying power of the old ways, the terrible inertia of the mind and heart. It is always frightening to move into something new. Evolution is a painful process.

For so long we have relegated the Divine to heaven and neglected to sanctify the earth. This is where Sophia comes in. She is at work *in* the world. Nature and all creation are sacred to her. She is the mediator between God and Man. Without her there is no growth, no love, no harmony or peace. She has no claim to power, but simply *is*. She *is* power. She does not rule over anyone. When she is not wanted, she disappears. She does not fight to defend herself. She does not punish us for disobedience, she simply leaves us to take the consequences of our deeds.

Sophianic power is not something that can be assumed or conferred. It exists as Power-of-Being, or Power-from –within, . .It does not dominate; it attracts rather than subjects. It has the erotic quality of fascination, love in the widest sense of the term. It is the power that creates, fosters growth and sustains life. It is not diminished by someone else's power, but rejoices in the unfoldment of any potential. It does not establish vertical power structures, but horizontal cooperative structures. . .It is leadership of a different order. We know it when we see it in operation. It has the answer to our conflicts.

Clearly it is not enough to visualize sophianic power, but it is an important first step. . .Images do help. Symbols are powerful. They work on the subconscious and prepare the ground for the paradigm shift we need.

We are now called upon to include the world in this bonding. This is the *kairos*. There is no other way.

32

Future

In the course of history, we have moved from tribes to nations to nation states to international connections, and now we are being called to a global state. That cannot happen without a new concept of love. For me, that love has to do with recognizing the god or goddess in every living thing. It has to do with recognizing that we are all part of one ecological system. For me, that manifestation of god in nature is the feminine principle. . .For me the feminine principle is that energy in matter.[1]

—Marion Woodman

We have awakened. Now the tide is turning and Sophia is re-emerging to restore balance and sensitivity to a spent and sick world. How will she do this? By impressing new goals upon hearts and minds as they open to her touch. Our modern world is challenged to repair damage done and to invest our healing energy in the human condition.

Mother Wisdom works to restore well-being through nurturing, sensitivity, and an expanded view of reality. Our caution is to be mindful that if we abandon the search for wisdom, feed ego, and misuse our spiritual self, we can lose our way. Spirituality in the twenty-first century demands:

● *A more caring attitude toward life in general.* Renewed respect for life-giving principles in areas of birth and death is just a beginning. Ecology, right use of resources, housing and food for all, appreciation of

---

1. Tami Simon, "Femininity and the Wisdom of the Body," an interview with Marion Woodman, *Magical Blend*, Issue 33 (Jan. 1992), www.magicalblend.com.

247

animals and nature, sharing, and equality are all aspects of this principle of economy coming to power within human consciousness. **Humanity must adopt themes and guidelines honoring life-sustaining attributes.**

● *Information to be shared.* True wisdom—more than knowledge rationally gained—appreciates the perceptions of the wise, beginning with respect for other ways of knowing, and the right for such to be expressed without shame or punishment. Respect for opinions of the disempowered is to be developed. **Information must become knowledge and as it is used sensitively, knowledge will advance to wisdom. We will advance to higher resonance as science and spirituality agree, and this will be soon.**

● *Excellence.* High standards are valued, but not perfectionism. Each of us must be credited for efforts, and rewards are to be benevolently shared. True wisdom—knowledge carefully adapted to one's culture, age, and companions—bears fruit only when used for the benefit of others as well as ourselves. **We come to understand not everyone gains inner maturity at the same time. We can advance only by compassion, not by judgment.**

● *Discerning adherence to guidance* as a means of self-respect and authenticity. We become courageous as we live out who we are openly and genuinely. We learn to listen attentively and hear with respect those who have traveled a different path. We come to see what each has to offer and learn from one another. **As guidance proves itself, we learn to trust our perception, and our intuition becomes more trustworthy.**

● *A new social consciousness* will emerge as we realize we truly are our brothers' and sisters' keepers. We discover we can love all children as our children and all parents as our parents, for indeed we are one. Look at your hand: each finger may think it is separate, but the hand knows itself as one with many parts. **As we gain freedom from our false identity—the ego—we gain alignment with the One.**

● *A deepening awareness of right relationship* with all kingdoms and with planetary life. We are only beginning (largely through biofeedback) to discover that plants are sensitive to our thoughts. Princeton Engineering Anomalies Research Institute placed 32 data-recording instruments around the world to be alert to changes in the Earth's collective "L" field (life field, also called the morphogenetic field).[2] According to the Princeton group, a couple of hours before the first plane struck the World Trade Center (Sept. 11, 2001) there was a significant perturbation in this field. **The world-wide collective consciousness knew danger to some portion of itself was on the way, even though our rational minds did not.**

● *Acknowledging our inner interconnection,* we will all be more respectful of others and learn both to listen and to speak more carefully. We are to develop qualities of harmlessness, right action, and right speech. A frequent injunction is that each speak his or her truth with honesty, gentleness, and tolerance for the truth of others when it differs; to live in such a manner as to "do no harm" fulfills this important step. **We come to honor the higher nature within each once we find it within our self.**

● *New patterns of action will result as a natural function of higher consciousness.* As we live in a kinder manner, we model a gentler, more genuine way of life. This is especially important for our youth, for the well-being of humanity, and for the future of our planet. **We come to accept it is just as damaging to the world around us to take offense as it is to give offense.**

As these shifts in awareness come to pass, our world will be quite different and the peace for which humanity longs will emerge. Each one of us walks an individual path challenged by the very personality he or she wears. A greater path also exists—seen or unseen. Here, the way is etched by awakened ones for the many. This collective flow then carries all humanity forward like a river flowing within its banks toward a divine destiny that awaits. Little understood by most, it hides within, beyond comprehension.

It is the soul that is being advanced in evolution, not the personality. In the past we have credited all of this to Christ-love, not understanding the wisdom (feminine) contribution. In coming to new awareness, humanity will right ancient wrongs and uplift the collective to an advanced understanding.

---

2. Morphogenetic Field. A term coined by Rupert Sheldrake of Great Britain as he studied the life field that exists around every living form. The concept is focused on etheric reality; major examinations and research are now being conducted by physicists as they venture into realms formerly known as mysticism or metaphysics. —Parrish-Harra, *Dictionary*, 184.

Good Karma

Challenges of discipleship demand
discernment, right action.
Learning to know little self (personality)
and its energies of operation
and recognizing energy of the Soul
require discrimination.
In light of guidance,
we bring in the Soul to inspire-
to breathe into external life
benefits of Soul.
Soul does not "play," it dances!
Soul does not judge, it discerns!
Soul does not personalize or flatter.
It requires and offers opportunities.
Soul serves to lead to greater challenges
that cause personality to refine its energies.
It is the good karma of one who wants to grow-
indeed, to have a challenge
and to practice divine qualities in the midst of this.

—Carol E. Parrish
Russia, 1996

The new that is in process will be resisted by tradition and old patterns of culture. Nevertheless, it moves steadily forward. Old crystallization dissolves slowly, but it will pass. It is hastened when fathers look with tender hearts at the hopes and dreams of their daughters and sons and support them in their search for wholeness. This is the father-love that is divine—the ideal love we all have sought from our Father.

Even though many people know and believe with all their hearts that these shifts need to happen in their own lives and in the greater life of the planet, what isn't always clear is what specific steps individuals can take in the middle of hectic, stress-filled lives that could possibly make a difference. They are hard-pressed to find either time or energy to become busy activists, no matter how heartily they sympathize with a cause.

The great question, then, becomes "How can I, as only one person with little time, talent, wealth, or influence, contribute to this river of change—or at the very least, keep from being an obstacle in its way?"

The wise and loving counsel of Sophia says the answer already awaits within you. Simply find and follow your heart. You don't have to go anywhere but there: you don't have to do anything but listen. *"And establish the counsel of your own heart, for no one is more faithful to you than it is"* (Sirach 37.13).

Jesus, in his service to both the higher world and humanity, became the Christ Sophia of humanity and stepped down the love-wisdom message. He demonstrated the wisdom way in the context of his time and set into motion a quest for learning to love, to release judgment, to balance heart and mind.

His message was appropriated by sincere thinkers who organized it into a set of rules and doctrines that for the most part replaced process with structure. If we are willing to allow this Master to move our attention from a rigidly structured solar plexus path to an experiential heart-centered path, we can explore the mystery of the heart with new insight.

In wisdom teaching there is a profound depth of awareness centered around the word "heart." It generally has been used since ancient times as a term meaning soul, but not in the simplistic manner the church uses today. Within the heart is the manger in which the ChristoSophia is to be birthed. At the point of stillness, waiting for the charms of the outer world to lessen their hold, is a space for the *more* to be realized. Humanity nears this point.

As we approach readiness we discover a need for stillness, for escape from the outer, or a thirst for silence. Can we learn to sit silently without mind demanding something? Can we spare a few minutes daily to "be with" the Unknown? Can we just sit, wait, allow, be—none of which is easy.

What is supposed to happen? Nothing, really. We just allow droplets of higher vibrating essence to fall upon our hardened personality, much like water dripping on a stone. In time, a bit of an indentation forms; after a longer time, a hollow is formed into which impressions can build up. The sensitivity of this hollow place responds through spiritual senses we mostly do not know we have. *"Called or Not Called, God is*

Present," said an inscription carved in stone over Carl Jung's door. Asked if he believed in God, Jung is said to have replied, *"I know! I have had the experience of being gripped by something stronger than myself, something that people call God."* [3]

Here in this manger new life quickens. At some point we will become more aware of those new frequencies that bounce off our heart and mind daily, but in the beginning it is enough to learn to wait on the Higher. Build the center and endure waiting. It is a kind of spiritual pregnancy.

We cannot hear the frequencies of the less dense planes until we have learned to hear silence, and in time we come to know communicating with the "No Thing" is everything. Great ones long ago discovered the wisdom of the process and had disciples who preserved this mystery. All traditions produced some who ventured far ahead of the masses, surpassing the religion that sought to guide them.

In each heart there is that stillpoint awaiting the coming together of the male and female in our energetic experience of Life. We develop one side of our nature and then focus on the other. In due time, a balance of power congeals within us to create what is referenced as stillness. This harmonious balance retains its ability to express in either mode as necessary. This is the marriage "made in heaven" by the divine. Out of this inner marriage comes a new spirituality: idealism, love, wisdom, and service. Thru this portal, from deep within comes a dedication to *Higher Good.* [4]

Whatever tasks we undertake now are charged with the higher qualities resulting from this union. Imagine a hurricane in your mind. The center is the point of stillness, the peripheral winds are the personality traits. Great power exists in the still, quiet eye, but it can rush outward to impact all with which it comes in contact. It is this point of stillness that births the love-wisdom vibration and develops the true human—we can call this the possible human or the true self or the transpersonal self—who is making the great journey.

---

3. Carl Jung, attributed, quoted by Seldes, *Great Thoughts*, 220.
4. "Higher Good" has a specific meaning in Agni Yoga teaching, similar to "Common Good," that which facilitates the evolution of humanity.—Parrish-Harra, *Dictionary*, 55.

Born from this stillness is the consciousness of unconditional love. Neither emotional nor sentimental, it just is. One becomes open to all of life and is enabled to live without judgment. As humanity rapidly comes of age, increased numbers of heart-centered lives will bloom and demonstrate humanity's evolving nature.

In Chapter 40, verses 3, 10, and 12 of The Aquarian Gospel of Jesus the Christ, Jesus says:

> [T]here is a silence where the soul may meet its God, and there the fount of wisdom is, and all who enter are immersed in light, and filled with wisdom, love and power. . .The silence is the kingdom of the soul which is not seen by human eyes. . .If you would find this Silence of the Soul you must prepare yourself the Way. None, but the pure in heart may enter here.

"Be still and know" is a radical spirituality. To be obedient to such a directive is not easy. To dare to sit and listen to whatever stirs and boils up from within can be a scary task. From here, the silent point of all potential, we receive the promptings of the inner nature that births ChristoSophia.

The purpose of silence is to become aware of this still place, of the God presence which expresses itself as our own inner being. As we consciously connect in this space to the Sacred Heart, the Still Small Voice, the Christ-within, the I Am Presence—however we would say it—we gather the droplets from that internal divinity.

As we strengthen this inner contact through communing with the silence, we learn to speak appropriately. The purpose of speech is to clothe thought. Disciples are taught: 1) to mean what they say and to say what they mean, and 2) to realize they are setting something into motion with each *word* they voice as well as with each act. As Christ's love merges with Sophia's wisdom, our thoughts and our speech reflect the creative word of the Mother-Father distilled from the essence of our soul.

33

Sacred

Feminine power is based on authenticity. It says, "this is who I am. I will live this truth. I cannot betray it. It is connected to the very roots of what I call Sophia." [1]

—Marion Woodman

Spiritual readers have become familiar with the sacred name "Shamballa," the center from which the will (masculine aspect) of God has emanated for centuries. During this rapidly closing era, other places are becoming known to be vital sacred centers as well.

Now we are discovering Miz Tli Tlan as the leading feminine center. It is emerging in South America, as are several other "sister" centers. [2] Such sacred sites serve as channels of divine impulses, stepping down the frequencies of "heaven," as the higher vibrating planes are best known in Western religious traditions.

Although more commonly referred to as dimensions or worlds in esoteric writing, each culture and tradition has its own language to acknowledge the frequencies that exist in the non-physical world. Sacred sites radiate an influence beneficial to the dense plane and beckon humanity to come hither. As we make our aura sacred, our homes, and in time our communities, vibrate in a sacred way also.

The body of Mother Earth, just like the body of human beings, receives energy through non-physical centers with corresponding physical

---

1. Tami Simon, "Femininity and the Wisdom of the Body," an interview with Marion Woodman, *Magical Blend*, Issue 33 (Jan. 1992), www.magicalblend.com.

2. José Trigueirinho Netto, *Calling Humanity* (Carmo da Cachoeira / MG, Brazil: Irdin Editora Ltda., 2003).

locations. In addition to the seven major centers (Earth's chakras), there are many minor ones. Often able to sense these points, ancients marked their locations, both on human bodies—we know these as meridians and acupuncture points—and on the body of Earth, where they became known as leys, ley lines, energy centers, power spots, or simply as sacred sites.

In Mexico prior to the rise of the Aztecs, the Toltecs were the educated of their time. Philosophers, artists, and innovators, many chose to devote their lives to the quest for enlightenment. The Maya were much the same. In many ways they resemble Tibetan lamas, European druids, and those of other indigenous cultures who believed all life to be an expression of the divine.

Many of the wise of such traditions actively used energy centers near them. Many of these have now become famous sacred sites. Certain places seem to be endowed with a quality or power that enables individuals to feel more alive. They seem to enhance dream activity, meditation, and healing experiences. Throughout history these energy centers have been chosen for cathedrals, temples, and healing ceremonies.

At many of these locations, dedicated communities preserved their teachings upon stelae, special stone markers, thereby seeking to communicate their cherished mysteries and stories to generations yet to be. Some developed astronomical observation points, others sacred burial grounds. Some sites were significant for certain herbs and fauna, others for healing springs or remembrance of myths or legends.

Stone pillars, formations, and pyramids still exist at many of these ancient places. The Mayan stelae and the standing stones of the British Isles are believed by many, even today, to be alive, continually vibrating life-giving energy. It is believed that these stones are "mirror-like" vibrations frozen in time. The Toltec goal, like many such systems, was to help devotees see themselves in the vibration of the stone, and by making this attunement, open to new awareness.

As artists, Toltecs used "the Word" to create. Don Miguel Ruiz wrote *The Four Agreements: a Practical Guide to Personal Freedom* [3] to record the teachings of the Toltecs and their clues for navigating "the big dream." Their teachings, and those of other indigenous people, tell us we are dreaming; it is time to navigate through the illusion. They say we do not stop dreaming until we become enlightened. Even when the body is left behind, each of us lives in illusion until we break free. Ancient wise ones emphasized the importance of waking up.

If we can accept such ideology, we realize each of us is a player in, and thus a reflection of, the dream of our society. This helps us understand that our materialistic society is surrounded by a world of illusion. Our group mind "floats" like a bubble in the great sea of consciousness. The debris of *materialism* [4] contaminates the sea about us until, hopefully, humanity itself will float clear, an enlightened collective.

Group illusions and hopes produce a lot of distortion. This collective illusion, called *maya*, (a Hindi word not related to the South American Mayan Culture) is the agreed upon hypnosis to which a group or society commits itself; maya includes all the values, both positive and negative, espoused by the group. In much of the world, movies and television amplify emotions and portray behavior judgments, rights and wrongs, what is good and what is not. We are all influenced as a part of the human group soul domesticated by "the dream." We are because we think we are. Our perception forms our drama, one experience after another; and to go free, to be liberated, we must become spiritually wise: we must wake up.

In two stanzas of his longer poem, *And It's Up to Us to Re-Enchant This Planet Earth*, Will Ashe Bason has beautifully expressed humanity's challenge—*our* challenge—as we progress inexorably into our own future.

---

3. Don Miguel Ruiz, *The Four Agreements: a Practical Guide to Personal Freedom* (San Rafael, CA: Amber-Allen Publishing, 1997).

4. Materialism is a belief system that nothing exists or matters except that which can be explored by the five senses. New sciences have already begun to challenge the concept, but too many people as of yet are over-identified with only the outer realities.

It's up to us to break the spell
that steals the colors from the world
and leaves it lifeless
It was our spell
we can break it. . .
We will dance the magic dance
and our bodies will remember
we will sing the magic songs
and together we'll remember
how to live together
how to love each other
how to ride the dragons
how to call the unicorns
Home

As each of us individually, and humanity collectively, becomes ready to activate our higher centers, soul is able to prompt us through enhanced inner awareness. Thus, under Sophia's tutelage, awakened ones are empowered to become co-creators in transforming the kingdom of Earth. Arthur Versluis says:

the soul of the world, or Sophia, is mediatrix between heaven and earth . . . sophiology mediates between an outward science and a science of the soul, between rationalism and its unutterable transcendence, between our present confused world and the serene delight of the spirit. [5]

Sophia beams sacred wisdom through the more enlightened ones for the benefit of all. Mother matter is to be transformed by the induction of spirit in such balanced formulas as represented in the mystical marriage of heart and mind, or of word and wisdom (Logos and Sophia), carried by the maturing harmonized children of the Most High. She heals duality, whether within the individual or within the world. The results will be a holy home, the new heaven and the new Earth as a sacred planet of spiritualized matter.

---

5. Arthur Versluis, TheoSophia (Hudson, NY: Lindisfarne Press, 1994), 188.

For the creation waits with eager longing for the revealing of the children of God; . .in hope that the creation itself will be set free from its bondage to decay and will obtain the freedom of the glory of the children of God. Romans 8.19, 21.

Sophia, the great mother principle is planetary partner to the father principle of creation. Though hard to understand, humanity as it penetrates the world of physics, frequencies, and spiritual quotients, is learning. Excitement builds as we advance in comprehension.

GAIA HYPOTHESIS:

is a modern grasp of planetary life as one entity wherein all species are coordinated and interacting for the well-being of the whole. The living planet exists as a single organism. The interactive system is becoming clear with more contemporary scientific tracking. It is now possible to see how systemic are the functions of the planet—water, winds, pollution, nature, all kingdoms.

SOLAR ANGEL. Each individual's Solar Angel is the agent that connects personality and soul, serving as a transformer to step the energy of higher realities down until the personality can handle it. The Christ (Love) is the Solar Angel for our planet while Sophia (Wisdom) is the wise World Soul leading Earth toward her part in the Greater Life of the Solar System. As World Soul, Sophia guides the collective consciousness of Earth toward its part in the Greater Life of the Solar System, of which the principal player is the Sun.

HIGH SELF. The Ball of Knowledge gleaned through past experience. Earth has a collective world soul called Sophia.

CONSCIOUS AWARENESS. Concepts humanity uses daily, accrued through education, experience, and cultures to all the people of the world. The mind or mental body of the Earth is humanity, and it functions within form.

PHYSICAL FORM. The dense form through which subconsciousness permeates, truly the psyche of each individual working together as one. This collective is beginning to be known as the S(ophia) Quotient.

"BECOMING A SACRED PLANET."

Planets that have been identified in arcane literature as sacred are seven in number—Vulcan, Mercury, Venus, Jupiter, Saturn, Neptune and Uranus.

"Clothed in the Radiance of the Sun"
by Sherry Robertson, Sarasota, Florida.

Meditation for Cleansing the Planet

◆ Please close your eyes now, and gently allow your attention to be focused within. Become as calm as you can. Enjoy the sense of resting in the serenity you are creating around yourself. Take a relaxing breath, and become aware that you dwell within an aura of creative light, unconditional love, and a never-ending stream of life divine. It is our goal to transform our private space into a personal temple of light as we are filled with a dedication to offer our love to the world in which we live.

◆ The sincerity of our thoughts creates holy intent as each accepts his or her self as an incarnated coworker of the higher world. Holy energies surround us as we perceive ourselves enclosed in a wellspring of lots-of-vital-energies. Rest safely in your heart center now, as it is a sacred center of peacefulness.

◆ The protective aura of the Divine Mother surrounds us as we pause from the busyness of the day to absorb her presence. We remind ourselves she is always present; we are always being tenderly nurtured, but now is a time for each to remember his or her own destiny.

◆ We begin by contemplating the confusion in the world; viewing it from afar. Become aware in an impersonal way of the pain, suffering, and loss of the world in general. Now love unconditionally this world you are viewing.

◆ See the physical beauty of our planet, but also see its emotional and mental confusion. We allow ourselves to create a response by gently sending love-caring forth from the heart. Feel qualities of compassion, mercy, and support radiating out from your heart center. Think "it's all right. I am here to help." Allow this feeling response to build throughout your body just as you would if you were moving across the room to reach out to a friend.

✦ Breathe deeply and contemplate "I am here to help heal this pain." Then with greater resolve repeat, "I am here to help." Direct healing power to go out to all the world—not just to friends or those you know.

✦ From deep within the heart now tell every point of consciousness on the planet of your strong desire to make a difference. Sit quietly and take your time. Address the soil, the minerals, the stones and sands; address the plants and trees, the animals, and then humanity, both those you know and those you do not.

✦ Breathe again, gently remembering you are an awakened elder, a brother or sister, and that you have purpose. You are a son or daughter of Sophia, of Mother Wisdom, and you have purpose. You carry love-wisdom, a radiance with which to illumine the path of those with whom you have contact. Now is the time to just radiate outward—see the light and love emanating in all directions.

✦ Recalling now your soul journey, feel your nature being revitalized; you are being renewed for continued efforts. Your own heart-mind streams forth your gifts and talents. The planetary life basks in great appreciation. Sense your own service coming closer to realization.

✦ From the great Mother of all, life pulsates through our inner nature, connecting us to our body and the physical world around us. We appreciate the opportunity we have to rejoice and give thanks.

34

Greatness

*In this age, more than any other, we need the divine boldness to affirm
that Christianity is not a matter of being good but of becoming God.*[1]
—Michael Casey, Monk of Tarrawarra

*I*t is fear of the Sophianic within us that has initiated the entire
concept of fear of greatness. The unknown dimension of ourselves is so vast it appears unfathomable. We have spent a few hundred
years now determining we are "the mind," and within this safe perimeter
we know what we *may* know and we know what we *may not.* Thus we have
erected a barrier to keep ourselves safe: we cannot, dare not, *may not,* pass
that line—or so we have convinced ourselves.

Life-long learning is a concept becoming common today among
many, but when the concept was birthed, it was shocking. Most thought
that the capability to learn was limited to the earlier years of life and that
our capacity to keep on learning and relearning was quite limited. We
know differently today, but most of us can remember the old adage, "you
can't teach an old dog new tricks."

Life thinks otherwise and continues to challenge us even to the
grave. In fact, some of our best learning occurs as we reach enough maturity to question, rethink, learn from our lessons, see the challenges life
brings, and decide to respond with new enthusiasm.

---

1. Casey, *Fully Human, Fully Divine,* 10.

The unknown contains a direct contact with our hidden potential. The quest for who we are triggers numerous small thoughts that buzz around our mind until we dismiss them or catch one to pull, like a thread, drawing new pieces into our consciousness. The more experience we have with this process, the more we get comfortable invoking the assistance of the creative. This is the same process used by artists, poets, mystics, and inventors as they examine possibilities. They probe the universe within themselves.

There is no limit to the mind of humanity except the limits we allow to be constructed by our prejudices and programming. The capacity to expand and become is preserved as we question, experiment, and ask, "what if." Curiosity leads the adventurer into uncharted space. Explorative thought creates pathways into what appears to the mundane world as "the unknown," but which is known in the higher realms as the chalice of "knowable things."

When we say, "I can't," or "I can't live without . . . whatever," we are turning off this creativity, within. When we say, "I can, I can, I think I can," or "I'll find the way," or "somehow it will work out," we accept divine potential, opening ourselves to opportunity when it stirs. We either reinforce the boundaries around our limited mind, or we become increasingly aware of the possibilities enfolded within our nature.

Our deepest fear is not that we are inadequate. Our deepest fear is that we are powerful beyond measure. It is our light, not our darkness, that most frightens us. We ask ourselves who am I to be brilliant, gorgeous, talented and fabulous? Actually, who are you not to be? You are a child of God. Your playing small doesn't serve the world. There's nothing enlightened about shrinking so that other people won't feel insecure around you. We were born to make manifest the glory of God that is within us. It's not just in some of us; it's in Everyone! And as we let our own light shine, we unconsciously give other people permission to do the same. As we are liberated from our own fear, our presence automatically liberates others ![2]

2. From unknown MS by Marianne Williamson as cited by Nelson Mandela, Inaugural Speech, South Africa, 1994.

When we come to believe we are one with the universe, we are actually allowing the consciousnesses of God Transcendent and God Immanent to co-work within our own creative nature. The unlimited consciousness of the whole can then respond with openness to the needs of the God Immanent. This concept is hard to communicate in English: we do better recognizing it in its reflection. The masculine personality gradually becomes accepting of being led by the feminine soul to be nurtured from infancy toward a new state of relationship: soul-infusion or spiritual maturity.

Many people, even women, are uncomfortable with the term divine feminine because of old negative programming. Believing themselves to be limited, less capable, or stagnant, they are intimidated. Some have been afraid; the price was too high, or they feared exploring their potential because this was not welcome in their society. When women enter a new and awakened state, it shakes the framework of the social order based on male dominated power structures. It is not only a matter of written institutionalized policies, but also of unspoken code. We are sailing beyond safe boundaries into the unknown. Much of our society is still struggling with such issues as we watch progressive and conservative ideologies clash.

Strong women dare: dare to question why women are considered inferior; dare to demand rights and equality; dare to see suffering, and challenge the privileged; dare to ask why women are of less value to the whole—especially as society depends upon female fertility to exist. These questions must continue to be asked because the secret to building a healthy humanity rests on the ability to look and to see, to seek and to find.

Women imprint their pain or confidence into the children they bear. No one likes to believe this, but cultural programs permeate body consciousness, waiting in mother matter to express as life progresses. We are coming to understand how the abused become abusers, not because they really want to abuse others or "get even," but because programming to respond to certain situations in a particular way lies imprinted on cellular consciousness. Many are horrified and mortified to find they have become that which they most feared and/or hated.

Just as most are afraid to move beyond actions accepted in society, they also fear what they may see if they look inward. Men expected those services that clearly could only be provided by women, or were traditionally "women's work." It was taken for granted that women would care for the sick, birth and suckle the male heirs, teach their children to be polite and orderly, clean, cook, and display their erotic nature at the demand of their husbands or bosses or other dominating males. When a woman could perform "male" activities better than the men around her, she found she encountered less resistance or hostility if she charmed, flattered, pretended ineptitude, gave undue credit to others, or used psychological manipulations to "make him think it is his idea." She is only now beginning to gain some small intermittent degree of public support when questioning masculine power, mental prowess, or command.

It is the co-working of masculine and feminine energies in people that is the healing space

This is exactly the situation with which the *inner* feminine of most males and many females—Jung's *anima*—has to contend in the psychological realms. This innate awareness has to deal with cultural restrictions on her exotic and creative powers. She must prove herself time and again through the validity of her impressions and talents, bring comfort to intimate areas of life, and come up with "logically sound" information, ideas, and concepts. Only with such "proof" will the mind release its tight control and give her a space in which to dwell.

Although this is true for either women or men seeking balance in our time, it is harder for men. Here exists the struggle between male dominated culture with its stereotypical "he-man" and the sensitive inner self that has awakened in a male body. Perhaps it is even more difficult for "straight" males of today as they fear being labeled effeminate, or gay. This judgment produces such a fearful response the mind naturally wants to avoid it. Such a reaction is itself indicative of hardcore homophobia still prevalent in society, and of lingering misogyny exacerbated by die-hard masculine fear of feminine qualities.

Some sensitive men can find a safe environment—most often in universities, monasteries, laboratories, artist's communities, or the theatre—from which to

explore unknown ideas. Some particularly talented ones, with unusually strong wills or extraordinary courage, dare to venture into more open expression of their sensitivity in spite of personal discomfort. I think particularly of bold creative artists, inventors, inspired thinkers, and others who have recognized their *anima* and devised ways to find acceptance. These are the role models needed for men now and for the future.

Society has granted the right to be sensitive to certain ones, but only with hindsight when they proved successful. We didn't really want our sons to be these, unless in addition to challenging cultural boundaries their efforts paid off financially, or at least in ego reward.

Indigenous people say the sensitive possess a special talent, the ability to walk between the worlds. This language is becoming more acceptable, as are such persons, whether called shaman, mystic, medium, or so forth, who go beyond the mundane and sense more to life than others. Today our collective readiness is creating more opportunities for our greater expression. Attributes of the sensitive and the rational are learning to work together in creative brainstorming, team working, and transformational techniques to name but a few. We are all learning we have various acceptable capabilities and some questionable ones as well. As these are examined and tried, even if limited, we all discover a bit of ability to "go beyond."

> *Sensitive men and women possess a special talent, the ability to walk between worlds*

As the feminine emerges in every corner of the world, many are struggling to respond. Old styles of leadership no longer work. We seek new ways of being, with an eye toward the future. Recently, H. E. Kofi Annin, Secretary General of the United Nations said, *"the future of this planet depends on women."* We must ask ourselves if we will use the power we hold to save the planet. Dare we leave behind our comfortable roles and create a new kind of "power response" to be heard around the world? Nothing less will do.

It is this interface—the co-working of masculine and feminine energies in people—that is the healing space. Here we are each needed to reconcile the push and pull of life itself. The dichotomy of being human is to be resolved. We will come to know ourselves, accepting and using well the powers of the mental nature while daring to welcome impressions at the edge of our mind that prompt new direction and wise possibilities.

In the Babemba tribe of South Africa, when a person acts irresponsibly or unjustly, he is placed in the center of the village, alone and unfettered. All work ceases, and every man, woman and child in the village gathers in a large circle around the accused individual. Then each person in the tribe speaks to the accused, one at a time, about all the good things the person in the center of the circle has done in his lifetime. Every incident, every experience that can be recalled with any detail and accuracy is recounted. All his positive attributes, good deeds, strengths and kindnesses are recited carefully and at length. The tribal ceremony often lasts several days. At the end, the tribal circle is broken, a joyous celebration takes place, and the person is symbolically and literally welcomed back into the tribe.[3]

She who dwells within rises to dance with *the he of outer personality* to bring each to greatness. She stirs our hopes, dreams, and wishes and resists the rational that would rain on our parade. Both are right; both can be wrong. It is important to remember "mind without heart is cruel, heart without mind is foolish." Gradually we discover we can release more and more restriction and become increasingly the creative individual walking between the worlds of limitation. Dare we be all we can be? Made in the image and likeness of the Highest, we are not complete until we do.

---

3. From http://globalvisions.org/cl/wwv the Wholistic World Vision Global Network Service comes the following email, subject: Appreciation As A Facet Of A Wisdom Culture.

*E*pilogue

Love-Wisdom leads us from darkness to light, from the unreal to the real, from chaos to beauty, from death to immortality.[1]

Who is this numinous Sophia? She is Mother Wisdom, come to guide us home. I know Sophia. She dances through my life, peeks through the windows of my mind, whispers words of wisdom, laughing and playing. Yes, I know Sophia, and she knows each of us—she desires everyone to know her. Eagerly she dashes here and there awakening, touching, shaking, and reshaping the world in which she dwells. It is her time; she assures us we are not alone.

To follow Sophia is the opportunity of our time. Remember she teaches what can't be learned intellectually. She privately guides and mentors when painful territory must be traversed. She leads to dynamic adventures requiring that we face our fears, learn to love, and dare to move more fully toward our potential.

Wisdom says: "I, Sophia, promise in my inner thoughts and from the depth of my heart, I understand and know. One must ask for me and I will come, but one must have Wisdom to know for what to ask—hear me. I wander the Earth looking for ones ready to know me. In soft-hearted graciousness I will appear to you as you travel your path, coming to meet you in your every thought. Just thinking about me brings understanding. Hope for Sophia and expect me to be with you. Just think of me, and pain and fear will lessen."[1] Christ Sophia, lead, guide, and direct me in thy service. So be it.

Every human being travels as far as they permit themselves into the adventure of life. Some gaze out the window from the safety of the known; some run along the beach and kick up some rocks; and others build a vessel and put out to sea.

I share these thoughts as a report to those who stay home, as a tale of adventure to those who roam the beach, and as a chart of the night sky to those who sail. Bon voyage!

---

1. From an ancient prayer, origin unknown.
2. Carol E. Parrish-Harra, Paraphrased from Wisdom texts and Seed thought meditation.

Oh, Spirit of mine,
>   Speak to me, so I will know my place within the universe.
>   Free my heart of all its guilt and sadness.
>   Forgive my mind its stubborn ignorance of your desires.
Oh, Spirit of mine,
>   I sacrificed you for many years; while my heart searched to
>   be loved.
>   Only to find the love I so desired, deep within myself.
>   It is autumn of my body's life.
>   Now I know, the searching, aching, longing of my spring
>   and summer was not in vain.
>   What a journey you have given me, so I can listen to you now.
Oh, Spirit of mine,
>   I feel the comfort of eternal energy, this universal connection;
>   It moves in these lake waters, like the life blood of earth.
>   I sit beside your shore, and drink you in, as my life blood
>   flows and ebbs.
>   This sand holding my body in place,
>   Each grain an energy unto itself,
>   Like each cell in my body, holding me together, so I can be.
>   The Sun's rays nourishing this earth, like my glands
>   Replenishing me day by day.
>   Trees surrounding me, like the bone, and muscle framing
>   my body,
>   So strong, yet flexible, and agile enough to bend and sway.
>   The wind, invisible like my breath, sometimes quiet, sometimes
>   Forceful, always in constant rhythm, giving me yet another
>   moment of Life.
Oh, Spirit of mine,
>   I feel now the spirit of eternity in one form or
>   another, loving
>   Me, touching me, showing me the way.
>   Even when I don't understand, I need not struggle anymore.
Oh, Spirit of mine,
>   Keep me in enough quietude so I will hear your voice, giving
>   me the courage to move to higher ground.

—K.K. Jonas

"Three Women"
© 1975 by Sulamith Wulfing (1901-1989)

I Am That I Am

"Knowingness does not require either thought or feeling because existence contains the quality of divine awareness. Life itself knows that it exists, but it gets caught up in its identification with its current form."
—David R. Hawkins MD, Ph.D. from The Eye of the I

☆ Our higher nature is constantly receiving streams of life-giving energy from the Source of all Life. Daily, according to our awareness, the energy likewise streams out from us in particular ways affecting life around us. Realizing this, we will consciously learn to use well the streams of life force that are provided for us from the higher worlds.

☆ Let us begin by invoking new life energy to our personality as we attune our outer nature to that inner part of our self where all is whole. We acknowledge our need for divine guidance in every aspect of our personality. We seek to become increasingly aware of this divinity in all our contacts. We affirm all life has purpose.

☆ Next we seek to conform our personality will to higher Will. We now choose to gain a sense of this inner Will, in order to help us build confidence in our higher nature, even in the midst of human struggles. Our intelligence is acknowledged as we will our mind to blend harmoniously with divine mind. We rejoice as inspiration flows from the higher into our receptive mental body. We know new awareness is stimulated; creativity abounds. We affirm we can, we can, we know we can.

☆ We realize we seek wholeness, abundance, healing and vibrant awareness that will assist us to hold harmony within even as change occurs without. We embrace the healing energy as a life giving stream of revitalization. We affirm a divine pattern is being woven of all experiences bringing them together for the uplifting of the whole.

☆ The interplay between mind and emotion, between the inner and outer, between body and essence, is divine science at work. The law of cause and effect become clearer as we integrate our daily experiences, becoming ever wiser. We affirm our allegiance to the laws of Life.

☆ We seek the clearing of miasma, glamour and illusion from the physical world in which we live. We seek clarity with dedication to personal integrity in all our relationships with the world of nature and humanity. We can claim it for we dwell in the Temple of the Spirit. We affirm we are beings of Love freeing ourselves from judgment, forgiving, and letting ourselves and others go free.

☆ The renewing stream of life force bathes our own nature and through us the world of nature around us as well. We dedicate ourselves to achieving an ever greater ability to utilize these divine capabilities. We affirm our true nature is made whole and holy.

☆ And so it is. Shanti.

Addendum

It is my pleasure to add to this volume an addendum that presents in shortened form the historical journey of Sophia through the ages as offered by one of the great Sophianic writers of our time, Robert Powell, Ph.D. Dr. Powell graciously agreed to the inclusion of material drawn from chapters 4 and 5 of *The Sophia Teachings: The Emergence of the Divine Feminine in Our Time* (New York: Lantern Books, 2001).

Robert Powell earned a Masters Degree in mathematics at the University of Sussex, England, and a Ph.D. from the Polish Academy of Sciences, Warsaw, for his thesis on the history of the zodiac. He is a trained eurythmist and movement therapist, co-founder of the Sophia Foundation of North America, and founder of the Choreocosmos School of Cosmic and Sacred Dance. Robert has written and lectured worldwide on the Sophia Teachings and Esoteric Christianity, and also on Astrosophy, the wisdom of the stars. Among the numerous books he has written are: *Chronicle of the Living Christ, Christian Hermetic Astrology, The Christ Mystery, The Sign of the Son of Man in the Heavens,* and *Divine Sophia, Holy Wisdom.* He is also the translator of the spiritual classic *Meditations on the Tarot.* In addition to lecturing and teaching Cosmic and Sacred Dance in North America and in several different European countries, he leads bi-annual pilgrimages to sacred sites. For further information visit the website: www.sophiafoundation.org.

For more in-depth study I would refer you to the entire volume *The Sophia Teachings: The Emergence of the Divine Feminine In Our Time* (also available as a six tape set) and *The Most Holy Trinosophia and the New Revelation of The Divine Feminine.*

Robert Powell has brought clarity to the modern Sophianic mysteries that is desperately needed. It is a pleasure to add this addendum to my efforts. Thank you, Robert, for your genuine love of Sophia and of humanity. Your efforts are greatly appreciated.

In the 2000 years since the birth of Christ, manifestations and actual revelations of Divine Sophia have occurred here and there. Certain individuals experienced Sophia as the mother of humanity in the period after the birth of Christ and before the New Age beginning in the twentieth century. Let us list the names of significant individuals who contributed to this Sophia tradition.

St. Augustine plays an important role because among the Church fathers he was the one most occupied with Sophia. St. Augustine was born in 354 CE in Africa and died in the year 430 CE. He distinguishes between two Sophias, one of whom is the uncreated wisdom, the uncreated Sophia, whom St. Augustine considers to be the Logos, the Christ, the begotten Son of the Father. The other is the created Sophia, divine wisdom, who was created at the beginning of creation. St. Augustine held that the uncreated Sophia is the illuminating light of existence, and that the created Sophia is the illuminated light. St. Augustine's distinction is one that has influenced many subsequent theologians and prominent figures in Christian history.

In the Middle Ages, we find an extraordinary revelation of Sophia through St. Hildegard of Bingen, who was born in 1098 and died at the age of eighty-one in 1179. Hildegard was from early childhood aware of being surrounded by divine light and was able to see beyond the natural world into heavenly realms of existence. Among St. Hildegard's most powerful and inspiring visions were those of Divine Sophia. For Hildegard, Sophia was on one hand the mother and soul of the world, and on the other hand she saw Sophia as the bride of Christ and the mother of the Church. Accompanying her vision, St. Hildegard heard a voice saying:

> *With Sophia I have rightly put the universe in order. God has established the firmament in wisdom and secured it by power of the stars. Both sun and moon are an adornment of wisdom. The firmament is the throne of all beauty. God furnished all this beauty for the divine glory as it was preordained in wisdom. Creation was Sophia's garment because Sophia clothes her own achievement in the same way as we human beings wear clothes.*

Very often the question is raised whether Sophia is an attribute of God as Divine Wisdom, or whether she is an actual person. Some think that the words of Sophia in the Books of Wisdom from the Old Testament show her to be Lady Wisdom, a personification of God's wisdom, who addresses humanity. However, if we study the actual words and indications of Sophia in the Wisdom Books of the Old Testament, it emerges quite clearly that Sophia is a *being*. We can summarize the Wisdom Books as leading to an understanding of Sophia as a *person* because in the Holy Scripture she is proclaimed as a spiritual nature with the qualities, attributes, and functions of a person, such as having reason and free will. Furthermore, she is described as being created female. She is different from

278

God and acts independently with respect to God. She is described as dancing before God. She advises God and she actively participates in the work of creation with God. With respect to the creation she is depicted as guiding, renewing, and ruling everywhere with reason, power, and goodness. With respect to humanity, she is described as admonishing, leading, and assisting us as mother, teacher, and beloved. Moreover, the Church fathers to the present, have often understood Sophia as a person, even if interpretations about her have varied. Some theologians identified her with the Logos and others identified her with the Holy Spirit. Mystics such as Hildegard of Bingen and Jakob Boehme make it quite clear that they had a direct, living experience of Sophia as an actual being, as a person, not simply as a personification of divine wisdom.

There are many depictions of Sophia as an actual being in the art of the Middle Ages. In Herrad von Landsberg's work, *the Garden of Delights*, from around the twelfth century, Sophia is depicted as queen of the seven liberal arts—grammar, rhetoric, dialectic, music, arithmetic, geometry, and astronomy. We see Sophia sitting on a royal throne in the center, surrounded by the seven liberal arts. A stream of water pours from each side of her body. Below her are the philosophers Plato and Aristotle, the recipients of the living water of Sophia's wisdom.

In Jakob Boehme's visions and experiences of Sophia, we find a powerful and extraordinary testimony to Sophia as a divine being existing in spiritual realms, with whom we can have communication and a relationship. Jakob Boehme was born the son of a poor farmer living in a little village near Gorlitz in Germany. During his first mystical experience, young Jakob felt himself bathed in a supernatural light and a blessed sense of peace that lasted for seven days. Around 1600 he had a second mystical experience while watching the splendid glow of sunlight on a pewter jug. It seemed to Boehme that he became aware of forces active within the jug that gave him insight into the foundation of things. After this second experience, Boehme had a number of visions and realizations that further deepened his insight. He remained silent about these visions until a third experience around 1610 seemed to unify everything. He was attacked from the pulpit by the Lutheran pastor of Gorlitz, who branded him as a heretic, and he was forbidden to write of his experiences. Boehme honored this prohibition for some years, but, urged on by his friends and by his own inner voice, he began to record his visions once again.

One of Jakob Boehme's most significant visions was that of an appearance of the Divine Sophia. This particular mystical experience took place when Boehme was under personal attack during his years of silence. Boehme indicates that his knowledge of Sophia increased after this vision, and he ascribes to her seven qualities or characteristics—keen, soft, firm, serious, clear, pure, and persuasive. For Boehme, Sophia is the exhalation or out-breath of God's power. She is God's mirror and the image of God's goodness. She dwells in pious souls, and is the friend, betrothed, bride, mistress, and teacher to those who seek her in the appropriate manner.

Due to his inspiring visions that testify to the Divine Sophia, Jakob Boehme has become known as the father of Sophiology in the west. As with Hildegard of Bingen, we see that Jakob Boehme was blessed with the grace of a revelation of Divine Sophia; he was someone who allowed his heart and mind to open to Sophia and to receive her instruction. Boehme's writings served as a seed impulse that had great influence not only upon the German cultural tradition, but that crossed over to England, and even extended all the way to Russia.

One key element in Boehme's teaching of Sophia concerns the profound relationship existing between Sophia and the Virgin Mary. Boehme was perhaps the first to have the intuition of an incorporation, or perhaps even incarnation, of the Divine Sophia in Mary.

The relationship between Sophia and the Virgin Mary is something that became of central importance for the Russian Sophiologists, although it's unclear whether or not they adopted this idea from Boehme. His testimony has nonetheless inspired numerous individuals since that time to turn to Divine Sophia, including John Pordage and Jane Leade in England. In Germany we find that Gottfried Arnold, the poet Novalis, and the great Idealist philosopher Friedrich Wilhelm Joseph von Schelling (1775-1854) were all inspired through reading the works of Jakob Boehme. Lastly, Vladimir Solovyev, the great Russian philosopher and founder of Sophiology in Russia, was also inspired and influenced by Jakob Boehme.

One of the most gifted clairvoyants of all time was Anne Catherine Emmerich, who bears witness in her works to Divine Sophia and her relationship with the Virgin Mary. Anne Catherine Emmerich was born in 1774 and died in 1824. At an early age she joined the Augustinian order. Later, at the age of thirty-eight, she received the stigmata. From this time onward she was confined to her bed in extraordinary suffering. She ate hardly anything, existing on the Host and water, but she received a continual stream of visions concerning the lives of Christ and Mary. Emmerich had a vision confirming the coming of one whom she described as the pilgrim. When Clemens Brentano arrived, she recognized him as the one from her vision, and he indeed remained with her, as had been prophesied, and wrote down her visions.

During this work together, Anne Catherine Emmerich began to receive visions day by day describing the life of Christ. History has been able to show that Anne Catherine Emmerich's visions are by and large authentic.

To highlight the remarkable power of Anne Catherine Emmerich's clairvoyance, mention must be made of the historic discovery of the Virgin Mary's house near Ephesus in Turkey. This discovery, that took place in 1891, was made solely on the basis of Anne Catherine Emmerich's visions describing its location. It has become a center of pilgrimage visited by people from all over the world.

Anne Catherine Emmerich's visions provide the most extensive description of the Virgin Mary that has even been revealed to humanity. From this we can also gain a feeling for Divine Sophia as a pre-existent being who, at a certain moment in time, entered into the soul of the Virgin Mary.

In the visions of Anne Catherine Emmerich we have also a testimony to Sophia as the wisdom of God, as a being who incarnated qualities of Sophia into the Virgin Mary.

A few years after the death of Anne Catherine Emmerich, the Russian philosopher Vladimir Solovyev emerged as the great prophet of the Sophia tradition in Russia. Solovyev, who was born in 1853 and died in 1900, accomplished much in his short life to bring Sophianic philosophy to the Russian people. With Solovyev we find a human being whose thinking is heart inspired and imbued with 1) a warmth of humanity, 2) a clarity of light, and 3) an intensity of purpose and direction—which makes him one of the most outstanding philosophers of the modern age.

Divine Sophia is the central idea in Solovyev's philosophy. On Ascension Day in 1862, Solovyev had a profound vision of the Divine Sophia. He was only nine years old. While attending the liturgy in the university chapel in Moscow, the heavens suddenly opened up and a majestic feminine figure wrapped in azure blue appeared to young Vladimir. This mystical experience was a powerful incentive for the young man to pursue a path of spiritual study that led him many years later to study in the library of the British museum in London. It was here that he immersed himself in many religious and spiritual works in his quest to understand the vision of Sophia he had had at the age of nine.

One day, while studying in the British Museum, Solovyev had a second vision of Divine Sophia, in which the face of Sophia appeared to him and he heard the words, "Go to Egypt." He followed the instruction from Sophia, made preparations, traveled to Egypt, and stayed in a hotel in Cairo. It was here in Egypt that he had his third and greatest vision of Divine Sophia. Solovyev describes his three mystical experiences of Sophia in a poem he wrote towards the end of his life.

Solovyev's great vision of Divine Sophia in the Egyptian desert became the central motivation and impulse for his whole life's work as a philosopher to the Russian people, and to working for the reunification of the Eastern and Western Churches. Solovyev believed it was a scandal for Christianity that the

Church was divided and that through Sophia there could be a reunification between East and West. His great impulse to work for peace and unity among all Christians lives on, and in the twentieth century there has finally emerged an ecumenical movement toward unity, so his work was not in vain.

Solovyev inspired many in Russia, among them poets and theologians. The tradition now known as Sophiology came to birth in Russia through Russian Orthodox priests who took up Solovyev's work and carried it further. Solovyev saw Sophia as the soul of the world, having three aspects, which allow her to unify, connect, and direct everything. She possesses a higher divine part, a lower earthly part, and a middle part, which creates and directs space, time, and causality.

Vladimir Solovyev is the last great nineteenth-century herald in the Sophia tradition extending from St. Hildegard of Bingen through Jakob Boehme and down to the modern age.

We have followed the Sophia tradition in the West from the time of the incarnation of Christ. Despite being held back from mainstream Christian development over the past two thousand years, Divine Sophia has continued to reveal herself to certain chosen individuals, culminating with Vladimir Solovyev in the nineteenth century. Now, in the twenty-first century, the first century of a new millennium, we can see a turning point, a beginning of a New Age in which Sophia is beginning to reveal herself to more and more human beings.

The Influence of Divine Sophia in the East

Interestingly, the Sophia teachings had a profound influence in the East. And the mystery of the Palladium leads us back to the East. The Palladium was a wooden statue of Pallas Athena, three cubits high, which had at its center a meteor that was believed to have fallen from heaven. This meteoric component is said to have conferred invulnerability upon the possessor of the Palladium. Buried in the depths below the city, guarded by vestal virgins, the Palladium was the source of the power of the city of Troy. But Troy lost its invulnerability when Odysseus, disguised as a beggar, secretly entered the city and recaptured the meteoric component of the Palladium. Due to the skillful maneuvering of Odysseus, the Greeks were able to enter the city and set fire to it.

The Trojan priest Aeneas rescued the wooden statue of the Palladium from the flames and thus prevented it from falling into Greek hands. The travels of Aeneas tell us of the further destiny of the Palladium. The Palladium came to rest in Rome, where, as in Troy, a special temple was built for it beneath the city, guarded by vestal virgins. This underground temple gave the city of Rome its power over the whole of the ancient world.

In the fourth century CE, the emperor, Constantine the Great, heard the prophecy of the sibyls that the city of Rome would collapse and its power would be lost. In an attempt to secure the future of the Empire, he decided to transfer the capital from Rome to Constantinople, the city named after him, with the idea of creating an even greater empire embracing both the east and the west. Constantine the Great carried out his bold plan and transferred the Palladium to Constantinople, where it was placed once again in an underground temple guarded by vestal virgins. The colossal porphyry pillar from the temple of Isis was also transported to Constantinople and placed above the Palladium.

The palladium is a Sophianic symbol. Let us recall that the Palladium was given to Ilias, the founder of Troy, by Athena, Greek goddess of wisdom. Through the power of the Palladium we have a Sun symbol, a burning light of wisdom beneath the earth that confers power upon its possessor. The light of that wisdom now radiated forth from Constantinople. On top of the porphyry pillar from the temple of Isis the emperor Constantine placed a golden statue of Apollo, but he had the face of Apollo made in his own likeness. We can see that Constantine suffered from megalomania.

A few centuries later, the statue was struck by lightning and half the pillar was destroyed. The rest of it still stands to the present day in the city of Istanbul, the current name for Constantinople. It is said the Palladium is still buried beneath this pillar. We wait, therefore, with great interest for any clues to the future destiny of the Palladium.

Early in the twentieth century some followers of Rudolf Steiner went to Istanbul and began excavations there to locate the Palladium, but without success. According to legend, the Palladium will one day be recovered and transferred to a Slavic kingdom in the north, to Russia. This points to the coming Aquarian Age in which, it is said, there will be a new culture, of which present-day Russia is the first sign—a culture that will blossom and flourish under the inspiration of Divine Sophia. This points to a Christianity of the new era, what we might call a Sophianic Christianity that will arise and flourish in Russian and the other Slavic countries.

What signs are there of a Sophianic Christianity in Russia? One of the greatest monuments to Christianity is the great basilica of Hagia Sophia, constructed by Emperor Justinian in Constantinople. For a long period of time Hagia Sophia possessed the largest dome in the world; the very name means Holy Sophia. Justinian was of the school that viewed Sophia as identical with the Logos, the Christ. So the Hagia Sophia in Constantinople, built not far from the site of the Palladium, is really a basilica dedicated to Christ as the wisdom of the world.

When Christianity spread to Russia in the year 988 CE, its orientation was not to the Roman Catholic world but to the Greek Orthodox tradition centered at Constantinople. The great temple of Holy Sophia in Constantinople also provided inspiration for the Russians, but they interpreted Sophia not as the Logos or Christ but as Divine Sophia, the feminine side of God. So from the very beginning of Christianity in Russian and Ukraine, we find a true Sophianic quality.

Sophia has been at the root of Russian Orthodox Christianity, even though within the Russian Church itself there was little understanding on a conscious level of the nature of Sophia, until the time of the philosopher and mystic Solovyev in the nineteenth century. The presence of the Divine Sophia in the Russian Orthodox tradition itself points to the future Sophianic culture that will emerge in Russia.

Vladimir Solovyev was the first within the Russian Orthodox tradition to reveal, on a conscious level, the mystery of Divine Sophia as the world soul, the mother, guide and inspiration of future humanity. Following Solovyev, we find two additional key figures in the development of Russian Sophiology. These two are the Russian Orthodox priests, Pavel Florensky and Sergei Bulgakov.

Florensky was born in 1882 in Tiflis in Georgia and was from youth an extraordinarily gifted child. He was a brilliant mathematician, yet he became a priest. In the 1930s, he was sent to a concentration camp on the White Islands in the far north of Russia where he was executed in 1937.

Florensky suffered an ignominious end, but now in contemporary Russia he is regarded as a hero. He was a truly spiritual individual, with a brilliant mind and a heart devoted to the divine. His major work on Sophia is called *The Pillar and Foundation of Truth.* In this work he describes Sophia as the soul of the world.

Florensky's Sophia teachings are drawn from the Russian Orthodox tradition, from the tradition of the early and whole Church back to its foundation, and from the Books of Wisdom from the Old Testament. Florensky tried to find a pure teaching of Sophia that would be acceptable within the Russian Orthodox Church. In this respect Florensky differs from Solovyev, who focused upon a purely Christian interpretation of Sophia from the Christian tradition without including any Gnostic elements such as we find in Jakob Boehme's work. Florensky also pointed to the central significance of the Virgin Mary as a manifestation and incarnation of the Divine Sophia. Although Florensky came to his perspective independently, his views concerning Mary as the incarnated Sophia are identical with the teaching of Jakob Boehme.

Florensky was a personal friend of the Russian priest Sergei Bulgakov (1871-1944), perhaps the most prodigious of the Sophianic theologians. At the time of the Bolshevik Revolution, Bulgakov was exiled from Russia and went to live in France, where he later became head of the Russian Orthodox Seminary in Paris. His works comprise the most comprehensive body of knowledge on

Sophiology. Bulgakov's purpose was, like Florensky, to present Sophia in a way that would be acceptable to his fellow priests and theologians of the Russian Orthodox Church. In this, as with Florensky, Bulgakov did not derive anything of his teaching from Gnostic sources outside of the Church, but concentrated solely upon the Church tradition. Nevertheless, in his exposition of the nature of Divine Sophia, Bulgakov later ran into conflict with the Moscow authorities and he was condemned on account of his Sophia teachings.

Bulgakov's views caused him to become viewed as a heretic. It was his idea that Sophia is the *ousia* (to use the Greek word), the substance that is common to the three persons of the Holy Trinity—the Father, the Son, and the Holy Spirit. This idea aroused the suspicion within Bulgakov's fellow theologians that Sophia could be put forward as a fourth hypostasis alongside the Father, the Son, and the Holy Spirit. Bulgakov wrote: "The three divine persons of the Holy Trinity have a life in common, that is, an ousia, Sophia. However, this does not mean transforming the Trinity into a Quaternity."

Bulgakov denies that the idea of Sophia being the common life of the Holy Trinity would transform it into a Quaternity. Nevertheless, it was for this that he was condemned. He continued to write and carry out his functions as a priest, but from this time onward his writings bore the stigma of heresy. There is hope within the Russian Orthodox Church that one day there will be a great council dedicated to Sophia. First held by Solovyev, the dream to unite East and West still persists.

Valentin Tomberg

Valentin Tomberg was of central significance for the Russian Sophia tradition, and he carried it a stage further. His teachings will occupy humanity for millennia, just as the teaching of the Holy Trinity within the Christian tradition occupied theologians from the fourth century down to the present time. Valentin Tomberg's teachings go a stage further and completely transform those of Florensky, based on the Wisdom Books of the Old Testament, where Sophia is recognized as the first created being. And as the first created being, she came forth from the womb of the Holy Trinity, and therefore has a relationship to each member of the Holy Trinity. Florensky elaborates three aspects of Sophia as the first created being. The first aspect is that of Sophia as the original substance of the creation in her relationship to the Father. Secondly, that Sophia is the wisdom of creation in relationship to the son, to the Word. Thirdly, that Sophia is the beauty and spirituality within creation in relation to the Holy Spirit. Valentin Tomberg goes a stage further, in that he speaks of Sophia not simply as having three aspects but of Sophia as being three *persons.*

He speaks of a Sophianic Trinity parallel or complementary to the Holy

Trinity with which most are familiar. In order to grasp some of the far-reaching implications of Valentin Tomberg's Sophia teachings, we must contemplate a Sophianic Trinity of Mother, Daughter, and Holy Soul.

Valentin Tomberg teaches that arising out of the primordial Godhead begotten from the Divine Father and the Divine Mother are the Divine Son and the Divine Daughter, Christ and Sophia, the Logos and Sophia.

And, just as we may understand that the incarnation of the Logos, the Christ, took place in Jesus, so, according to Jakob Boehme and the Russian Sophiologists, there also took place an incarnation of Divine Sophia into Mary.

Valentin Tomberg teaches that the heart of the Divine Mother is to be found in the center of the Earth and that the plant kingdom resonates with the very heartbeat of the Mother. The Divine Daughter is the wisdom of the cosmos extending from the realm of the fixed stars down to the planets and the Moon. This awe-inspiring image of Sophia as the world soul can be found in the Book of Revelation, where she is depicted as a woman clothed with the Sun, with the Moon under her feet, and upon her head a crown of twelve stars.

Between the Divine Mother in the center of the Earth and the Divine Daughter Sophia as the world soul, weaves the Holy Soul, the third aspect of the Divine Feminine Trinity. The Holy Soul is the creator of community, who ensouls and elevates groups of human beings in the progress of unfolding evolution. An example of this is the spiritual tradition of Israel that conceives of the Shekinah as the soul of the community of Israel. Here Shekinah corresponds to the Holy Soul weaving between the Divine Daughter and the Divine Mother. In this Sophia teaching of the Divine Feminine Trinity—Mother, Daughter, and Holy Soul—we reach the pinnacle of the Sophia tradition of Russia.

Through a spiritual awakening of humanity to the Divine Feminine, a turning point in spiritual evolution is coming that will signify the beginning of a transformation and spiritualization of the whole Earth.

Agni Yoga Society. *Mother of the World: Selections from the Books of the Agni Yoga Teachings for the New Era*. NY: Agni Yoga Society, 1956.

Bailey, Alice A. *The Externalization of the Hierarchy*. NY: Lucis Publishing Co., 1982.

Baker, Douglas. *Karmic Laws the Esoteric Philosophy of Disease and Rebirth*. Wellingborough, Northampton, UK: The Aquarian Press, 1977.

Bendit, Phoebe D. and Laurence J. Bendit. *Our Psychic Sense: A Clairvoyant and a Psychiatrist Explain How It Develops*. Wheaton, IL & Adyar, India: Theosophical Publishing House, 1967.

Borg, Marcus. *Meeting Jesus Again for the First Time*. San Francisco: Harper, 1994.

Brown, Dan. *The Da Vinci Code*. N Y: Doubleday, 2003.

Bulgakov, Sergei. *Sophia: The Wisdom of God*. Hudson, NY: Lindisfarne Press, 1993.

Campbell, Joseph with Bill Moyers. *The Power of Myth*. NY: Doubleday, 1988.

Casey, Michael. *Fully Human Fully Divine: An Interactive Christology*. Liguori, MO: Liguori/Triumph, 2004.

Demetry, Nicholas and Edwin L. Clonts. *Apocalypse of Peace*. [Unpublished Manuscript].

Drayer, Ruth A. *Wayfarers, The Spiritual Journey of Nicholas and Helena Roerich*. Las Cruces, NM: Blue Waters Press, 2004.

Economou, George D. *The Goddess Natura in Medieval Literature*. Notre Dame, IN: University of Notre Dame Press, 2002.

Ellsberg, Daniel. *All Saints: Daily Reflections on Saints, Prophets, and Witnesses for Our Time*. NY: Crossroad Publishing, 1999.

Firestone, Tirzah. *The Receiving*. San Francisco: Harper, 2002.

Freke, Timothy and Peter Gandy. *The Jesus Mysteries: Was the "Original Jesus" a Pagan God?* NY: Three Rivers Press, 1999.

Gardner, Lawrence. *Realm of the Ring Lords*. Gloucester, MA: Fair Winds Press, 2003.

Greene, Liz. *The Astrological Neptune and the Quest for Redemption*. York Beach, ME: Samuel Weiser, Inc., first paperback ed. 2000.

Goleman, Daniel. *Emotional Intelligence.* NY: Bantam Books, 1995.

Guiley, Rosemary Ellen, ed. *Harper's Encyclopedia of Mystical & Paranormal Experience.* Edison, NJ: Castle Books, 1991.

Hall, Manly P. *Orders of the Quest: The Holy Grail.* 2d. printing. Los Angeles, CA: Philosophical Research Society, Inc., 1976.

Harpur, Tom. *The Pagan Christ: Recovering the Lost Light.* Toronto, Ont., Can.: Thomas Allen Publishers, 2004.

Heline, Corrine. *Mystery of the Christos.* Santa Monica, CA: New Age Bible & Philosophy Center, 1961

Hindes, James H. *Renewing Christianity: Rudolf Steiner's Ideas in Practice.* Hudson, NY: Anthroposophic Press, 1996.

Hoffman, Glynda-Lee. *The Secret Dowry of Eve: Woman's Role in the Development of Consciousness.* Rochester, VT: Park Street Press, 2003.

Howell, Alice O. *The Dove in the Stone: Finding the Sacred in the Commonplace.* Wheaton, IL and Madras, India and London, UK: Theosophical Publishing House, 1988.

———. *The Web in the Sea: Jung, Sophia, and the Geometry of the Soul.* Wheaton, IL and Madras, India and London, UK: Theosophical Publishing House, 1993.

Jowett, George F. *The Drama of the Lost Disciples,* 10th ed. London, UK: Covenant Publishing, 1980.

Lansdowne, Zachary. *The Revelation of Saint John: The Path to Soul Initiation.* York Beach, ME: Red Wheel/Weiser, 2006.

LeShan, Lawrence. *The Medium, The Mystic, and The Physicist: Toward a General Theory of the Paranormal.* NY: Ballantine Books, 1974.

Luke, Helen M. *Such Stuff As Dreams Are Made Of : the Autobiography of Helen M. Luke.* NY: Parabola Books, 2000.

Lovelock, James. *The Ages of Gaia: A Biography of Our Living Earth.* Oxford, UK: Oxford University Press, 1995.

Maslow, Abraham. *Religions, Values and Peak-Experiences.* NY: Penguin Books, 1976; Harmondsworth, Eng: Penguin, 1986.

Mollenkott, Virginia Ramy. *The Divine Feminine: The Biblical Imagery of God as Female.* NY: Crossroad Publishing, 1983.

Muktananda, Swami. *Play of Consciousness, A Spiritual Autobiography,* 4th ed. South Fallsburg, NY: The Syda Foundation, 1994.

Nash, John. *The Soul and Its Destiny.* Bloomington, IN: Author House, 2004.

———. *Quest for the Soul: The Age Old Search for Our Inner Spiritual Nature.* Bloomington, IN: 1st Books, 2004.

Netto, José Trigueirinho. *Calling Humanity.* MG, Brazil: Irdin Editora Ltda., 2003.

Pagels, Elaine. *Beyond Belief.* NY: Random House, 2004.

———. *The Gnostic Gospels.* NY: Random House, 1989.

Parrish-Harra. Carol E. *The New Dictionary of Spiritual Thought*, exp. 2d. ed. Tahlequah, OK: Sparrow Hawk Press, 2002.

———. *The New Age Handbook on Death and Dying.* Tahlequah, OK: Sparrow Hawk Press, 1982.

———. *Reflections.* Compiled by Maggie Webb-Adams. [selected poetry by Carol E. Parrish-Harra]. Tahlequah, OK: Sparrow Hawk Press, 1997.

Pataki, Raphael. *The Hebrew Goddess.* Detroit: Wayne State University Press, 1978.

Pirani, Alix, ed. *The Absent Mother.* London, UK: Mandala, 1991.

Powell, Robert. A. *The Sophia Teachings: The Emergence of the Divine Feminine in Our Time.* NY: Lantern Books, 2001.

———. *Divine Sophia Holy Wisdom,* 2d. ed., Nicasio, CA: Sophia Foundation of North America, 1997.

———. The Most Holy Trinosophia and the New Revelations of the Divine Feminine. NY: Steiner Books, 2000.

Prater, Rick. *Bridge to Superconsciousness.* Mariposa, CA: Source Publications, 1999.

Ray, Paul H., and Sherry Ruth Anderson. *The Cultural Creatives.* NY: Harmony Books, 2000.

Robinson, James M., ed. The Nag Hammadi Library. San Francisco: Harper & Row, 1988.

Roerich, Helena. *Letters of Helena Roerich Vol. I.* NY: Agni Yoga Society, 1958.

Rowlett, Martha Graybeal and Margaret Starbird. *The Feminine Face of Christianity.* Wheaton, IL: Quest Books, 2003.

Ruiz, Don Miguel. *The Four Agreements: a Practical Guide to Personal Freedom.* San Rafael, CA: Amber-Allen Publishing, 1997.

Saraydarian, Torkom. *The Science of Meditation.* Sedona, AZ: Aquarian Educational Group, 1971.

———. *Breakthrough to Higher Psychism.* Cave Creek, AZ: T.S.G. Publishing Foundation, Inc., 1990.

———. *Christ—The Avatar of Sacrificial Love.* Sedona, AZ: Aquarian Educational Group, 1974.

Scholem, Gershom. *On The Mystical Shape of the Godhead.* NY: Schocken Books, 1991.

Shlain, Leonard. *The Alphabet Versus The Goddess: The Conflict Between Word and Image.* New York: Viking, 1998.

Spretnak, Charlene. *Missing Mary: The Queen of Heaven and Her Emergence in the Modern Church.* Houndmills, Basingstoke, Hampshire, UK: Palgrave Macmillan, 2004.

Starbird, Margaret. *Mary Magdalene, Bride in Exile.* Rochester, VT: Bear & Co., 2005.

———. *The Goddess in the Gospels: Reclaiming the Sacred Feminine.* Rochester, VT: Bear & Co., 1998.

———. *Magdalene's Lost Legacy: Symbolic Numbers and the Sacred Union in Christianity.* Rochester, VT: Bear & Co., 2003.

———. *The Woman With the Alabastr Jar: Mary Magdalene and the Holy Grail.* Rochester, VT: Bear & Co., 1993.

Starhawk. *The Earth Path: Grounding Our Spirits in the Rhythm of Nature.* NY: HarperCollins, 2004.

Terrenus, Aurora. *The Shroud of Sophia.* Santa Cruz, CA: Publishing House of the Holy Order of Wisdom, 1988.

VanDerLeeuw, J. J. *The Fire of Creation.* Adyar, India: Theosophical Publishing House, 1947.

Versluis, Arthur. *TheoSophia.* Hudson, NY: Lindisfarne Press, 1994.

Whitehead, Leslie D. *Life Begins At Death.* Nashville & New York: Abingdon Press, 1969.

Woodman, Marion and Elinor Dickson. *Dancing in the Flames: the Dark Goddess in the Transformation of Consciousness.* Boston & London: Shambhala, 1996.

Internet Sites

Barry Dunford. *Barry Dunford's E-Zine.* www.sacredconnection.ndo.co.uk.

Eduseek. www.mystae.com.

Encyclopedia Mythica. www.pantheon.org.

Gard Jameson. www.citynet.com.

Light of Christ Community Church and Sancta Sophia Seminary. www.sanctasophia.org.

Wholistic World Vision Global Network Service. www.globalvisions.org.